Bonnie L. Parkhouse holds a Ph.D. in athletic and business administration from the University of Minnesota. Currently she is an assistant professor and director of the sports management program at the University of Southern California. Her research in the sport management field appears in distinguished physical education, commercial, and management journals. In addition, she has written numerous articles on such topics as equality in sport for women and sanity in sport. Dr. Parkhouse is a former executive director for the National Association for Girls and Women in Sport (NAGWS) and the Association for Intercollegiate Athletics for Women (AIAW). **Jackie Lapin** is one of the nation's most respected women sportswriters. A contributing editor to *Women's Sports,* she was awarded the Los Angeles-Anaheim Baseball Writer's scholarship while a student at the University of Southern California. Lapin covered sports for the Washington Post, the Detroit Free Press, and Associated Press, before electing to free lance for such publications as *Sports Illustrated, Sport, New West, Ms., Playgirl,* The New York Times, and The Los Angeles Times, among others.

Parkhouse and Lapin have recently completed another book, *The Woman in Athletic Administration.*

Bonnie L. Parkhouse & Jackie Lapin

Women Who Win
EXERCISING YOUR RIGHTS IN SPORT

A SPECTRUM BOOK

PRENTICE-HALL, INC., Englewood Cliffs, N.J. 07632

Library of Congress Cataloging in Publication Data

PARKHOUSE, BONNIE L
   Women who win.

   (A Spectrum book)
   Includes bibliographical reference and index.
   1. Sports for women—United States.   2. Women's
rights—United States.   3. Sex discrimination in
sports—Law and legislature—United States.   I. Lapin, Jackie, joint author.   II. Title.
GV709.P24   796'.01'9   80–10248
ISBN 0–13–962365–5
ISBN 0–13–962357–4 pbk.

*To the future of those who play in the
gymnasiums and on the athletic fields
of the world with the hope that humanistic
sport opportunities may soon become a reality for* all
student athletes.

© 1980 by Prentice-Hall, Inc., Englewood Cliffs, New Jersey 07632

A SPECTRUM BOOK

10   9   8   7   6   5   4   3   2   1

Printed in the United States of America

PRENTICE-HALL INTERNATIONAL, INC., *London*
PRENTICE-HALL OF AUSTRALIA PTY. LIMITED, *Sydney*
PRENTICE-HALL OF CANADA, LTD., *Toronto*
PRENTICE-HALL OF INDIA PRIVATE LIMITED, *New Delhi*
PRENTICE-HALL OF JAPAN, INC., *Tokyo*
PRENTICE-HALL OF SOUTHEAST ASIA PTE. LTD., *Singapore*
WHITEHALL BOOKS LIMITED, *Wellington, New Zealand*

Contents

Preface

To hear some men tell it, Title IX of the 1972 Education Amendments ranked right up there with the fall of the Roman Empire and the collapse of the Ming Dynasty. Title IX, they seemed to think, spelled doom for the American way of life, not to mention every one of the nation's 36,000 athletic programs. On the other hand, extremist feminists hailed it as the savior for all womanhood, the first step in preparing young women to take their rightful place in the world.

From coast to coast, girls' and women's athletics have come of age. No longer is sweating a sin, nor are female athletes social outcasts. A whole new vocabulary has sprung up to suit the times; grandfathering a rule has become grandmothering, red-shirting is red-blousing, and letterman is now letterperson. Instead of female athletes having to mold themselves to meet society's expectations, society is now making concessions to them.

Whether it has been the courts and Title IX, pressure by athletes, parents, and coaches, or the women's movement that has brought about such sweeping reforms, a vast new world awaits the little girls on today's playgrounds. For them it has become a reality; at least there exists a potential for equal opportunity.

Equality is a right and not a privilege guaranteed to every individual as are life, liberty and the pursuit of happiness in the Declaration of Independence. But the struggle is far from over.

Since the regulations went into effect, what has really happened? Certainly the doomsayers have been proven wrong, but is Title IX really doing what it was designed to do? There is little question that millions of dollars more than ever before are being poured into athletic programs for females and that those programs are expanding opportunities. Every newspaper and women's magazine in the country has pointed out the increased funding, yet many have failed to report the alarming backlash of Title IX. The National Federation of State High School Associations maintains that the participation of high school girls in athletics has actually *declined* since Title IX went into effect. The Association for Intercollegiate Athletics for Women (AIAW) has revealed that in the year Title IX was passed, 79 percent of the administrators who represented women's programs were women and 21 percent men. Three years later, only 55.7 percent were women and 44.3 percent were men. This trend has also had a decided effect on coaching. Because of financial pressures, administrators frequently combine male and female teams under one male coach. For this and other reasons, women coaches are becoming an endangered species.

Many women administrators are wondering whether Title IX was a blessing or a curse. Says one, "How can I use Title IX as a threat with the administration at my school when no school has ever been taken to court by the Department of Health, Education and Welfare? The men just laugh at it."

Yet a spokesman for the Department of Health, Education, and Welfare (HEW), Larry Velez, says that is a sign of progress. "How can you take a school to court when it complies with your demands? We have not had one school yet which has failed to enter into negotiations and make the necessary changes," he explains. That is not to say that some institutions currently under investigation might not end up in the courts. The University of Michigan alone has four complaints filed against it—obviously revealing an unwillingness to comply unless under duress.

Men have not been the only people who have held women's athletics back. Women athletic directors' and coaches' reluctance to get involved, their collapsing under pressure, and their disorganization and fragmentation have obstructed progress.

"Women are ready to throw in the towel," says Claire Nolan, an athletic director in Waltham, Massachusetts. "Women won't stand up for what they believe in. Women coaches here fought for higher salaries and when they got them, they no longer wanted the jobs. So the men took over. Men laugh at us because we change rules all the time. All the state tournaments have men coaches and are directed by men, while women take a back seat. When will they have the courage to fight?"

When indeed? No one will fight for your rights and the rights of your students but you. If you allow discrimination against female athletes to exist because you remain reticent, you are perpetuating the problem. In becoming a coach and teacher, you accepted the responsibility of providing a meaningful athletic experience for your students. Inherent in the job are the three A's—awareness (of discrimination), assuming responsibility (for correcting it) and action.[1] They are the stepping stones to equality.

Equality is a right, not a privilege. However, it has become apparent in "this land of opportunity" that equal opportunity becomes a reality only if we act when that right is denied. Women can't stand by and quietly wait. We must stand up for our rights. We must exercise our right of free speech—be willing to speak out when our rights are denied. Becoming aware of existing discrimination, knowing the avenues for correcting it, and committing oneself to action are the essential strategies that are addressed in this text.

Mary Alice Hill had the courage to tackle the system. She filed one of the very first suits in women's athletics and won. When it was all over, she could say:

> I'm really excited about the decision. This has far-reaching implications for women in all job positions. I'm really pleased that the judge took so much time to write a document that will do an awful lot for women all across the United States.
>
> I've always thought I had a very strong case, and the only times I guess I've lost faith is when I've been down because the wheels of justice turn so slowly. Now with the appeals it will be at least another year and a half. If you can get something resolved out of court, it's so much better because it takes so much time, energy and money. If it weren't for my lawyer, Judith Ward Maddox, who took the case on a contingency [she would be paid only if Hill won], I would never have been able to do it.
>
> One of the most important things about this case is that since 1974, women in athletics have not had tenure, and as a result it is very difficult to put your head on the line when trying to enforce Title IX or bring equality into your program. Now women can safely speak up.[2]

Hill felt the success of her case could be traced to her lawyer's attempts to argue the case only on the facts, whereas the universities' representatives clearly revealed their emotional involvement—their anger that this woman had dared to challenge the system—which is ironic because men often charge women with being unfit for administrative positions because of their emotionalism.

Obviously, as Hill notes, the fastest and most effective method of bringing about equality is staying out of the courts, but an implied threat of a suit can be a tremendous incentive to bring a program into line. Two women filed suit against the University of Illinois, and with an out-of-court settlement, managed to boost the women's budget in four years from $83,000 (including physical education) to over $500,000 for women's athletics alone.

However, in general, more doors can be opened with a smile than a fist. That is why this book is dedicated to finding peaceful, creative methods to bring about change and influence attitudes. By making a concerted effort to gain equality through negotiation, cultivation, and communication, a firm foundation for the future can be built. Justice in the spirit of compassion, fairness, and human—rather than male or female—rights is a much healthier and more civilized approach than attempting to gain justice by the letter of the law. Unfortunately, equal opportunity is becoming more of a reality today because women are being forced to express their dissatisfaction through litigation. The courts should be the absolutely final recourse. Although reason is ideally the most positive way to obtain equal opportunity when there is no alternative, it is far better to force compliance than perpetuate inequality or discrimination.

Acknowledgments

A special recognition of Louise Jenkins is in order for the knowledge, technical preparation, and encouragement she provided.

Our sincerest gratitude also goes to these people who so graciously gave their time and effort for this book: Shirley Almeda, Nena Amundson, Vivian Barfield, Marna Bauer, Ruth Berkey, Laurie Billis, Ben Byers, Jane Davis, Jay Davis, Margaret Davis, Linda Dempsay, Joanne Dixon, Pam Erwin, Linda Estes, Nancy Eyler, Lila Farr, Sue Feamster, Gooch Foster, Linda Garrison, Sue Garrison, Larry Geracioti, Marythea Grebner, Kit Green, Lee Green, Ruth Halsey, Nancy Hamilton, Pat Harvey, Mary Jo Haverbeck, Karen Hellyer, Barbara Hedges, Mary Alice Hill, Judie Holland, Judy McInnes, Karol Kahrs, Sharon King, Anne Krummes, Virgil Luberdon, Joyce Malone, Sharon McAlexander, Kaye McDonald, Marlene McMullen, Sherry Moody, Lauren Moore, Linda Moore, Nettie Morrison, Jean Mylen, Carole Oglesby, Jo Oliver, Jan Palchikoff, Nick Pappas, Jim Perry, Richard Perry, Lea Plarski, Carlos Reeder, Fran Schaafsma, Becky Sisley, Lionel Sobel, Judy Stiehm, Neale Stoner, Pam Strathairn, Judy Sweet, Barbara Swihart, Vicki Toutz, Tom Tutko, Barbara Twardus, Tom White, Barbara Wilson, Don Winston.

CHAPTER 1

Equality: Exercising
Your Rights

In 1972 Mary Alice Hill was hired to run the athletic program at Colorado State University. Her enthusiasm dimmed shortly after the ink was dry on her contract when she realized there was only $5,500 allotted for all the institution's women's teams competing in six Rocky Mountain states. That money, budgeted out of the instructional funds, compared to $1.5 million provided for the men's program. She approached her coaching staff to see if they felt as she did: They deserved more. With their sworn support, she began to lobby for an additional $20,000. It was surprising when she got it, but what happened afterward was even more surprising.

Hill began to notice that whenever she taught, there seemed to be a person from the physical education department sitting in on her classes. Since she had been selected the most outstanding teacher in the department by the students, this surveillance seemed unusual. In the course of the year, she was evaluated not less than 18 times. Nevertheless, she was speechless when at contract renewal she was told she was being terminated because of 18 charges of such earth-shaking proportions as the following, among others:

> Failing to park her car in the proper place.
>
> Not dressing properly for class.
>
> Not having her parking sticker on her window.
>
> Not posting her office hours.
>
> Letting her track team out five minutes early.

When she approached her department chair to ask if she could appeal, he told her, "That would be very, very unprofessional." Then that is what she would do, she decided. Three times over the next three years she went before appeals boards. She won all but the last case, whereupon she filed a lawsuit that is discussed later in the book.

During the appeals and subsequent court appearances, Hill, who estimates she spent $35,000 in legal fees, tried to find a job elsewhere, but she had been branded a "troublemaker." The Colorado State administrators discouraged any prospective employer from hiring her. She began to fear that she would never find another job in athletics again.

Meanwhile, she seldom slept nights. Several times her car was broken into, her two German shepherds would take off into the darkness after some unnamed intruder, her phone would ring and the only sound would be heavy breathing. Six times in one year she changed phone numbers and each time, her harassers would locate it. Someone even tried to run her car off the road.

Dr. Vivian Barfield, currently women's athletic director at the University of Minnesota, left her position at Colorado Women's College to accept a job at the University of Massachusetts offered to her by an old friend, the dean of physical education. Barfield contended that she had turned down a teacher-coach-administrator job until it was amended to be a full-time administrative position that included the following conditions:

She would serve as assistant athletic director and be administratively equivalent to the associate athletic director.

She would be included in all policy making within the department, covering both men's and women's athletics.

She would have a five-year contract and an expense account to use as she saw fit for traveling to athletic meetings and conventions.

A week before she was to report to the school, she received an 18-month contract and a promise that it would all work out. Upon arrival at the school, she discovered she had no expense account and she would be subordinate to the associate athletic director. She requested to see her job description, but the personnel department refused. Her friend, the dean, agreed to requisition the job description, which turned out to have been written by the athletic director. It clearly illustrated that she was literally powerless, a mere figurehead in the department. Subsequently, Barfield began writing memos to the dean and athletic director requesting a meeting to discuss her rights and obligations. None was ever acknowledged; instead, she received a note from the athletic director suggesting he rewrite her job description. Eight or nine times in the ensuing months she received unacceptable job descriptions that did not meet the conditions under which she had agreed to take the job. Meanwhile, the story was beginning to hit the local newspapers.

Eventually, Barfield sought out the campus ombudsman. Coupled with the publicity, this brought some reaction from the department. The dean drew

up a new job description, which, aside from a few minor exceptions, was the equivalent of that of the associate athletic director. Barfield accepted it, the athletic
director refused to sign it or recognize it, and since
the dean was away on vacation for a month, it just
sat on the dean's desk. On April 1, 15 months from
the day she was hired and three months shy of the
end of her contract, which was soon extended for 18
more months, she made final a reasonable job description with the department. Her comments at the time
reflected her long and hard battle, "I just hope this
isn't an April Fool's joke."

Meanwhile, Barbara Quinn, coordinator of wom-
en's athletics at the University of Nevada, Las Vegas,
was getting herself into some hot water. When she realized that illegal recruiting practices that were going
on in the men's department were being carried over
into the women's program, she tried to put a stop to
it. However, she was overruled. Being ethical and law-
abiding, she turned her school in to the AIAW ethics
and eligibility committee for penalizing. As a result,
she was completely stripped of her administrative
powers, and her job became unbearable. At year's end,
her contract was not renewed. Quinn has been fighting
her dismissal in the courts, but for more than a year
afterward, she could not find a job. The year out of
work ate up her entire savings. She is working again
now, but it has been a hard trip back uphill.

These women discovered a universal truth: The
price for believing in one's rights and fighting for them
is costly. They need only remember the harassment
suffered by Martin Luther King and the sacrificing of
his own life for the sake of civil rights. Although the
issues may not be as igniting, they are still central to
American life. Instead of the black race, they are concerned with women. As in so many other causes, the

women who are the first to speak up become the martyrs. Yet to endure and stand strong, as each of these women have, and gone on to other jobs where they demonstrate they cannot be shuffled aside and discounted, is a tribute to womanhood and a forecast of a bright future for women in the field. These women must suffer the initial indignities so that others after them will never know discrimination.

Until recently, the Declaration of Independence, solely predicated on the premise of equality, has been a myth to women in athletics. It is well-documented that nowhere in society has discrimination been so rampant and blatant as in athletics. The stories are all familiar—the men get millions for programs and the women get nothing; the men get uniforms, the women get hand-me-downs; the men practice from 3 to 6 P.M., the women from 5 to 7 A.M.; the men have the use of a trainer, the women get a roll of tape. Somehow these accounts seem endless. Still, years after Title IX, they keep rolling in. Why? Because laws cannot change attitudes. The law may say women are entitled to equal opportunity, but society challenges: "OK, let's see if they can take advantage of it." Meanwhile, society is lifting none of the real covert roadblocks. Women must either learn to hurdle them or take them head-on in order to collect the prize at the end of the race. Change will not come until women begin demanding change. As Mary Alice Hill, Vivian Barfield, and Barbara Quinn discovered, the only way to gain actual equality is to challenge the system. By law each of them was entitled to equal rights, but it did not become a reality without a fight—knocking down the roadblocks.

Equality is a right, not a privilege. But unfortunately, in this "land of opportunity," equality can only truly exist when it is mandated by law and when people

© 1979 United Features Syndicate, Inc.

denied their rights take action. To wait quietly for equality to be bestowed on women is to wait for eternity. Survival for the woman athlete means ACTION—exercising her right of free speech. There is little question that women are getting the least of their needs met at schools where they have been afraid to speak up. Although there is an inherent risk of being fired when women administrators and coaches take up the cause, there is a greater risk when they do not—a risk of integrity, dignity, and pride. To become aware of existing discrimination, plot an avenue of correction and then make a commitment to action is to show the courage that will one day make women truly equal.

EQUALITY: WHAT IT MEANS

A girl in Detroit whose basketball is flat and whose uniform is patched, may well have equality—that is, if the boys are playing basketball under the same circumstances.

To a boy in Iowa, where the girls' team gets most of the attention, equality may be getting the same page one spread on Saturday morning that the girls have.

To a young woman at a major midwest university, it is receiving the same benefits that the $700,000 provided for her male counterparts will bring them. For her, it could mean a training table, quality uniforms, shoes, travel accommodations, flying to events, and games against top level teams that require guarantees, but, according to the school, she is not entitled to any of it.

The law defines and provides direction about what is legally permissible. Generally, equality can be looked at in several ways.

If there is identical money, identical number of teams, and identical treatment for members of both sexes, that is complete *equality.*

If a male basketball player wears bigger shoes and is given a more durable uniform which costs more than the female player, but she is still provided a uniform and shoes that suit her needs (though they are not as costly), that is equal opportunity. All athletes have the same *opportunity to compete and to have the same benefits.*

If the program is one where there are only five teams for girls and 10 teams for boys, but there are half as many girls in the school, that is a *comparable* situation. Similarly, comparability occurs when the school decides to offer softball for girls instead of base-ball.

If women athletes have to share a training room, that is equitable provided the training room is not placed inside the boys' locker room where the girls cannot get to it or find it difficult to use. As long as the opportunity provided for females is *fair,* it offers *equity.*

Within the law, some of these terms are inter-changeable and others are not. Note how equality is defined by each law when utilizing it to your benefit. For example, the employment regulations call for com-plete equality in pay, benefits, etc. The laws regarding students (Title IX) permit equal opportunity or com-parability.

Christine Grant in *Equality in Sport for Women,* (American Alliance for Health, Physical Education and Recreation, 1977), an excellent resource book says, "While equality may be the ultimate objective, perhaps equity should be the immediate objective. With regard to achieving equity at a given institution, perhaps all proposed actions could best be evaluated by examining them in light of the following crucial questions:

Will the action enable the disadvantaged to move expeditiously in a positive direction toward equality?

Will the action in any way further disadvantage the previously disadvantaged group?"[1]

These two questions are key, because, as we see in the definition of equity, some institutions can provide equality, but flout the intent of the law. Their interpretations do more to disadvantage women than the existing conditions before the law. The "spirit," the "letter," and the "intent" of the law are three conflicting concepts which impose their individual interpretations on the term "equality."A school can comply with the letter of the law that provides equal opportunity by cutting back what is generally considered a major women's sport, volleyball, to "minor" status (part-time coach, less money) because the men's volleyball team is considered minor. Thus, they have made all things equal, but obliterated the intent of the law to give women better funding and better coaching, and the spirit of the law to upgrade women's athletic experience. Says noted Title IX expert, Candace Lyle Hogan, "Some women stand to lose as much as they could gain from false interpretations of Title IX which do not incorporate its spirit of fairness and affirmative action."[2]

Actually, it is the courts which will eventually provide the "correct" interpretation of the law, a process which takes years. The guidelines of Title IX, the bills passed by the Congress, are only a starting point. The courts may choose far stricter interpretations than those of agencies like HEW. In the interest of progress, there is another option. Administrators can decide now, rather than wait for the courts to make such decisions.

Instead of issuing panic-stricken cries by male athletic directors that Title IX and the like will "destroy" sports in America—male sports, mind you—they can embrace the regulations graciously and begin to find a workable solution.

Roswell D. Merrick of AAHPER analyzes the men's fears thus, "Men's sports programs have been living high on the hog for many years in many ways. They're knocking Title IX because it won't allow them to keep on doing what they are doing wrong."[3]

A Michigan Congressman, M. Robert Carr, further notes of the male dominance in sports, "Discrimination against a class or caste of people is always profitable for those that are perpetrating the discrimination. Slave owners doubtlessly worried about the ramifications that the emancipation of the slaves would have on the Southern economy."[4]

Like the slave owners, male athletic directors have deceived themselves to think that their system is financially sound and that it provides for the "poor underprivileged." Male administrators fail to acknowledge that their own programs are financially in hot water and that they really do not support women's sports. Student fees largely pay for women's programs, not gate receipts from the men's program.

Male administrators do not deny that discrimination exists. Many just do not see anything wrong with it. For them, it is economically and philosophically feasible. Instead of being concerned with athletics' contribution to a student's education, some men see sports as a means to fame and fortune.

PHILOSOPHICAL IMPLICATIONS
OF EQUALITY

It is largely male administrators who decide what is equity within their institutions, men who have long been exposed to the male athletic model. The law has not concerned itself with whether the school must offer a soccer team for women. It has only held that if that soccer team is available to men, it must also be available for women. It says that all philosophies and practices must be applied *uniformly.* Thus, it would only follow that these male administrators would select practices and philosophies common to their male athletic experience. Where does that leave the women in athletics? Should they not choose a philosophical view on equality?

Most assuredly they must. But will the law allow women to forge their own path? With the money that is earmarked for women's sports, must women put it toward those aspects of the program that have always been considered important by men? Just because the men have it, should the women? Women would do better to seek what they want and need because they want and need it. Is the law really making women equal or just enslaving them further? Although HEW denies it is mandating a philosophy, it may actually be doing just that. Telling women what they *must* have instead of asking them what they *want* is eliminating the basic spirit of legislated equality, since those being equalized have no voice or choice in the pattern or model others have established over the years.

The best approach may be the one taken by the following three women:

Patsy Neal—"Just because opportunities are available, or just because equal funding is one of the rights extended to women, does not necessarily mean the quality of the women's programs is going to improve. Spending money just to spend it, or having programs just because you have the 'right' to have them is detrimental in the long run. Budgets and programs should be planned on need and interest. Premature spending of money and over-expansion of programs without adequate and knowledgeable coaching can lead to a worse program than that being run when finances were negligible."[5]

Barbara Hedges, USC—"It's not my intent to always compare with what men are doing, but rather to say: What is the best program for the women compared to the women's needs?"

Judie Holland, UCLA—"The spirit here isn't 'We have to do this to comply with Title IX,' but rather, 'We've got a whole section of the student body—namely women—and we ought to be doing more.' As a woman in athletics, I don't rely on Title IX to do my job for me."

Even many men administrators and coaches have encouraged women to shape their own future. Tom Tutko, the noted sports psychologist, remarks:

I take the position that women are far healthier than men in the whole area of athletics. Why are they trying to be crazy? Why are they conforming? Women can really change athletics dramatically—and change it in a healthy direction. This will happen if they reinforce more participation, more education, more fun, and more involvement of people. You start with a broader base that is positively educationally oriented. By doing what the men are doing, women are admitting the men are right. And by doing so, they put themselves in an inferior position.

THE EQUALITY YARDSTICK: MEASURING IT

Athletics

1. Does the school provide equal opportunities on all levels of commitment (intramural, varsity, club, junior varsity)?
2. Are the number of sports and teams provided for women comparable to that provided for men?
3. Do the selected sports reflect "the interest and abilities" of the persons of that sex?
4. Are athletes given equal quality and quantity of equipment, supplies, and uniforms?
5. Do athletes receive an equal number of contests in like sports, schedules with games against comparable quality teams, and reasonable dates and times for those games?
6. Are scholarships provided for men and women athletes in comparable numbers?
7. Where the institution offers only one team, are women given a fair chance to make the team or are choices a foregone conclusion?
8. Is tutorial help equally accessible to male and female athletes? What about books?
9. Is the season of sport schedule one that is fair to athletes of both genders?
10. Do athletes have comparable locker rooms and facilities within locker rooms (athletic lockers, etc.)? How about weight rooms and storage areas?
11. Do athletes of both sexes have equal access to facilities for games and practices at reasonable hours?
12. Is the department conscious of and responsive to the needs and desires of athletes of both sexes? Is an interest survey conducted?
13. Is the administration solidly behind both programs?
14. Are all athletes provided a comparable number and calibre of coaches?

15. Do athletes have equal access to training and medical facilities and services?
16. Is the budget comparable and adequate for female athletes?
17. Are athletes treated equally with regard to housing and dining facilities?
18. Are athletes furnished comparable publicity? Are adequate funds allotted to publicizing women's events?
19. Does the women's program have equal use of support services?
20. Is the same insurance coverage provided for men and women?
21. Are adequate laundry services given to both programs?
22. Do both programs receive funding from the same source or are women forced to raise funds?
23. Are fund-raising projects geared to supporting both programs?
24. Are both programs provided equal custodial services and cooperation?
25. Are all games refereed by an adequate number and a sufficient calibre of officials? Are they paid equally regardless of sex?
26. Are all athletes exposed to available teaching aids (cameras, video tapes, tennis ball machines, etc.)?
27. Are the paperwork and procedures nonsexist?
28. Do recruiting practices discriminate against either sex (discounting differences stipulated by the governing bodies)?
29. Do the programs have a similar philosophic approach to sports?
30. Are the awards comparable? Are students of both sexes entitled to award banquets?
31. Do women's teams have the same opportunity to belong to a conference as the men's?
32. Is the administrative structure such that women athletes are represented adequately by women administrators? Are those women administrators given the authority to accomplish their jobs?

Subtle Ways to Discriminate

1. Does the administration give equal support?
2. Do women get asked why they need to go by bus when they can drive the station wagon?
3. Are women administrators treated like secretaries?
4. Are women's opinions ignored?
5. Are women omitted from activities in the department only to find out about them when they read about them in the paper?
6. Are women consulted on matters concerning their departments?
7. Are people going around women administrators to get what they want?
8. Are sign-ups for coed golf teams in the men's locker room?

Employment

The following is an excellent list taken from *Equality in Sport for Women.*

1. Are men and women given equal opportunities to apply for open positions?
a. Is news of vacancies readily available to both women and men, i.e., are jobs advertised in places where women would have easy access to them as well as in places where men would have such access?
2. Are men and women paid the same salaries for essentially the same work for coaching?
3. Do both sexes have equal opportunity to assume coaching or supervision duties (including selling and taking tickets, keeping score, conducting open recreation programs, etc.) for extra pay?
4. Are men and women given the same decision-making power regarding the conduct of athletic programs?
5. Do men and women in athletics have comparable teaching loads and/or released time?

6. Are both sexes represented in administrative positions for the programs?
7. Are men and women given similar contracts with regard to length of appointment, fringe benefits, etc.?
8. Are monies for professional travel, coaches' clinics, scouting trips, recruitment, etc. distributed equally between men and women?
9. Are secretarial help and clerical assistance available equally to men and women coaches?
10. Do both sexes have equal opportunities for teaching at preferred hours of the day?
11. Do men and women have equal opportunities to schedule their practice and competitive events at the preferred times?
12. Do both sexes receive the same fringe benefits with regard to insurance, retirement contributions, etc.?
13. Are men and women given comparably sized, located, and equipped offices?
14. Are numbers of men and women distributed equitably throughout the professional ranks?
15. Do both sexes receive promotion and tenure after like years, performances, etc.?
16. Do men and women both have access to the same number of support staff in their positions, e.g., assistant coaches, trainers, information directors, managers, custodial help?
17. Do women and men share equally in the "extra duties" expected of school personnel, e.g., committees, supervision?
18. Are men and women given equal opportunities to assume leadership positions within the department?
19. Do both sexes have equal access to such fringe benefits as coaching uniforms, use of school owned vehicles, access to recreational facilities, passes to athletic contests, membership in golf and country clubs, discounts on clothing and sporting goods, etc.?
20. Does the institution have an affirmative action plan? Is it available for public examination? Has the institution activated this plan?[6]

CHAPTER 2

Legal Vehicles

Just as ignorance of the law is no defense in a court-room, ignorance of the law pertaining to women in athletics will only make women vulnerable to discriminatory practices. The more women know about their legal rights, the more leverage they have in demanding them. However, women should only turn to legal action when all other avenues have been exhausted. Recitation of the law may often be as effective as a threat of a suit. Administrators may simply need reminding that they are in violation of the law. For that reason, women should know what laws guarantee them rights.

TITLE IX—THAT ALL WOMEN AND MEN ARE CREATED EQUAL

The greatest sports battle of the century has not been the Ali–Spinks fight, the Billie Jean King–Bobby Riggs match, or any one of the Super Bowls. It was the one fought in Congress, the courts, and the Department of Health, Education and Welfare (HEW) over Title IX—thirty-seven seemingly innocuous words:

"No person in the United States shall, on the basis of sex, be excluded from participation in, be denied the benefits of, or be subjected to discrimination under any education program or activity receiving federal financial assistance . . ."

It has been said that Title IX is the greatest accomplishment for women since 1920, when they were accorded the right to vote. The reactions to Title IX have widely varied:

God Bless You, Title IX!—for those who view it as an unprecedented opportunity.

God Bless Who, Title IX?—for those who see it with ambivalence.

God _____ You, Title IX!—for those who curse the day Congress ever decided women should be treated like people.

Title IX is not the work of a few people. HEW received and considered 9,700 comments before adopting the final guidelines in 1975. All of the nation's 16,000 public school systems and 2,700 colleges and universities have felt the impact. The vast application of the Title IX regulations is mind boggling itself. Notes Ernest C. Casale, athletic director at Temple University, "As is always the case, it is one thing to develop regulations which look good from a legalistic or bureaucratic point of view, but it is another thing to apply these rules to a real-life situation. This is obviously the case with Title IX. There is a tremendous divergence of athletic programs and these regulations have had to apply to the smallest elementary school as well as to the largest collegiate institution; to an institution which sponsors twenty sports as well as to an institution which sponsors four sports; to a collegiate institution which has an athletic budget of four million dollars as compared to one which has a budget of one hundred dollars; and to an institution which has a nationally oriented program as compared to one which is strictly local in outlook."[1]

The critics claim that Title IX regulations are vague, ambiguous, and hard to interpret to specific circumstances. Many administrators fear that it will lead to arbitrary withholding of governmental funds or a substantial decline for men's athletics, since no additional federal funds are forthcoming to equalize the women's programs. The women would just as soon not see Title IX have an adverse effect on men's programs either, yet former Immaculata basketball coach Cathy Rush comments, "Women don't need favors, just fairness. If colleges profess to be helping all students and then cut the football budget 9.5 percent and the other sports by 40 percent, it's unrealistic to expect 'minor' sports for men *or* women to contribute much."[2]

Former Marquette basketball coach Al McGuire does not see women's athletics as a threat to the men's program. "If a women's program is handled right, it can carry its own weight. It's like anything else, you can whine and cry poverty, or you can go out and sell the hell out of your program like a Cathy Rush does. With a few more great leaders the women might even catch up with men in some areas—assuming they want to. How long will it be before the first under-the-table payola scandal over a 6 foot 6 inch women's volleyball spiker?"[3]

Unfortunately, McGuire, who made that statement in 1975, did not know how prophetic he was. That is one of the unfortunate aspects to Title IX. With more money comes an increasing pressure to win. With the pressure to win comes underhanded recruiting practices and other undesirable and unethical activities. The win-at-all-costs spiral begins.

According to Caspar Weinberger, the former HEW Secretary, "The goal of the final regulations in the whole area of athletics is to secure equal opportunities for men and women while allowing schools and colleges the flexibility in determining how best to provide such an opportunity."[4] Nevertheless, there is a backlash to Title IX that is having a very negative effect on those opportunities.

Distortions and misrepresentations of the law are devastating. Separate athletic departments are told they are mandated by Title IX to merge (untrue), athletic directors are given ultimatums to provide equal (not comparable) budgets for both programs.

The National Collegiate Athletic Association is seeing dollar signs in the mandated growth of women's athletics, and thus has attempted to usurp the AIAW, by coming very close to voting to host women's championships. That way the NCAA could be the beneficiary of the television revenues and could represent itself as a body governing women's athletics to international organizations.

Merging—or mainstreaming, as it has sometimes been called—is having a very deleterious effect on women administrators. Where they once ran their own programs, women find themselves in subordinate roles, outside the conference room when key decisions are being made. (Title IX forbids merging if it has an adverse effect on women, but who is to judge that—the institution?)

This unfortunate trend can be seen in the number of women who represent their schools at the AIAW Delegate Assembly. A study by the AIAW revealed that in 1973 when Title IX became law, 79 percent of the administrators who represented women's programs were women and 21 percent men. Three years later, only 55.7 percent were women and 44.3 percent men.

Incidences are increasingly occurring, which seem to limit opportunities in the name of equality. Boy's wrestling teams are eliminated, for example, because the girls do not want to compete in wrestling and the money can be used elsewhere. Scholarships are only awarded for women in the same sports where they are awarded for men; thus, women cannot get them for field hockey or volleyball. Male administrators are forcing women's programs into established male sports leagues or conferences, regardless of the increased distances women's teams are compelled to travel and other disadvantages such as poor-quality competition at those conference schools.

Then, of course, there are those situations where males have assumed positions on female teams. In Illinois, the state championship winning girls' bowling team had four boys and one girl. Five boys have dominated the field hockey team in New Bedford, Mass. Two boys not good enough for the boys' baseball team in Newton, Mass., went out for the girls' softball team. What about the girls who could have had those berths?

In the interest of uniformity, coaching classes geared to women have disappeared. Many separate-sex practices that benefited women have been eliminated since Title IX.

Facilities, once uncrowded, are like the freeway at rush hour. Teams are practicing at outrageous times. Unqualified coaches and athletic directors are being forced into positions in order to satisfy the needs of students.

Administrations are using Title IX to gratify the public, but not to solve the problem. They grant substantial sums to upgrade the program once, but fail to follow up with adequate monies in the succeeding years.

Male and female teams are being combined under one coach, usually male, thus giving the coach a double burden. Assuming he had enough to do before the merging, at least half the students are deprived of his time. Since coaches of women's teams have begun being paid equally to men, males are enthusiastically scooping up those jobs, putting qualified women coaches out of work.

Decisions are being made according to what is expedient and economic, not thoughtful and fair. The men complain that the women plan to live it up on big brother's credit card and lock the doors when they see them coming. Even much of the good that comes from the growth and change is tainted. When Judy Sweet was chosen athletic director for the combined male-female program at the University of California, San Diego, she received hate mail!

Yet none of this can obscure the victories that Title IX has wrought.

Hundreds of thousands of young women are competing in organized contests under the same circumstances that their fellow male students have for many years. They have decent transportation, uniforms and equipment, training and medical services, travel opportunities, facilities, scholarships, awards, recognition, coaches, schedules, etc. Their lives are filled with the joy of competing.

Besides the additional money, there have come enormous intangible advantages because of changing attitudes. When women's teams win championships at the University of Texas, Austin, the tower is lit up in an orange glow as it is when men's teams are victorious. At a high school in Huntington Beach, California, a victory flag is hoisted aloft in the quad for girls' wins as well as boys'. Male athletes—from the very young to college age—are exhibiting new respect for female

competitors. This note was found in a school library
waste basket:

> Dear Mary:
>   I watched you pitch during the 6th period girls'
> PE class yesterday. For a girl, you sure can throw! I
> think that's neat. My father said I could call someone
> to go with us for a ride and banana splits. How about
> it?
> Bobby

A San Antonio plebe, Peggy Feldman, was the only
Navy entrant in the eastern AIAW regional swimming
championships and single-handedly placed the school
13 out of 43. For her achievement she received a gold
varsity letter N (the first awarded to a woman), was
cheered by 4,200 midshipmen and was shoulder borne
through the dining hall—a tradition long established
to exalt Navy's athletic heroes.

Male coaches are even openly praising female athletes in predominantly male sports. In Rock Hill, South
Carolina, an outstanding girl became the third top hit-
ter on her high school baseball team, leaving her coach
to comment, "I haven't been much in favor of girls
playing on boys' sports teams, but she sure is making
me eat a lot of things I've said in the past." A 16-year-
old pitcher, Robin Petrini, pitched four innings for her
boys' varsity baseball team in South San Francisco.
After five runs (two earned) were scored off of her,
the coach noted, "If you look at the stats and analyze
the ballgame carefully, there shouldn't have been a
run scored off Robin. . . . The defense let down a cou-
ple of plays and it cost . . . she did a good job." It sounds
like something he would say about any other member
of his pitching staff, and that in itself is a big step in
the right direction.

Additionally, sports stereotypes are breaking

down—girls can play baseball and soccer without feeling masculine. Boys can play badminton and field hockey without feeling like "sissies." Athletes of both gender are helping each other to succeed, instead of scorning each other. New trusts and understandings are emerging.

For the first time in history, female athletes are getting women role models. The initial wave of female competitors is coming out of the colleges to become coaches, thus providing girls with women who can truly relate to their own competitive experience. Coaching classes are opening up for females, as are athletic administration programs. Competency is growing rapidly. Women are, in some schools, taking on decision-making responsibilities.

And, on top of all of this, Title IX is having a positive and rational effect on men's athletics. As *Newsweek* columnist Pete Axthelm remarks, "One shudders at the images, for example, of college officials flying tourist class or the Alabama football traveling squad being trimmed below the size of Genghis Khan's horde—all in the name of sports for women."[5]

The Law

The detailed Title IX regulations became effective on July 21, 1975. All high schools and colleges receiving federal monies were required to be in compliance by July 21, 1978, or risk losing the subsidies. It specifically forbids discrimination against students and employees on the basis of sex. The only exemptions granted under Title IX which apply to intercollegiate and interscholastic athletics are those for privately funded schools that receive no government money and for public single-sex schools. HEW's Office for Civil Rights (OCR) is the agency which reviews and investigates any com-

plaints, though all governmental departments which
grant financial aid to educational programs may enforce the laws. Complaints can be made in the form
of a letter to the Secretary of HEW or the OCR, and
can cite patterns of discrimination as well as individual instances. They may be filed by individuals or organizations, which are not required to identify the persons subjected to discrimination. Although complaints
should be filed within 180 days, the HEW may extend
the time if "good cause" is demonstrated.

The investigation of a case cannot begin until
HEW is supplied with the following information in
the initial letter of complaint:

1. Name and address of person(s) or group filing the complaint
2. Who (what person or group) has suffered discrimination
3. Names and addresses if there are three or fewer victims
   of discrimination
4. When the discrimination occurred
5. A description of the discriminatory act(s)
6. Initial complaints filed within 180 days of the act of
   discrimination.

Provided the institution receives any general institutional aid, the entire school may be investigated. Not
only does HEW have the power to review any records
that have a bearing on the complaint, but the institution is required to keep on file for at least three years
a description of any changes made as a result of the
required "self-evaluation."

In October, 1976, new provisions for handling
cases were devised, including a deadline of 210 days
from the filing of the complaint for HEW to close the
file on the case. In the event the institution refuses to
comply with the government's requests the OCR may

cut off all federal grants or refer the complaint to the Department of Justice with a recommendation for pressing suit. The institution may be ordered to cease its discriminatory practices and provide equitable relief or remedial action. (OCR may also delay new awards while seeking voluntary compliance.) As of the date of publication no *individual* has successfully brought suit against an institution under Title IX. Although institutions are forbidden from firing, discriminating against, or harassing complainants or those participating in an investigation, the names of those persons are likely to be released to the school during the investigation.

> Office for Civil Rights
> Department of HEW
> Washington, D.C. 20201
> or Regional HEW office.

The Challenge

In February, 1976, the NCAA filed suit against HEW in Kansas City, Kansas, stating, "The standards by which DHEW . . . purport to determine whether a particular educational institution is providing equality of opportunity, are so vague and indefinite as to permit virtually unfettered and unimpeded discretion to DHEW and a violation of due process requirements of the First and Fourteenth Amendments to the Constitution of the United States, in that they provide the member institutions of the NCAA with no meaningful standards by which they can be assured of compliance with the law."[6]

Throughout the birth of Title IX, the NCAA had spent as much lobbying against it as the AIAW did on 17 national championships. When at last the amendment was passed, NCAA continued to fight. Walter Byers, the executive director, had called Title IX, "The most injurious piece of legislation on college athletics to come out of Washington yet."[7] When the organization filed its comments on the guidelines, president Alan Chapman of Rice University sent a letter to Caspar Weinberger, HEW Secretary, taking this position:

"Briefly stated, the NCAA believes the proposed regulations, insofar as they purport to relate to athletics, to be entirely without requisite foundation in legislation and to be so vague, ambiguous and obviously lacking in comprehension of the realities of administration of college athletics as to represent a deterrent, rather than an aid, in the development of athletic opportunities for women . . . The vague injunctions of the proposed regulations, if issued, will effectively place college administrators in the position of attempting to comply, on their own particular campuses with their own particular mixes of facilities, student populations, and budgets, with standards so generalized that no administrator will enjoy even reasonable certainty that his institution will be deemed in compliance by HEW investigators. This is arbitrary government in its most naked form. . . ."[8]

A year later, that statement was followed up by the letter the NCAA mailed to its members at the time of the filing of the lawsuit. It further amplified:

"One may legitimately ask why, if the NCAA favors development of quality of opportunity in intercollegiate athletics, it would file a legal action seeking to invalidate Federal regulations which purportedly have the same objective. The answers are, first, that the DHEW regulations contain what the NCAA regards as a number of unreasonable arbitrary standards in measuring equality of opportunity . . . Second, the regulations are designed to permit and foster interference and 'second guessing,' in every aspect of university life, by Federal enforcement personnel. The NCAA believes that NCAA member institutions should have the right, within their own community and through their own personnel and counsel, to determine their legal or other obligations with respect to provision of equality of opportunity, free from interference of the Federal bureaucracy.

"Another, and perhaps equally important, reason for the Council's action is the fact that once DHEW is permitted to establish a foothold in the regulations of intercollegiate athletics and other aspects of college life, as it is purported to do with the present regulations, there is no assurance (indeed history is to the contrary) that DHEW will not increase, make more complex, and enforce with ever greater arbitrariness regulatory standards which it, in its wisdom, deems appropriate."[9]

Yet even these statements did not get to the crux of the matter. The NCAA feared that Title IX would rob big time football of its profits and cause its decline. Remarked Byers in a moment of frankness:

> The thing that causes most of the problems in college athletics today is the pressure on the football team to win and to make money. This is what leads to recruiting violations. It's what leads to short coaching tenures. It causes most of the unpleasant things associated with college sports. And Title IX just adds to the emphasis and pressure. It adds heavily.
>
> This one sport supports most (men's) sports at most colleges and universities. If you bring in women's sports too, the burden on football—and the pressure—are increased that much. Considering the problems football already has with (recruiting) violations and so forth, you can see that adding to the emphasis on winning in college football takes up contrary to the way we should be going.[10]

Thus, the NCAA suit sought to extract revenue-producing sports from the clutches of Title IX, maintaining that since those athletic programs did not receive *direct* support from the government, they should not be required to comply. However, HEW's stance was that the courts have consistently upheld the ruling that an athletic department is an integral part of a school's educational program and is subject to the same equal opportunity laws.

The case was dismissed by a judge in 1978 because, he said, the NCAA lacked the standing to sue since it was not injured by the regulations. U.S. District Judge Earl E. O'Connor stated, "If the . . . regulations impose upon the NCAA no duties of compliance, it necessarily follows that the NCAA cannot be injured."[11]

This does not mean the battle is won. On the contrary, the NCAA does not give up easily. Although the regulations have been finalized, they can be amended in the future. Title IX supporters will need to watch carefully for any potential threats to the potency of the law and guidelines, and take action should it be necessary. The following are the guidelines as they existed in May, 1979.

Guidelines—Sections 86.41 and 86.37

Separate and combined sex teams—"A recipient may operate or sponsor separate teams for members of each sex where selection for such teams is based on competitive skill or the activity involved is a contact sport (boxing, wrestling, rugby, ice hockey, football, basketball, and any others where the major activity is bodily contact.)"

In the event the institution does not provide separate teams in noncontact sports, but only a single team, according to Title IX, that institution must allow the

members of the excluded sex to try out if "athletic opportunities for members of that sex have previously
been limited."

When an institution has a single sex team in a
noncontact sport, it need not take any action unless
it has been determined that the excluded sex has an
interest in that sport. At that time, the institution has
the choice of allowing the students of the excluded
sex to try out for the team or supplying a second separate sex team. However, if the school offers teams for
both sexes, it may, according to HEW interpretation,
prevent a person from one sex from trying out for the
team of the other sex.

If by opening a team to both sexes in a contact
or noncontact sport a school does not accommodate
the abilities of members of both genders, the institution
is required to offer separate teams in that sport. For
instance, a school does not fulfill its obligations if it
eliminates all the women's teams and instead opens
the tryouts on men's teams to them, because only a
few women would make the cut. That is not accommodating women's "interests and abilities."

Nowhere do these regulations stipulate that
schools provide single coed teams exclusively, only that
whatever is provided for one sex must be provided for
the other if there is interest on the part of that sex.

If a school sponsors both a girls' golf and tennis
team in the fall and one girl chooses to go out for the
girls' golf team in the fall and the boys' tennis team
in the spring, the school is not required to let her try
out because the girls' tennis team meets the needs of
the *majority* of the girls at the school. (However, if
the girls' seasons have been relegated to what may be
a less desirable season, the school might be open to a
discrimination complaint.)

Institutions that provide a girls' noncontact sport

such as volleyball, but no team for boys, do not have to allow boys to compete on that team unless athletic opportunities at that school have been limited for boys in the past.

Limited opportunity can be ascertained by measuring the *total* program for males against that for females, with consideration for student interest and abilities. This means examining the Title IX laundry list (noted elsewhere) for inequities, determining whether enough teams to meet students' interests have been offered and whether those teams were adequately funded and staffed. A school cannot establish that limited opportunities existed or did not exist based on a team-by-team comparison. Thus, they cannot say boys' volleyball opportunities were limited if there did not previously exist a boys' volleyball team *but* the boys had 15 other sports, while girls only had two. Similarly, it cannot be said that there were limited opportunities in school that offered only 6 girls' teams and 8 boys' teams. Girls did have a "comparable" opportunity to compete.

The guidelines direct institutions to "determine the interests of both sexes in the sports to be offered by the institution and, where the sport is a contact sport or where participants are selected on the basis of competition, also determine the relative abilities of members of each sex for each sport offered, in order to decide whether to have single sex teams or teams composed of both sexes. (Abilities might be determined through tryouts or by relying upon the knowledge of athletic teaching staff, administration, and athletic conference league representatives.)"

The interests of the prospective participants can be ascertained through periodic interest surveys. HEW encourages schools to provide the broadest program that they can afford in order to satisfy the needs of students. It does not tell schools what sports to sponsor, only that its provisions must be equitable.

It should be made abundantly clear to administrators that when a female is allowed to compete on a male team, that they are getting further away from providing an equal sports program for women in that sport. Where that once was appropriate, schools should be looking forward to offering separate-but-equal teams or combined teams with the same number of coaches and athletes as two separate teams would otherwise have.

The Laundry List. Title IX stipulates that an institution which operates or sponsors interscholastic, intercollegiate, club, or intramural sports must "provide equal athletic opportunity for members of both sexes." Those factors commonly used to determine whether that opportunity is available are:

1. whether the selection of sports and levels of competition effectively accommodate the interests and activities of members of both sexes;
2. the provision of equipment and supplies;
3. scheduling of games and practice time;
4. travel and per diem allowance;
5. opportunity to receive coaching and academic tutoring;
6. assignment and compensation of coaches and tutors;
7. provision of locker rooms, practice and competitive facilities;
8. provision of medical and training facilities and services;
9. provision of housing and dining facilities and services;
10. publicity.

It is imperative that institutions compare these and other criteria which could also be considered during a Title IX review and take remedial action. There does not have to be "equal aggregate expenses" for teams of both sexes provided the equal opportunity is available. (Example, the boys' baseball equipment is more expensive than the girls' softball equipment, but they are equally well equipped.) It matters little whether the inequalities occur on two separate sex teams or one combined team—males and females must be entitled to the same benefits. Equality of opportunity must be present regardless of how much money is spent. However, failure to provide the necessary funding will be seen as a violation. The source of monies is irrelevant.

Scholarships.   Women must be given the opportunity to grant the same ratio of scholarships provided to the men's program. The regulation reads,

(1) To the extent that a recipient awards athletic scholarship or grants-in-aid, it must provide reasonable opportunities for such awards for members of each sex in proportion to the number of students of each sex participating in interscholastic or intercollegiate athletics.

(2) Separate athletic scholarships or grants-in-aid for members of each sex may be provided as part of separate athletic teams for members of each sex to the extent consistent with this paragraph and 86.41 of this part.

Assume, for example, that a program has 90 women and 180 men participating. One half of those men (90) are on scholarship. The institution should then, theoretically, offer half (45) of the women scholarships. The originating source of those monies may be the institution general fund or the student body treasury.

Proposed New Guidelines.   In December, 1978, HEW responded to all those institutions that demanded a clarification of the previously established guidelines.

It issued new, more comprehensive regulations which created an enormous stir and re-ignited the anti-Title IX sentiment that had begun to die down. Over 600 institutions wrote evaluations and requests for changes prior to the February 10, 1979, deadline. Secretary Califano had stated that a final version would be issued by Spring, 1979.

The new guidelines did not negate the previous ones, but merely added some measuring sticks. They stated that a school which can show its per-athlete expense for both male and female athletes is equal will not be subject to investigation, but one where there is a great differential will likely be reviewed.

The way this was figured was to add up all the female athletes and divide that number into the total dollars spent on the women's program. The same was done for the men's program. If the resulting figure was equal, the school's athletic department was in compliance.

However, this is not as simple as it seems. Equality was to be determined by the financial parity of certain specific expenses that directly effect the athlete: Scholarships, recruiting, equipment and supplies, travel expenses, per diem and publicity. The question is how does one equate the expensive equipment needed in football with that relatively inexpensive variety used in women's field hockey? That is why the male athletic establishment was up in arms. True equality by this standard necessitates coming up with large amounts of money to bring women's sports to the funding level of football or taking dollars from football for spending on women's athletics.

Final Policy Interpretation. In December, 1979, nearly nine months late, HEW issued its final policy interpretation. These guidelines, probably the most clear and understandable version thus far, did much to appease the pro-football, anti-Title IX lobby, while still leaving the teeth in the law.

HEW, under new secretary Patricia Roberts Harris, stated it revised the regulation because, "most institutions based objections to the proposed Policy Interpretation in part on the assumption that failure to provide compelling justification for disparities in per capita expenditures would have automatically resulted in a finding of noncompliance. In fact, such a failure would only have deprived an institution of the benefit of the presumption that it was in compliance with the law. The Department would still have had the burden of demonstrating that the institution was actually engaged in unlawful discrimination." Thus, HEW determined that noting actual compliance factors was for more valuable to both the schools and government evaluators.

Essentially, the guidelines, reprinted in whole in the appendix, provided more flexibility in judging what is discriminatory behavior. However, the specific measuring sticks by which one can judge discrimination are defined clearly for the first time.

Additionally, the interpretation allows for disparities in expenditures for football game management and equipment costs, etc., but still does not exempt the sport from close scrutiny. States HEW, "If sport-specific needs are met equivalently in both men's and women's programs, however, differences in particular program components will be found to be justifiable."

These guidelines negated the previously proposed regulations demanding per capita equal expenses. Instead, they returned to the previously stated premise of providing "proportionately equal amounts of financial assistance . . . for men's and women's athletic programs," which is outlined earlier in this chapter. It allows for disparities if they can be explained by taking into account "legitimate, nondiscriminatory factors" such as a larger number of out-of-state athletes on men's teams. (Many institutions charge a higher tuition for out-of-state students.)

In the December 1979 interpretation, HEW chose to replace expenses with practices as the major standard by which to judge a program's compliance. Though this creates a more subjective evaluation, it allows for the flexibility needed to more fairly judge each unique situation.

Rules for Athletic Contests. Also in December, 1978, HEW issued a statement permitting different rules or entirely different sports or versions of sports for males and females. This essentially endorses policies by states that encourage high school girls to play a 6-person, half-court style of basketball instead of the men's traditional 5-person game.

Administrative Structures. In September, 1975, HEW issued the statement that "changes in current administrative structure(s) or coaching assignments which have a disproportionately adverse effect on the employment opportunities of employees of one sex are prohibited by regulation." A year later, it further noted that separate men's and women's departments were acceptable. There was no necessity to merge in order to comply with Title IX. Thus, the agency addressed the common practice of giving previously visible, autonomous, decision-making women who ran their own departments subordinate roles in a combined department. An institution must first analyze whether it is eliminating key women's positions or demoting female administrators in the process of merging. If these problems are occurring, the school has a responsibility to grant opportunity for training and greater experience to upgrade women for important decision-making positions.

Employment. Title IX does several things that the Civil Rights Act and the Equal Pay Act also do. It prohibits employers from paying men and women differently for equal skill, effort, and responsibility under similar working conditions. It prevents jobs from being classified for male or females. And it forbids institutions from using different standards based on sex to evaluate applicants, calling for affirmative action measures. Additionally, Title IX states that a school cannot recruit and hire employees solely from sources which discriminate against one sex. Any attempt to hire only women to coach girls and men to coach boys is open to review by HEW, though other factors may weigh heavily for or against a case for discrimination.

EQUAL PAY ACT OF 1963

This act prohibits any discrimination in salaries and fringe benefits on the basis of sex in *all* institutions. School administrations have numerous subtle ways of justifying paying women less than men. Some of these tactics include:

Paying people with military experience more

Paying heads of households more

Paying male coaches more because they are non-tenured where female coaches are tenured

Paying men athletic directors more because they are full professors

Paying men coaches more because they spend more time recruiting (though this justification is quickly changing in light of the recent AIAW decision to pay women to "assess talent")

Paying men more because they are paid as coaches where women are paid as physical educators

Giving men, and not women, extra duty pay or release time to coach

Paying women less because they are "not under substantial pressure" from the community.

These are all discriminatory practices. The Equal Pay Act stipulates that persons in jobs that require equal skill, effort, and responsibility under similar working conditions be given the same pay. "Substantially similar" skills are measured by the experience they require, training, education, and ability. Effort refers to the degree of mental and physical energy which is demanded by the job. (A woman who has a sport as physically demanding as a man cannot be paid less.) Perhaps the most easily identifiable discriminatory practices are those which do not take into account equal responsibility. A woman coach who has an equal number of contests, equal number and length of practices, equal number of students in her charge, equal budgets to administer, etc., cannot be paid less than her male counterpart. Small differences in responsibilities (she has three less athletes than he does) should not matter in estimating proper pay scales. A case in Delaware in U.S. District Court in 1974 established that a high school violated the Equal Pay Act for paying a male baseball coach more than a female softball coach, because their jobs were "substantially the same." Should an institution decide to correct the matter, it may not lower the salary of the man to be equitable to a woman. The law stipulates her salary must be increased to meet his. However, there are certain restrictions on the application of the Equal Pay Act. The two parties being compared—male and female—must be located in the same school or building. A school

district cannot be cited if a women coach in school X
is not paid equal to a man coach at school Y.

Although merging departments may well prove
disadvantageous in the long run for women because
they may lose power and decision-making authority,
it does have positive implications for equal pay. In
merged departments it is far more easy to document
inequalities, because, on premise, some men and
women have equal roles within the unit. Any complaints should be directed to the local Wage and Hour
Division of the Employment Standards Administration
of the Department of Labor. This agency will review
the institution based on a complaint filed by any individual or organization on behalf of the employee. Organizations can also file class or pattern complaints
without identifying individuals. A complaint can be
filed at any time, but the recovery of back wages is
limited to a two-year statute of limitations for a non-
willful violation and three for willful. Patterns of discrimination and individual complaints can be cited.
The institution is responsible for keeping records
which apply to the possibility of employment discrimination and the government has the power to review
them. Although 95 percent of the complaints are resolved through voluntary compliance, the Secretary of
Labor has the right to file a suit against any agency
that does not comply. Individuals may also do so,
should the Department of Labor decline. The employee
may be awarded salary raises, back pay and interest.
No institution can harass or discriminate against an
employee who has filed a complaint, assisted with an
investigation, or instituted proceedings. Unless the issue comes to court, the name of the complainant may
not be revealed to the institution without the person's
consent.

Wage and Hour Division Employment Standards Administration

Department of Labor

Washington, D.C. 20210

Field, Area, or Regional Wage and Hour Office.

TITLE VII OF THE CIVIL RIGHTS ACT OF 1964

This provision protects employees from any type of employment discrimination (hiring, upgrading salaries, fringe benefits, training, and other conditions of employment) based on race, color, religion, national origin, or sex in an institution with 15 or more employees. (Religious institutions are exempt with regard to the religion of their employees.)

Some of the ways institutions have circumvented these regulations are to:

discount women's degrees and experience

hire and promote only men with considerable experience in the field, thus discriminating against competent women who have had the handicap of not being given the previous experience

using men to coach women's teams

employing male officials when there are an equal number of qualified female officials

failing to promote women while promoting men with lesser qualifications and experience

failing to include women in the hiring process

hiring only women to coach women and men to coach men (bypassing qualified women coaches who apply to coach men's teams)

giving women shorter contracts

giving women different types of contracts than their male counterparts (tenured versus coaching) not providing pensions and other benefits for women

giving male coaches more release time than women

using "special" inessential and discriminatory criteria for promotions—the candidate for athletic director is required to be a former football coach

giving the male more support services so that he may devote more time to coaching

providing a tiny office for women coaches and large separate offices for male coaches

failing to grant women an opportunity to attend professional meetings and in-service clinics while men are paid to do so

requiring women to do additional chores (such as laundry) and not paying them extra for them.

The most effective way to win a lawsuit filed under the Civil Rights Act is to gather statistics that prove the institution discriminated against an entire class of people (women), not just a single individual. If the community or school district has a working population of 40 percent male and 60 percent female, the institution or district must reflect that make-up in its hiring. So, if women only represent three percent of the athletic directors in the district, those are considered "anemic statistics."

One aspect of the Civil Rights Act is that it says that jobs may not be classified, labeled, or advertised as "men's" or "women's," unless there is a "bona fide occupational qualification," which is demonstrated by the institution. Locker room or equipment managers come under this category in order to protect the athlete's right to privacy.

A complaint form, obtainable from the Equal Employment Opportunity Commission (EEOC), can be filed with the agency within 180 days of the discriminatory act. Under this statute, individuals and organizations may make the complaint on behalf of themselves or a class, citing a pattern as well as individual case. Members of the EEOC may also file complaints, though the government cannot conduct an investigation if no charges have been filed. The school is notified within 10 days of the filing of a complaint. However, once the complaint has been filed, the EEOC may investigate part or all of the institution, including its records which are relevant in determining whether violations have occurred. Should there be a necessity to go to court, the EEOC will file suit against private institutions, while the Attorney General will do so against public schools. Individuals may also take legal action. The court may order the institution to stop its unlawful practices, initiate or step up its affirmative action program, reinstate the employees, and award back pay for up to the two years prior to the filing of charges. As in the Equal Pay Act, the institution is prohibited from harassing the participant in these matters. Although the charges are not made public by the EEOC, the name of the person filing the complaint is revealed to the institution at the time of the investigation. However, the complainant is free to make public statements.

Equal Employment Opportunity Commission
2401 E St. NW
Washington, D.C. 20506
Regional Office

EXECUTIVE ORDER 11246

Unlike the others discussed here, Executive Order 11246 is not a law. It is a related number of regulations the government established under which institutions

that are considered contractors must abide in order
to receive federal funds.

The order, which applies to all institutions that
have government contracts of over $10,000, prohibits
them from discriminating against any employees or
job applicants based on race, color, religion, sex, or
national origin. This order differs from Title VII in
that any institution which has a contract of more than
$50,000 as well as more than 50 employees is compelled
to file written affirmative action plans (including nu-
merical goals and timetables for recruiting, hiring,
training and upgrading women and minorities) with
HEW. Thereafter, the school must note in its advertise-
ments that it is an equal opportunity employer. Under
the executive order, women *must* be granted preg-
nancy leave without being penalized. Applicants for
jobs or promotions may be tested using only exams
that can be proven to be relevant and nondiscriminatory. Schools are also required to provide in-service
training and experience for those who wish to seek
promotions.

Although the Office of Federal Contract Compliance Programs (OFCCP) of the Department of Labor
has jurisdiction over this area, it allows HEW's Office
of Civil Rights (OCR) to enforce the regulations. Complaints should be filed by letter to either agency or the
Secretary of Labor or HEW. It is more effective to file
a class action complaint when citing the Executive Order and seek redress for individual complaints through
the Equal Employment Opportunity Commission. Individual complaints with class action implications are
occasionally handled under these regulations. The
complaint must be filed within 180 days, though an
extension may be granted if "good cause" is shown.
Another positive aspect to the order is that HEW may

conduct an investigation without a complaint, but this is only where government contracts are over $1 million. All of the institution's records must be made available to HEW upon investigation. Should the institution fail to comply, OFCCP or OCR has the power to suspend or terminate federal contracts, prevent future awards, or refer the issue to the Department of Justice, whereupon it may end up in court. The school may be ordered to raise salaries, provide back pay for up to two years for a nonwillful violation and three for a willful violation, or take other remedial action. Participants in complaints are protected from harassment, though the name of the complainant is usually provided to the school. The government is compelled not to disclose the results of the investigation, but neither the complainant or the institution is so bound. Write to the OCR.

TITLE VII (SECTION 799A) AND TITLE VIII (SECTION 845) OF THE PUBLIC HEALTH SERVICE ACT

This law has special application for women who wish to enter sports medicine or athletic training programs at an institution. It prevents discrimination in admissions, internships, and employment at schools which receive a grant, loan guarantee or interest subsidy to health personnel training programs, or which are receiving a contract under Title VII or VIII. HEW will conduct an investigation upon receipt of a letter addressed to the Secretary of HEW or the OCR. Both individual and class action complaints are acceptable, but must be filed within 180 days (with an extension for "good cause"). This investigation may extend beyond the segment of the institution directly receiving federal aid, and will include an examination of all pertinent records. The response to noncompliance includes termination of federal monies, elimination of all future awards, or court action, at which time the institution may be ordered to cease discriminatory practices and provide equitable relief. Persons may not be singled out for their involvement in complaints, however names of those filing complaints is likely to be revealed during an investigation. Write to OCR.

EQUAL RIGHTS AMENDMENT

In March, 1972, the House and Senate approved the proposed Equal Rights Amendment (ERA) which has been an enormous source of controversy. It read,

"Equality of rights under the law shall not be denied or abridged by the United States or by any State on account of sex. The Congress shall have the power to enforce by appropriate legislation the provisions of this article. This Amendment shall take effect two years after the date of ratification."

Therein lies the problem. At the time of publication, the ERA was three votes short of the number of states needed to ratify it. Its supporters were seeking an extension. The battle raging over the ERA was exemplified by the debates that occurred in Congress. Proponents claimed that the ERA left no room for "rational classification—different treatment—based on sex," that it mandated "identical treatment." According to Richard Alan Rubin in the Syracuse Law Review, The House Committee on the Judiciary claimed that the "identical treatment" interpretation would be "undesirably rigid and that lawmaking bodies should still be permitted to make reasonable classification in order to reflect differences between males and fe-

males. . . ." Rubin further noted that experts felt that
the amendment would preclude "separate-but-equal"
treatment that has previously been upheld by the
courts in cases regarding women's sports. " 'All legal
distinctions made between men and women, no matter
how reasonable and necessary,' may be unconstitutional," he quoted authorities.[12]

Thus, according to the experts, states may not
make laws which prohibit boys and girls from playing
on the same teams, either contact or noncontact sports
(see state laws) in high schools or colleges. The ERA
could force totally mixed competition. Unfortunately,
those exceptions to the ERA which allow differences
do not apply to athletics.

On the other hand, after the passage of the ERA
there could be absolutely no footdragging by institutions in providing equality for women athletes. Women
would have the power of a Constitutional amendment
behind them.

Many of the critics' fears may never come to pass.
As with all such laws, the real application of the
amendment will not be fully known until some of the
cases hit the courts. However, some trends can be seen
in the suits that are related in these pages, already
decided in states which have state Equal Rights
Amendments.

WOMEN'S EDUCATIONAL EQUITY
ACT OF 1973, H.R. 208

This act provides monies for training and educating
women so that they may assume equal status within
society. It specifically provides grants to:

encourage the development of new and improved
curricula

demonstrate and evaluate curricula in model educational programs

help originate and maintain programs concerning
women at all levels of education (elementary through
career and postgraduate)

distribute materials for use in education programs
and mass media

offer training programs for parents, educational
personnel, youth and guidance counselors, community
leaders, and government employees

furnish aid for the development of women's resource centers

provide improved career, vocational, and physical
education programs

promote community education programs and programs on the status, roles, and opportunities for women
in society.

The Women's Program Staff which administers
the program makes small grants of under $15,000 and
large grants ranging from $35,000 to $200,000. In 1979,
over $9 million was distributed, approximately half
of the monies in continuing grants and half in new
awards. The agency's allotment is increasing by about
$1 million each year. One recent award was to the Colo-
rado Commission on Women to provide sports materials and an "action center, for young women to explore
their sports potential." A small grant went to a Title
IX facilitating organization in California called "Project Equity." Administrators indicated some Title IX
monies are available, but that the states are expected
to carry most of the financial burden. Eastern Kentucky
received a related award for developing instructional
models for physical education teachers in coed programs to eliminate sex bias.

Joan Duval
Women's Program Staff
U.S. Office of Education
Room 3121
400 Maryland Ave. SW
Washington, D.C. 20201

STATE LAWS

In the spirit of fairness and equality, four states responded to Title IX by opening all teams to both sexes.
The result was that boys dominated all the teams and
fewer girls than ever could compete. In Indiana, the
first and second place volleyball teams (which were
originally female) had one and three boys, respectively.
In West Virginia, the first place girls' bowling team
was solely composed of boys. One state, Michigan, had
to reverse itself to prevent boys from competing on
girls' teams. Massachusetts passed a regulation, commonly known as 622, which permits mixed competition
even in contact sports. As a result, a young girl named
Tammy Lee Mercer played on her high school football
team. Now she is faced with extensive experience in
football, no money to attend college, and certainly no
college football scholarship—that would be heresy. In
the Massachusetts state volleyball championships, a
team with five boys entered. The other schools in the
tournament refused to play it, not so much because
it was a coed team, but because the team played by
coed rules (completely different net height than under
girls' rules). Claire Nolan, athletic director for Waltham High School, one of those schools that was protesting, anguished, "It was horrible to have to present
the championship trophy to a school that hadn't even

© *1979 United Features Syndicate, Inc.*

played a game." It was only in 1973 that Oberlin College was censured by the Ohio Athletic Conference for letting women swim in exhibition meets. How far we have come!

What has occurred here is that equality has backfired on women in athletics. If girls must be permitted to compete on boys' teams to acquire the opportunity to compete, why not boys on girls' teams? Many school districts are now offering "girls' teams" and "student teams"—combined sex. But if the girls' teams are not protected by Title IX, they are open for usurpation by males.

A tug of war is developing within the law. Fifteen states have passed state equal rights amendments—Alaska, Colorado, Connecticut, Hawaii, Illinois, Maryland, Massachusetts, Montana, New Mexico, Pennsylvania, Texas, Utah, Virginia, Washington, and Wyoming. Within the borders of these states, the state ERAs (applicable only in public institutions), negate Title IX's effect because boys must be allowed to participate on girls' teams regardless of whether opportunities for them have been limited in the past. Conversely, of course, girls do have a better chance to compete on boys' teams when there is none provided for them in that sport. But is this advisable? A girl in Longmont, Colorado, played basketball on the girls' team during one season and then went out for the boys' team the following season. When she was told that was not permissible, her parents took the case to court and won because the court claimed that under the ERA she was being discriminated against. Under such provisions, administrators will be saying their prayers that young women choosing to go out for wrestling and football are not severely injured. (This incidentally could prove to be a serious insurance problem in the future.) Says one former Colorado administrator, "Girls' volleyball is going to be made up of six boys and a girl manager again. Instead of taking 400 steps forward with Title IX, we're back to the 1920s in girls' sports. We're just going to have to make sure districts in states that have ERA laws have good lawyers." All this is not to say the ERAs are poor laws—on the contrary, they insure many rights that Title IX cannot guarantee and they have a greater enforcement potential. However, they must be examined in the context of the paradox they provide women in athletics.

While these states have been protecting women's rights through state constitutional amendments, others through their state high school associations have sought to do so with the state athletic code. California, for example, has passed what is commonly called Rule 200, a rule that nearly got the entire city of Los Angeles kicked out of the California Interscholastic Federation for failing to comply at first. The rule is as follows:

(a) Student team: Whenever the school provides only . . . (one varsity) team . . . for boys in a particular sport, girls are permitted to qualify for the student team(s).

(b) Boys' Team: Whenever the school provides a (varsity) team . . . for boys and a (varsity) team . . . for girls in the same sport, girls shall not be permitted to qualify for the boys' team(s) in that sport, nor shall boys be permitted to qualify for the girls' team(s) in that sport.

(c) Girls' Team: Whenever the school provides only . . . (one varsity) team . . . for girls in a particular sport, boys shall not be permitted to qualify for the girls' team in that sport unless opportunities in the total sports program for boys in the school has been limited in comparison to the total sports program for girls in that school. Permission for boys to qualify for the girls' team must be secured through petition by the school principal to the State CIF Federated Council.

(d) Mixed Team (Coed): Whenever the school provides a mixed or coed team in a sport in which the game roles designate either a certain number of team participants from each sex, boys shall not be permitted to qualify for the girls' positions on the mixed team nor shall girls be permitted to qualify for the boys' positions on the mixed team.

(e) These limitations are binding upon all CIF Sections, although not intended to prohibit any student from qualifying for a team for which he or she has previously competed.

This regulation serves to protect opportunities for girls to compete. Is this constitutional? California attorney general Evelle J. Younger issued an opinion on the rule in September of 1977:

1. Sections 200(a) and 200(c)

Regulation 200 consists of five subparts and each will be examined separately. Section 200(a) allows girls to qualify for a boys' team whenever their school does not sponsor a comparable team for girls. On its face, this section creates no problem since all students are permitted to qualify for the team on an equal basis, and there is thus no classification.

Section (c) prohibits boys from qualifying for a girls' team in a sport in which only one varsity team is provided unless the total boys' sports program has been limited in comparison to the total girls' sports program. Section (c) imposes more restrictive conditions under which boys may qualify for the girls' team where their school sponsors no comparable team for boys. The question arises whether the juxtaposition of (a) and (c) creates an invalid classification in that boys are not offered the same opportunities as girls to compete for a place on opposite sex teams. C.I.F. asserts, and has provided documentary support for, the proposition that whenever boys are permitted indiscriminately to try out for girls' teams, the boys dominate the teams and restrict the opportunities for girls to participate. We are not aware of any facts or opinions to the contrary. It therefore can be persuasively argued that if the schools are to fulfill both the statutory and constitutional requirements of providing girls with equal opportunities to participate in sports, such a restriction on boys' participation must be imposed. A C.I.F. representative and athletic director of a California high school states that the only girls skilled enough to compete on boys' teams are the potential Olympic and professional champions. She believes that these girls, by sharing their unusual talents with other girls, set the standards of excellence to which other female athletes should aspire. This official asserts that the mere presence of an outstanding girl athlete on a girls' team improves the quality of the other girls' performances. If these highly skilled athletes are siphoned off into a different program, the girls' program loses the inspiration these competitors provide and the level of competence for the program as a whole is perforce set by participants who are "second best." The defection of the most highly qualified girls to the boys' program also can have a demoralizing effect on the remaining girls and tend to increase the stereotype that girls' athletics are inferior to boys' athletics. Thus the rule is directly related to maintaining the highest possible standards in the girls' program in order to meet the government mandate of providing high quality athletic programs for girls.[13]

Younger concluded: "Thus there appears to be a demonstrable substantial relationship between the government's objective of providing equal athletic opportunities and the regulation which requires girls to compete, if possible, on girls' teams. Accordingly, we conclude that a court would hold that Bylaw 200(b) is constitutionally permissible."[14]

It also needs to be pointed out that a 1976 CIF survey revealed that 84 percent of the women coaches in the state supported Rule 200. The CIF reported opposition to the regulation came from coaches of boys' teams who wanted top quality competitors regardless of sex.

Lionel S. Sobel, noted specialist in sports law and legal counsel for the western region of the AIAW, and Richard Weintraub of the Constitutional Rights Foundation point out:

> A rule which permits women to try out for "men's" teams, but which prohibits men from trying out for "women's" teams may appear to deny equal protection. However, it can be argued that there is a rational basis, and perhaps even a compelling interest, for such a rule; because without it, virtually all women might be excluded from teams engaged in all sports where strength or speed are important abilities. Assuming that this is a rational or compelling reason for a rule which prohibits men from competing on women's teams, the rule would be perfectly constitutional. Thus, the United States Supreme Court has approved certain laws which appear to benefit women over men, if their purpose is to afford women equality in fact. *Schlesinger* vs. *Ballard,* 419 U.S. 498 (1975). The Supreme Court has even affirmed a decision which held that a South Carolina statute which limited admissions to one of that state's eight colleges and universities to women only, because certain courses taught there were thought to be especially helpful to women, had a rational basis and thus did not deny equal protection. *Williams* vs. *McNair,* 316 F.Supp. 134 (D.S.C. 1970), affirmed, 401 U.S. 951 (1971).[15]

The Supreme Court has taken the first step in defending women's programs from the encroachment of males. In May, 1979, a 19-year-old from Newport, Rhode Island, filed suit in a Providence courthouse against the Rhode Island Interscholastic League for barring him from competing on the girls' volleyball team. Donald Gomes was granted a spot on the team after a lower court judge ruled he had been discriminated against since there was no volleyball team for boys at Rogers High School. A federal appeals court reversed the decision and the U.S. Supreme Court stood by the ruling, turning down a bid by Gomes to play the last two games of the season on the girls' team.

PHILOSOPHICAL AND LEGAL IMPLICATIONS

The Argument for Girls on Boys' Teams

"Denying young women what is given to men is not only illegal, it is immoral," comments University of New Mexico athletic director Linda Estes. Her remarks are the heart of an argument to allow girls to compete on boys' teams. Those girls not provided a team of their own should be allowed to try out for the boys' teams, undoubtedly, but should girls have the opportunity to go out for boys' teams when there already exists a girls' team at the school? Many top level women athletes say yes. Their rationale is that their needs are not being met on girls' teams. Notes Tom Tutko and Patsy Neal:

> Most top women athletes find that there are not enough other highly skilled women athletes with which to practice, or else that individuals with the same caliber of skill are so geographically scattered that the distances make it impossible to get together to practice. Highly

talented girls and women must therefore seek out other ways of improving their performance. Generally they decide to practice against men because of the latters' quick reflexes and high skill levels, and, of course, because of their availability. Boys and men are usually very cooperative in helping the highly skilled female athlete.[16]

Los Angeles Times sportswriter Charles Maher makes an even more vivid argument:

In the case of allowing girls on boys' teams, the principle is this: Any athlete, regardless of sex, should be able to advance as far as his or her talent will permit, unless exceptional considerations are present. Few would object to keeping girls off boys' football teams in the interest of preventing injury. In the absence of such risk, however, sex is or should be irrelevant. Girls should no more be denied opportunity to seek the highest level in tennis than in drama.

As it happens, boys' varsity teams offer the most advanced competition in most sports. If we exclude girls from these teams, we deny them full expression of their talents. And we do so, quite simply, for sexist reasons.[17]

It can be said by proponents that coaching is superior in men's programs simply because male coaches are more experienced. The question then becomes, "Should women be denied access to better coaching?"

Sobel and Weintraub note the following as the legal justification for girls to compete on boys' teams:

"(1) Even if participation in sports is a privilege, rather than a right, girls have the legal right to enjoy, on an equal basis with boys, those privileges which public schools do grant their students. Thus, if participation in organized sports is a privilege granted by public schools, girls have a legal right to enjoy that privilege equally with boys.

(2) In non-contact sports, the risk that girls may be injured while competing against boys is no greater than the risk they may be injured while competing against other girls. Moreover, even in contact sports, risk of injury depends primarily on weight, height, and experience, and these factors should be considered with respect to each participant, boy or girl. Schools are not truly considering the risk of injury when they permit light, short, inexperienced boys to compete against bigger, more experienced boys, while prohibiting qualified girls from doing so simply because of their sex.

(3) Psychological damage is speculative only. No student of either sex has ever been shown to have actually suffered any such damage as a result of sex-integrated athletic programs, and many experts believe that no such damage would ever in fact be suffered. Moreover, the potential for psychological damage exists, if at all, only because of stereotypes and prejudices which society has concerning appropriate roles for boys and for girls and concerning the significance of winning. Society should not in fact have these stereotypes and prejudices, and they would vanish in time, were girls and boys to compete against one another routinely. Thus, the risk of psychological harm, if any, would vanish as well, as a result of such competition.

(4) If the benefits of athletic competition justify the expense of providing it for boys, then such benefits equally justify the expense of providing athletic competition for girls as well. Where financial resources are limited, the question is how to distribute them fairly among those students who desire to participate in organized sports. There is, however, no justification

for distributing all of the available resources to one class of students, boys, to the exclusion of another class, girls.

The Argument Against Girls on Boys' Teams

Obviously, the first and foremost argument is that women are physiologically handicapped compared to the strength and power of male athletes. Although an experiment in mixed teams in contact sports in New York ended with the girls noting that they experienced no harmful effects physically, emotionally, or socially, neither the courts not physicians can actually agree on whether girls have the capacity to meet males equally on the athletic field without being physically damaged. This not only means an additional risk to the girl, but very likely also means she does not have what it takes to compete on an equal basis. If a female makes such a team, she is usually going to sit on the bench, and the team will be dominated by males. Gilbert Funk, the director of physical education and athletics in Colorado Springs notes:

> . . . Colorado does sanction four coed sports. They are baseball, golf, cross country, and pentathlon. In my estimation the experience has been a complete flop. We do have some girls that go out for each of these activities and in rare cases will make the varsity team, but it is not in the best interests of girls. (He was seeking to add softball and girls' cross country as sanctioned sports as an alternative.) As you can see, we have made no progress as far as coed sports are concerned, but I think we have learned here that it is best to keep them on a separate basis. The only place I can visualize a coed activity on an interscholastic basis is in mixed doubles teams in tennis. I am very much in favor of

the girls' sports program and marvel at its progress, but there is no way we can remedy the difference in physical ability.

The major objections by female coaches is that once girls are able to compete on boys' teams, the girls' program will be drained of its top talent just when it is gaining credibility. Says Barbara Wilson, head of the CIF advisory council on girls' sports, "We fought for a long time to establish a solid program and now that we have it, we want the girls to stay in it."

William W. Russell, one-time CIF commissioner comments further, "Title IX requires parity in athletic opportunities for girls and boys. If the girls' program is to be upgraded, how in the world can it be done if you let the top athletes on girls' teams play on boys' teams? We believe the top girl quite often wants to play on the boys' team. It's more glamorous. She becomes something apart from the other girls. OK, but when you have a girls' tennis team competing for the league championship, you want the top athletes on your team, not on the boys' team."[18]

Tutko and Neal see this as a serious threat to the growth of women's programs. They hold: "It has also been pointed out by some people that when girls and women wish to participate on men's teams this implies that the women's programs are inferior, either because of insufficient competition for the highly skilled girl or woman, or because of the complete absence of any program at all for the skilled female athlete. This concept of inferiority has already been so ingrained in our way of life that now when this myth is finally about to be dispelled, it is absolutely necessary that women do not fall back into this image by modifying their demands for top-level programs for girls and women."[19]

Once girls are admitted to boys' teams, there is little in the way to prevent the boys from taking over girls' teams without a Rule 200. (Remember Rule 200 has not, as of this printing, been tested in the courts.) Many states consider it unconstitutional to limit the opportunities of either sex. However, as Barbara Wilson notes: "If girls' basketball were opened up to boys, I would no longer have a girls' team. There are boys playing on weekends who are far superior to girls if you look at height, jumping ability and shooting.

"If we said to the girls, 'You can try for any of the teams, girls' or boys', and to the boys, 'You only have one choice; you must go out for the boys' teams'— well, most educators think that is not fair to the boy."[20]

The incidences noted at the beginning of this section bear out the fears of administrators.

Another case against opening girls' teams to boys is that institutions may begin to feel that that fulfills their obligations under Title IX, and therefore, only provide girls' teams in sports not commonly played by boys. This would have the exact opposite effect that Title IX was intended to have.

Women administrators and coaches also predict the exploitation of the female athletes on the part of male coaches. One irate female athletic director comments, "Many times girls are encouraged to go out for and be on the boys' teams because they happen to be outstanding female athletes and they are better than some of the boys in their school. They are encouraged by male coaches because they are interested in seeing to it a girl gets her 'rights' because they don't care if it is a boy, monkey, or girl that plays on their team so long as they can help them win."

Despite polls that reveal today's students like the idea of mixed teams, Tutko and Neal comment, "The real problem today is not that girls and women want to compete with or against boys and.men. Quite simply, the female wants to *compete, period.* Most girls and women prefer 'separate but equal' programs in order to have the optimum chance to participate in sports."[21]

The AIAW discourages women from competing on men's teams at schools where women's teams are available by prohibiting them from entering the national championships. However, if they compete on a men's team because there is no women's team at the school, they are not penalized.

Like the AIAW, the National Federation also takes a stand against girls on boys' teams:

> Boys and girls are not the same, but they are equal. And high school athletic programs must accommodate differences as they provide for basic quality. . . . Continuing study by the National Federation proves boys and girls are not the same in the realm of athletics and cannot be treated the same. We have comparisons of swimming times and track and field performances for several years that show boys consistently do better than girls in these activities. The exceptions are rare. However, comparisons of performances in activities which emphasize flexibility and balance could suggest opposite results.
>
> But these results have nothing at all to do with basic equality. Athletic ability is not a determining factor of basic rights, any more than sewing, cooking, plumbing, accounting, painting, or piano playing are or should be. But the results do reveal the need to design an athletic program which recognizes differences in the sexes.
>
> Experience shows that on the high school level the approach which best deals with the differences of the sexes, best meets the challenge of providing opportunities, and best deals with the reality of practical and financial limitations, is an approach which provides separate athletic programs for boys and girls.[22]

Additional legal justifications against females competing on male teams comes from Lionel Sobel and Richard Weintraub:

"(1) Participation in sports by boys or girls is a privilege, not a legal right. Since girls do not have a legal right to participate in sports at all, they certainly have no right to compete against boys where rules prohibit them from doing so. Furthermore, since participation in sports is a privilege and not a right, there is nothing legally improper about rules which restrict that privilege in some fashion, such as rules prohibiting girls from competing against boys.

(2) Even if the most outstanding girl athletes could compete successfully against boys, they should not be permitted to do so, because their participation in all-girl programs is important to the success of those programs. High quality competition is important to generate spectator interest, and it is also important to attract participants. If the most outstanding girl athletes participated in the "boys" program, there would be little spectator interest in the competition between the more average girls; and the girls' program would be less interesting and attractive to the more average girl athletes themselves. Thus, permitting the most outstanding girls to compete against boys would result in fewer girls participating in sports, not more, even if boys did not then seek to participate in previously all-girl programs.

(3) Because, as a general rule, high school girls are shorter and lighter than high school boys, and because of physiological differences between the sexes, including differences in their bone, musculature, and ligament strengths, there is a substantial risk of physical injury to girls who compete against boys in sports.

(4) Separating the sexes in athletic competition

is necessary in order to prevent psychological damage to both boys and girls. Girls who compete against boys may suffer psychological damage, because the boys' superior athletic abilities will prevent the girls from winning. Boys, on the other hand, would realize no psychological achievement in defeating girls, and may even be psychologically damaged if they were to lose to girls.

(5) It would be very expensive to permit girls to compete against boys in athletic programs which were previously for boys only, because girls would require, for example, separate dressing and showering facilities staffed by female attendants, specially designed and manufactured uniforms and protective equipment, and chaperones for overnight trips."

Charles Maher, the *Los Angeles Times* sportswriter is also a lawyer. Based on his assessment of the controversy over Rule 200, he arrived at the following conclusion:

> In the case of keeping boys off girls' teams, the principle may be illustrated by a parallel:
> Many schools offer remedial programs for students below the academic norm. These programs are not open to average students. A boy can't take a course in remedial reading, for example, just because he'd like to be a star in one class.
> Girls' athletics may be analogized to such remedial programs. Through no fault of their own, girls are below the athletic norm for boys. First, they have been undertrained. Until recently, they were hardly involved in organized team sports. Second, they have a natural physical handicap. Generally, they aren't as strong as boys.
> These two factors fully justify making girls a protected class by offering a sports program for their sex alone. Boys require no such protection. Occasionally,

a gifted girl will be good enough to play with the best
boys in tennis or golf or whatever. But there is certainly
no immediate prospect of a female takeover.

Girls may seem to have the better of it if they can
play on boys' teams while boys cannot play on girls'.
But, in terms of positions realistically within reach of
girls, such is apparently not the case.[23]

The issue is not really what form that equal opportunity takes for females in athletics, whether it be separate-but-equal or integration, but that true equality pre-
vail. To advocate that one approach is superior to
another is not for the authors to say, since there appear
to be a variety of workable methods. What is successful
or a failure really depends on the individual situation—
on the administrative competence and the philosophy
of the program. Separate-but-equal may be merely a
facade at East City High, but, on the other hand, may
be a reality at West City High. Despite the legal compli-
cations, it really will be necessary to judge each program independently, or wait until the courts take a
firm stand on the issue.

The authors cannot dictate philosophy. This must
be left to the discretion of the individual institution.
Neither can a judgment be made on what is right or
wrong, which is a legal question or a matter of litigation.

CHAPTER 3

Court Decisions

The law does not have its full impact until the court begins to interpret its application. Court decisions are the real determinants that tell the organizations, agencies, and citizens of this country what is permissible under the law and what is not. Knowing the law is an important lever for women in athletic administration, but knowing the trends in court decisions provides an even better foundation for fighting discrimination. It is useless to try to fight a case when similar cases have already been lost in preceding litigation; by the same token, it is far easier to win a case that has a precedent. Being familiar with the law and its application can weigh heavily for a woman when she presents her arguments to school boards and institutions.

Court decisions have a varying degree of importance nationwide. The lower the court, the less application it has over a wide area. For example, one case that had a tremendous impact on the media occurred in Ohio where a school district sued the state high school association because two girls wanted to try out for the boys' basketball team since no girls' team existed there. The case got wide publicity because Judge Carl Rubin wrote in his decision for the girls, "It has always been traditional that boys play football and girls are cheerleaders—why so? Where is it written that girls may not, if suitably qualified, play football?

"It may well be that there is a student today in an Ohio high school who lacks only the proper coaching and training to become the greatest quarterback in professional football history. Of course, the odds are astronomical against her, but isn't she entitled to a fair chance?"[1]

Undoubtedly, Judge Rubin's comments caught the nation's fancy, and many who were quick to get excited interpreted the ruling to mean that all girls everywhere have a right to go out for contact sports. Not so. The decision was handed down in the U.S. District Court and it only has application in Ohio. However, the judgment may influence cases elsewhere in the nation. The rulings which have a bearing on the entire nation are those by the Supreme Court, and no cases on women's athletics have yet reached that plateau.

CASES RE: GIRLS ON BOYS' TEAMS

Certain trends have emerged since 1971, the date of the first case involving this issue. They are perhaps best noted by Richard Alan Rubin in the Syracuse Law Review,

"A female athlete who brings an individual or class action to compel mixed competition in a noncontact sport will have the greatest chance of success if the school has no separate program for women in that sport. However, the likelihood of a favorable result diminishes substantially if she has been provided with 'separate but equal' opportunities, if she brings a class action, or if the suit is to compel mixed participation

in a contact sport. Needless to say, the combination of any of these circumstances will reduce the chances of success further. In every case the plaintiff's task will be to rebut the notion that physical and psychological differences warrant different treatment and to expose the countervailing inequities of the present system."[2]

Nearly all of the cases brought by girls who wished to compete on boys' teams maintained that the prohibition against their participation represented a violation of their rights guaranteed by the Fourteenth Amendment. The Amendment provides that no state shall "deny to any person within its jurisdiction the equal protection of the laws."

Sandra Wien, a law student at Cleveland State University College of Law, explained in the Cleveland State Law Review the ways the court uses to determine if a person's rights have been abridged under the Fourteenth Amendment:

A "reasonable relationship" test is generally applied: Does the classification bear a reasonable and just relation to a permissible one and if the classification bears the required fair relationship to the purpose, the constitutional mandate will be held satisfied.

However, in two circumstances a more stringent test is applied. When the "state action" affects "fundamental rights or interests," such as voting or education or when the classification is made on a basis "inher-

ently suspect" the "most rigid scrutiny" is required.
Thus, state action distinguishing on the basis of race
or ancestry embodies a "suspect classification," and the
burden shifts to the state to show a "compelling state
interest" to uphold its constitutionality.

Changes in society's attitude toward women have
forced a reexamination of the premises underlying the
"suspect classification" doctrine. Although it is presumed reasonable for a state to distinguish between
individuals on the basis of their ability or need, it is
impermissible to distinguish on the basis of congenital
or immutable biological traits of birth over which the
individual has no control. Such conditions include not
only race, clearly within the suspect classification doctrine, but, it is asserted, include also sex. Sex has been
recognized as a suspect classification in at least two
decisions which found no "compelling state interest"
in limiting individual opportunities on the basis of sex.[3]

Hollander vs Connecticut
Interscholastic Conference, Inc.
(Superior Court, 1971)

A high school girl brought suit in 1971 because
she was forbidden to compete on the cross country
team. She lost her bid for a permanent injunction
against rules which discriminated against girls in in-
door track and cross country when the judge, John
Clark FitzGerald, held that the courts should not be
the ones to determine the reasonableness of the league
rules unless the plaintiffs could show that the rules
were not supported by reason or "adopted in good conscience." Women may be protected from physical involvement, he held.

FitzGerald caused a furor when he further commented, "The present generation of our younger male
population has not become so decadent that boys will
experience a thrill in defeating girls in running con-

tests, whether the girls be members of their own team or of an adversary team. It could well be that many boys would feel compelled to forgo entering track events if they were required to compete with girls on their own teams or on adversary teams. With boys vying with girls . . . the challenge to win, and the glory of achievement, at least for many boys, would lose incentive and become nullified. Athletic competition builds character in our boys. We do not need that kind of character in our girls. . . ."

Gregario vs. *Board of Education of Asbury Park* (Superior Court, 1971)

At a school that provided no girls' tennis team, a female student sought to get on the boys' team. When refused, she filed suit. The court noted that not all discrimination is illegal, because the board of education could legally choose to safeguard the female's psychological well being. The judge also questioned whether the right, as it was defined, to equal use of school facilities, was a Constitutional right.

Reed vs *Nebraska Activities Association* (U.S. District Court, 1972)

Debbie Reed requested permission to compete on the boys' golf team because her school did not offer a team for girls. She was granted an injunction in April 1972. The judge commented,

"One justification advanced by the defendants for the rule prohibiting girls from playing golf with and against boys is that golf, unlike education, is a privilege, rather than a right. Even assuming that interschool competition in golf is not educational, the privilege-right distinction is not viable. . . . The issue is whether she can be treated differently from boys in an activity provided by the state. Her right is not the right to play golf. Her right is the right to be treated the same as boys unless there is a rational basis for her being treated differently. The burden on that issue rests upon the state—the defendants. . . . If the program is valuable for boys, is it of no value to girls?"

Brenden vs *Independent School
District* (U.S. Court of Appeals,
1973)

Initially the case was heard in a U.S. District court when Peggy Brenden sought to gain admission to the boys' tennis team and Tony St. Pierre to the cross-country skiing and distance running teams, which were not offered to girls. The case was decided in the girls' favor largely because both of them proved that they *could* compete equitably with the boys and that their sex was the only factor which precluded their competition. The school district set out to show that its rules were in consideration of the physiological differences in males and females and that separate programs was in their best interests, to insure "equitable competition." The court somewhat agreed, but noted that the skills of the women who sued merited their placement on the boys' teams, since they could compete equitably.

This decision was upheld a year later by the U.S. Court of Appeals. The court noted that the reference to gender had no substantial relationship to the league purpose, which was to insure that persons with similar skills and capabilities compete against each other. The athletes had illustrated that they did have the skills and capabilities, and since no other program existed for them to utilize their ability, deserved the right to compete with the boys. The lower court had suggested that had the women brought a class action suit, instead of individual suits, the decision might well have been reversed, since most females could not compete equitably with males, as it was argued in court.

Bucha vs *Illinois High School Association* (U.S. District Court, 1972)

When Sandra Lynn Bucha first filed suit to be admitted to the boys' swim team, there was a rule prohibiting interscholastic swimming competition for girls. During the period preceding the case that rule was changed, but she, on behalf of other girls so situated, maintained that she was being discriminated against by not being allowed the same access to the boys' team. It seemed that the girls' swim team was conducted in a low-key intramural style with few of the benefits accorded the boys' team. Being forced to compete on that team or none at all was discriminatory, she maintained.

Bucha lost this case largely because a program for females was provided, despite the differences. The court, noting testimony in Brenden, allowed the differences based on the stated physiological and psychological dissimilarities.

The judge remarked in his decision, "Since the instant inquiry probes only the rationality of separate programs for the sexes, this court takes judicial notice of the fact that at the pinnacle of all sporting contests, the Olympic games, the men's times in each event are consistently better than the women's. In the hearing on the motion for a preliminary injunction in this matter, it was shown that the times of the two boy swimmers sent to the state championship contest . . . were better than those ever recorded by either of the named plaintiffs. Moreover, plaintiffs claim that the physical and psychological differences between male and female athletes are 'unfounded assumptions' is refuted by expert testimony presented and received in a case which palintiffs [sic] themselves cite in their favor. All of these facts lend substantial credence to the fears expressed by women coaches and athletes in defendants' affidavits that unrestricted athletic competition between the sexes would consistently lead to male domination of interscholastic sports and actually result in a decrease in female participation in such events. This court finds that such opinions have a rational basis in fact and are constitutionally sufficient reason for prohibiting athletic interscholastic competition between boys and girls in Illinois."

Haas vs. *South Bend Community School Corporation* (Supreme Court of Indiana, 1972)

Johnell Haas made a "B" boys' golf team at her school, but the high school association refused to permit her to compete in the matches under its jurisdiction. Again, acting as an individual, she was vindicated by the State Supreme Court, after appealing a first defeat. The lower court held that the prohibition was reasonable because of the difference in ability between the sexes and because it denied both genders, not just one, from competition in mixed competition; therefore, it was not discriminatory. The State Supreme Court reversed the decision because it was shown that few schools in the state provided teams for girls at all, and precluding them from participating on male teams effectively prevented them from competing at all. "Although the difference in athletic ability is a justifiable reason for separation of male and female athletic programs, the justification does not exist when only one athletic program is provided." The court also struck down the argument that if girls could participate on boys' teams, it left the girls' program open to domination by boys, simply because no girls' teams existed. The judge further commented, "Due to the apparent superior level of athletic ability possessed by most males, it will probably be difficult for most females to qualify for the team. However, this factor, by itself, can have no bearing upon the issue of a female's right to the opportunity to qualify. Until girls' programs comparable to those maintained for boys exist, the difference in athletic ability alone is no justification for the rule denying 'mixed' participation in noncontact sports."

Morris vs *Michigan Board of Education* (U.S. Court of Appeals, 1973)

In a very similar case to Haas, two young girls wanted to represent their school in tennis and since there was no girls' team, that meant getting a berth on the boys'. And as it did for Haas, the court ruled for Cynthia Morris and her friend. However, in reviewing the case, the Court of Appeals modified the lower court's stand. Instead of allowing girls to compete on *all* boys' teams, it held that the injunction should provide for girls to compete on all *noncontact* boys' teams.

Ritacco vs *Norwin School District* (U.S. District Court, 1973)

Roxanne Ritacco and her mother filed a class-action suit charging that the girls' rights were violated by a rule that required separate girls' and boys' teams in noncontact sports. The court ruled in favor of the defendant because (1) Roxanne had already graduated when the case got to court and, therefore, was not a member of the class and (2) according to the court, "Superficially, the maintenance of separate sports teams suggest the possibility of a denial of equal protection of the laws, but sound reason dictates that 'separate but equal' in the realm of sports competition, unlike that of racial discrimination, is justifiable and should be allowed to stand where there is a rational basis for the rule."

Gilpin vs *Kansas State High School Activities Association* (U.S. District Court, 1974)

In a case that closely parallelled the Brenden case, Tammie Gilpin was granted an injunction from the rule that prevented girls from competing on boys' cross-country teams. As in Brenden, the judge cautioned that had she brought a class action suit, the outcome might have been different. However, the issue was not "other" girls, but this particular girl, so the application of the injunction applied only to her. Here too, skill was a factor. The judge commented, "As a result of her school's action (failure to provide a girls' team), plaintiff through no fault of her own, must either compete on a team comprised primarily of boys or not at all. She decided the opportunity afforded by her school was better than no opportunity at all, and despite stereotyped notions of female inferiority, she has proven herself capable of competing with the other members of her team." The court also noted, "The Association does not contend that Tammie Gilpin is not personally qualified to compete with boys in cross country competition, or that such participation would in any way be either physically or emotionally harmful to her or the other male participants, but it reasons that such participation could, in some nebulous manner, jeopardize the overall development of the state's girls' athletic programs. The Court finds this reasoning constitutionally infirm."

The Commonwealth of Pennsylvania vs Pennsylvania Interscholastic Athletic Association (Commonwealth Court of Pennsylvania, 1975)

The Commonwealth challenged the constitutionality of the high school association's rule forbidding mixed teams, under the state's Equal Rights Amendment. The Court invalidated the regulation. First, it stated that the Pennsylvania Interscholastic Athletic Association (PIAA) was subject to the scrutiny imposed on it by the ERA because it utilized state-owned schools funded by the taxpayers. Therefore, the court held, although students have no fundamental right to participate in high school sports, once the state decides to permit such participation, it cannot discriminate against any person. "Moreover," noted the judge in his decision, "even where separate teams are offered for boys and girls in the same sport, the most talented girls still may be denied the right to play at that level of competition which their ability might otherwise permit them. For a girl in that position, who has been relegated to the girls' team, solely because of her sex, 'equality under the law' has been denied. . . . The existence of certain characteristics to a greater degree in one sex does not justify classification by sex rather than by the particular characteristic. . . . If any individual girl is too weak, injury-prone, or unskilled, she may, of course, be excluded from competition on that basis, but she cannot be excluded solely because of her sex without regard to her relevant qualifications." The judgment went on to specify that there was no valid reason for girls to be excluded from football or boys' basketball.

Darrin vs *Gould* (Supreme Court
of the State of Washington, 1975)

Two sisters brought a class action suit against the
Washington Interscholastic Activities Association for
preventing them from playing football on their high
school team. One of the girls was 14 years old, five
feet nine and 212 pounds. The other was 16 years old,
five feet six and 170 pounds. Both of them met the pre-
requisites for competing, including physical exams,
medical insurance, and practice sessions. Additionally,
the male football coach supported their opportunity
to play. The girls lost their case in the lower court,
where testimony centered around the issues of the
physical handicap of females and the opening up of
female teams to males should the rule be found unconstitutional against the state ERA. The Court handed
down its decision that the girls might have won their
case had they sued for individual rights instead of initiating a class action. Two years later, 1975, the Supreme
Court of Washington reversed the decision. The judge
ruled that no school district could constitutionally deny
two of its fully-qualified high school students an opportunity to play on the football team entirely on the
grounds that the students were female. It found the
state had no compelling interest other than to see to
it, "equality of rights and responsibilities under the
law shall not be denied or abridged on account of
sex."

Carnes vs *Tennessee Secondary*
School Athletic Association (U.S.
District Court, 1976)

A high school senior brought action against the
high school association to allow her to play on the boys'
baseball team, thereby circumventing its rule against

girls playing contact sports with boys. She was granted the preliminary injunction because the court was critical of the association's willingness to let injury-prone boys compete while denying healthy girls the chance. It also felt that preventing her participation would cause her an irretrievable loss. Lastly, the judge questioned whether baseball should be considered a contact sport.

Hoover vs *Meiklejohn* (U.S. District Court, 1977)

Donna Hoover was selected as a member of her Colorado school's all-male junior varsity soccer team. In September of 1976, the principal of the school demanded that she be dropped from the team because it violated the Colorado High School Activities Association rule limiting soccer teams to boys. She sued for her rights in a class action and won. The Court was extremely biting in its decision. ". . . the evidence also shows that the range of differences among individuals in both sexes is greater than the average differences between the sexes. The failure to establish any physical criteria to protect small or weak males from the injurious effects of competition with larger or stronger males destroys the credibility of the reasoning urged in support of the sex classification. . . . Any notion that young women are so inherently weak, delicate or physically inadequate that the state must protect them from the folly of participation in vigorous athletics is a cultural anachronism unrelated to reality." The judge was no less harsh on the issue of constitutional rights: "The applicability of so fundamental a constitutional principle as equal educational opportunity should not depend upon anything so mutable as customs, usages, protective equipment, and rules of play. The courts do not have competence to determine what games are appropriate for the schools or which, if any, teams should be separated by sex. What the courts can and must do is to insure that those who do make those decisions act with an awareness of what the Constitution does and does not require of them. Accordingly, it must be made clear that there is no constitutional requirement for schools to provide any athletic program, as it is clear that there is no constitutional requirement to provide any education. What is required is that whatever opportunity is made available be open to all on equal terms." The high school association was given the choice to discontinue all soccer teams, field separate teams for each sex with substantially equal support, or let both sexes play on the same team. Lastly, the judge commented, "Should equality of opportunity be measured according to style of play? Must there be 'measure for measure' in each sport? Will girls be hurt by playing soccer with boys? The courtroom is not the place and the adversary process is not the method by which these questions should be answered. Fundamental principles of participatory democracy must not be trivialized by elevating every public controversy to a constitutional level."

Yellow Springs School District Board of Education vs *Ohio High School Athletic Association* (U.S. District Court, 1978)

Two young girl basketball players threatened to sue the school district if it did not let them compete on the boys' team, since no girls' team existed there. Under that pressure the district agreed to bring charges against the high school association which forbade mixed competition in contact sports. Although at the time of writing the case was being appealed, it was decided in favor of the girls. The judge, as previously noted, remarked that the greatest quarterback in pro football history could well be a female who has never had a chance to develop her skills. The ruling did not mandate all coed teams, but simply stated all girls must have the opportunity to try out for teams, regardless of the sport, if they are physically qualified. Said the judge in his decision, "There may be a multitude of reasons why a girl might elect not to do so (go out for a boys' team), reasons of stature or weight or reasons of temperament, motivation, or interests. This is a matter of personal choice. But a prohibition without exception based on sex is not." The high school association had maintained that it modeled its rules on Title IX, but the judge opined that the Title IX regulations were unconstitutional "insofar as they suggest that mixed gender competition, creation of separate teams for girls and boys . . . or creation of an all-male team in contact sports are independent and wholly satisfactory methods of compliance."

Re: Other Cases Concerning Women Athletes

Kellmeyer vs *NEA, AAHPER, NAGWS, AIAW, and others* (U.S. District Court)

This case was settled out of court. Eleven women athletes at Broward County Community College and Marymount College in Florida filed suit against the organizations stating they had their rights to equal opportunity denied by a rule that prohibited women who received scholarships from competing in champion-

ships. After much legal debate, the agencies gave in
and permitted scholarship winners to compete.

Cape vs *Tennessee Secondary*
School Athletic Association (U.S.
Court of Appeals, 1977)

Victoria Ann Cape sued the state high school association for forcing girls to play six-person, split-court
basketball which she maintained breached her rights
under the Fourteenth Amendment. Cape held that she
had a right to play "boys' rules" and that the prohibition against guards shooting deprived her of the opportunity to obtain a college scholarship. Indeed, she had
been told by several colleges she was not a "worthy
recruit" for that reason. Although she filed suit under
both Title IX and the Fourteenth Amendment, only the
latter proved effective (See Cannon vs University of
Chicago). The United States District Court decided in
Cape's favor, stating, "Protection of weaker and less
capable athletes from harming themselves by playing
the strenuous full-court game of basketball is a legitimate objective. However, there are several problems
with the defendants' argument that the classification
by sex bears a rational relationship to this objective.
The use of sex as a criterion for achieving this objective
is both under-inclusive and over-inclusive. Because
there are surely some boys who could benefit from the
split-court, less-strenuous game played by the girls, the
classification fails to include all the weak and incapa-
ble athletes. Similarly, there are female athletes, including the plaintiff, who are willing and able to play
the full-court game. . . . Furthermore, the proof shows
that plaintiff is deprived of the greater health benefits
enjoyed by male players under the full-court rules. And
finally the proof established that the plaintiff, due to

shooting prohibition applied to guards, has a lesser opportunity to attain a college scholarship than she
would if she could play under the full-court rules.
Thus, the Court concludes that plaintiff's injury is significant."

One year later the U.S. Court of Appeals over-
turned the decision. The judges alleged that the split-
court rules were justified by the difference in the
female's physiology and capabilities. "It takes little
imagination to realize that were play and competition
not separated by sex, the great bulk of females would
quickly be eliminated from participation," they noted,
"and denied any meaningful opportunity for athletic
involvement. Since there are such differences in physical characteristics and capabilities we see no reason
why the rules governing play cannot be tailored to accommodate them without running afoul of the Equal
Protection Clause."

Cannon vs *University of Chicago*
(U.S. Circuit Court of Appeals,
1976)

Although neither of these cases actually dealt with
women's athletics, they have a significant bearing on
them. The decisions in these two cases take conflicting
views on whether women may utilize Title IX as a
private right for litigation. The judge in Cannon vs
the University of Chicago maintains that since the government provided a method for corrective action
through HEW, individual women are not entitled to
sue under the statute. In Piascik vs the Cleveland Mu-
seum of Art, the judge took the exact opposite position,
saying the law "implies" women have such a right.
The issue may be resolved in the appeals to follow.

Hill vs *Chamberlain et al.*
(Colorado State University), (U.S.
District Court, November, 1977)

The case of Mary Alice Hill is noted on the opening page of this text. She was fired by Colorado State several times before filing suit against the institution for $3 million. Part of her suit contended the university "utilized subjective non-job related criteria" in its evaluation of employees which adversely affected women. The school maintained that it terminated her because she failed to fulfill an agreement to obtain her doctoral degree. Hill claimed she was the only person on the staff required to sign such an agreement. She brought suit under both Title VII of the Civil Rights Act of 1964 and the Executive Order 11246 employment clauses and the First Amendment, claiming she had been denied freedom of speech since she viewed her firing as an attempt to keep her from speaking out on behalf of the women's program in budget hearings. A Denver judge awarded Hill $65,000 under the First Amendment violations—$50,000 mostly for damages to compensate her for the time from the point she was fired until the case went to court, and $3,000 each from two professors of physical education, a university academic vice president, a chairman of the physical education department, and dean of the College of Humanities and Social Sciences. Although the amount was considered to be "excessive" by the U.S. District Court judge who ruled on the appeal, he also found evidence of sex discrimination in violation of Title VII of the Civil Rights Act of 1964 and awarded her monies to cover back pay only. Judge Richard P. Matsch noted, "Not only was the plaintiff treated less favorably by other faculty members because of her position as a symbol of sexual equality, she was also a victim of a system which had a disparate impact on females."

CHAPTER *4*

Methods of Compliance

As the saying goes, there is more than one way to skin a cat—or more appropriately—more than one way to put a stop to discrimination. Many of the agencies mentioned in previous sections interact with each other and overlap in their duties. Thus, it is often appropriate to file complaints with several agencies. In other cases, a complaint may be referred from one agency to another, or two agencies may work jointly on a reported violation. The sooner the complaint is filed, the better; preferably within 90 days of the discriminatory act because some of the agencies have that as a deadline. Do not worry about where to file first. All complaints should be filed simultaneously for the best results. Even though an agency may specialize in pattern or class action complaints (where facts illustrate a "pattern" of discrimination for a whole segment of people), it never hurts to file an individual complaint anyway. The agency in its review may discover a pattern of discrimination, but it takes the individual complaint to bring it to the office's attention.

EQUAL PAY—SALARY, HOURS, ETC.

1. Equal Employment Opportunity Commission—Complaints may be filed in any of the commission's five litigation centers, eight regional offices and local district offices (Albuquerque, Atlanta, Austin, Birmingham, Chicago, Cleveland, Kansas City, Mo., Los Angeles, Memphis, New Orleans, New York, San Francisco, Washington, D.C. Write the Washington Office or look in the phone book for the address of the appropriate bureau.) The following agencies are also designated authorities to handle individual complaints:

1. Alaska Commission for Human Rights
2. Colorado Civil Rights Commission
3. Connecticut Commission on Human Rights and Opportunities
4. Delaware Department of Labor
5. District of Columbia Office of Human Rights
6. Illinois Fair Employment Practices Commission
7. Indiana Civil Rights Commission
8. Michigan Civil Rights Commission
9. Minnesota Department of Human Rights
10. New Hampshire Commission for Human Rights
11. New Jersey Division on Civil Rights, Department of Law and Public Safety
12. Oregon Bureau of Labor
13. Pennsylvania Human Relations Commission
14. South Dakota Human Relations Commission
15. Utah Industrial Commission
16. West Virginia Human Rights Commission

The EEOC has a specific form that is used for filing charges of discrimination. This may be filled out individually or with the aid of a person in the local office. The agency generally handles individual cases and some patterns of discrimination, while HEW's Office of Civil Rights deals almost exclusively with class action complaints. A copy of the complaint is provided to the institution, after the EEOC has determined that it has some substance. A representative will review all the facts by mail or in person from both defendant and complainant. Should the charges prove to be erroneous based on the facts, the case will be dismissed. If, however, the commission is in agreement that the institution has been discriminating, it will seek a settlement with the administrators. Failing that, the individual has the right to go to court. Some cases may be sent back to the state's Fair Employment Practices Commission or State Civil Rights Commission before they are handled by the EEOC, but the practice of also filing with that agency may speed up the process of compliance.

2. Wage and Hour Division of the Department of Labor—This agency may sue an institution for an employee's back pay. Complaints, which can be in letter form, should be filed with any of the 350 offices nationwide. The address of the local office may be found listed under U.S. Government in the phone book.

3. Office of Federal Contract Compliance—Complaints should be filed in letter form with this agency, but they will be referred for investigation to HEW's Office for Civil Rights. The OFCC seeks pattern cases rather than individual ones. Office of Federal Contract Compliance Programs, Employment Standards Administration, Department of Labor, Washington, D.C. 20210.

4. HEW's Office for Civil Rights—Any person may phone in, walk in or write a letter of complaint to one of HEW's regional offices (Atlanta, Boston, Chicago, Dallas, Denver, Kansas City, Mo., New York, Philadelphia, San Francisco, Seattle) or the national headquarters in Washington. This agency prefers to handle pattern or class action complaints, though it still considers individual problems.

The procedure is to review the facts, usually notify the institution (this depends on which law is being violated), and then seek a conciliation. Should that fail, HEW holds a hearing at which time the defendant may state its case. No further monies are awarded to the institution during this process, but no monies are cut off until the judiciary makes a ruling. The institution has the option of appealing the decision to a five-member reviewing body. If the board upholds the initial decision, all funds are withheld from the school beginning 30 days after that date.

5. State Fair Employment Practices Commission—Aids at the FEPC offices will assist a person with drafting a complaint. The addresses for the local offices will generally be listed under the state (California, State of . . .) in the industrial relations section of the phone book. They may also be obtainable from the state Attorney General's office.

6. State Civil Rights Commission—These can also be located in the same manner as the FEPC. However, formal complaints are not necessary; a letter will suffice.

7. District Affirmative Action Committees

Title IX Type Violations. Unequal treatment of athletes, not reflecting the interest and abilities of women athletes, etc.

1. Regional and national HEW offices.

2. State Department of Education—Some states have laws in the education code that prohibit discrimination against students of one sex or race. Thus, the state may well be charged with the ability to bring suit against violators. Usually, a letter is enough to bring the problem to the attention of the state superintendent of schools. It might also be directed to the state

Title IX coordinator. State Title IX Offices may offer: Technical assistance in responding to OCR guidelines; programmatic assistance in athletics, physical education, vocational education, pupil personnel services and mathematics; awareness training in identifying discriminations and responding to social content concerns in instructional methods and materials.

3. Local Title IX facilitating agency (such as Project Equity in Southern California)—This type of organization can offer to help an institution come into compliance before legal action becomes necessary. Offices can usually be located by contacting the state department of education.

4. Local or district Title IX coordinator—On some occasions one school may be out of sinc with the entire district which is trying to comply. The most effective tactic may simply be bringing it to the attention of the district Title IX coordinator that violations are occurring and that complaints have been filed with HEW, etc. The pressure the complainant brings to bear on the district will find its way back to the principal.

Job Discrimination. Women being overlooked for promotions, failing to hire an adequate number of women, women being excluded from internships, conditions of employment, etc.

1. EEOC—As noted under Equal Pay
2. HEW—As noted under Equal Pay
3. Office of Federal Contract Compliance—As noted under Equal Pay
4. FEPC—As noted under Equal Pay
5. State Civil Rights Commission—As noted under Equal Pay
6. District Affirmative Action Committees

WRITING THE COMPLAINT

Some of these agencies have their own complaint forms, but others do not. In lieu of a printed form, a person has the task of constructing a solid case in a letter illustrating that discrimination occurred. In other words, she must play the part of a lawyer. The most effective complaints are those where the person can show that she was not the only person discriminated against, that others of her sex received the same treatment. By citing "anemic statistics," as well as numerous other situations similar to her own, she can note that a "pattern or practice" of discrimination has developed at the institution. It is not necessary to have a full knowledge of legal language, merely a knowledge of what the law says. The complaint in its simplest form as noted by the ACLU in it's document "Sex Discrimination in Athletics & Physical Education," must include:

1. The names of the individual complainants.
2. The law that was violated. Cite every law that may be applicable such as the Fourteenth Amendment, Title IX, Title VII, Executive Order 11246, the Equal Pay Act, state ERA (if there is one), state public accommodations law (if there is one), state fair employment practices law, other state laws, the written rules or policies of the school itself (check its affirmative action plan if it has one), etc.
3. The precise nature of the discrimination they suffered. Tell the whole story, to the extent you are sure of the facts, including dates, times, people, and places. For example, don't say only that "Mary Smith was not permitted to try out for the varsity track team." You should include facts as to how she applied, who turned her down, dates, reasons given, her background and experience, the fact that there is no women's team or that it is inferior, the details of how it is inferior (less equip-

ment, fewer opportunities for competition, inferior coaching, different level of funding), how she is disadvantaged by not being given the opportunity to try out (i.e., exposure, publicity, opportunity to increase skills, scholarship or pro opportunities).

4. Broader aspects of discrimination, such as lack of affirmative recruiting and funding inequities. If these are relevant to your charge, show how the class of women is disadvantaged by the rule, policy, or system in question. If the school has an affirmative action plan that is not being enforced, describe how it is not being enforced. For employment issues, you may also want to show that the existing plan is legally inadequate.

5. Data and statistics on women in general as it relates to your charge. For example, relevant physiological data about women athletes, or data relating to the increased participation of women in athletics, or the increased availability of scholarships for women athletes.

6. The remedy you propose, whether it's simple (permit women on the men's team) or complex (change the structure of the physical education or athletics department). If you propose affirmative action, submit an outline of what it should contain. If you are dealing with a non-employment related issue, much of the material from the employment area is still relevant, for example, recruiting requirements.[1]

You cannot legally counsel the school or anyone to answer your questions or provide you with information except in the context of a lawsuit (in which you have "discovery" rights to "relevant" information); so it may be that some of the information you need is simply not obtainable at this stage. That should not deter you from proceeding with your efforts, including filing a charge. The charge does not have to be exhaustive; so long as it contains enough information to support your allegation persuasively, it will be adequate.

THE REVIEW

There are also some things a person can do to facilitate an investigation of discrimination by a governmental agency. The Women's Rights Project of the American Civil Liberties Union recommends:

1) Know when HEW is coming. Advise the school EEO officer and the local regional HEW office that your group wants to be notified of any scheduled on-site investigation by HEW. Personal contact with the HEW office to acquaint their representative of your concerns will facilitate communication.
2) Establish your group as a resource group to which HEW can refer easily and quickly for information and the women's perspective on the situation.
3) Do your homework. You must present a cohesive and comprehensive summary of your complaints and proposed changes. Written materials, including tables, charts, affidavits should be carefully prepared. The HEW staff is limited in terms of staff and time. The case you make may have a large impact on the scope and direction of an HEW investigation.
4) Present your case. Where the facts you have are sufficient for a "reasonable suspicion" tell the investigators frankly that the information you have, while not conclusive, indicates a possible violation. It is up to HEW to conduct the investigation. You should provide help and direction, but make sure they conduct a thorough investigation. In many instances they will have easier access to information than your group.
5) Meet personally with the investigators. You should also recruit a number of supporting organizations to present separate testimonies before the investigators.
6) Establish contact with relevant congresspeople—the representatives for the district in which the institution is located and those who are members of the committee that controls appropriations to the institution. Inform

them of your concerns and areas you think should be investigated.

7) Bring complaints about the course of the investigation to the attention of sympathetic congresspeople as well as the regional and Washington offices of HEW.

8) Obtain copies of the report prepared on the HEW investigation. As quickly as possible, submit your comments on the report, pointing out inadequacies and inaccuracies where they exist. You should also point out what's right with the report—if anything.

9) Weigh whether it is in your interest to have some organizing activity or press coverage during the HEW investigation.[2]

LEGAL ADVICE AND FILING SUIT

The most effective enforcement tool in *all* cases of inequity is for a private litigant to hire an attorney. The attorney is familiar with the pertinent legislation and the governmental roadblocks that often hinder nonlawyers. Legal advice is often expensive, but organizations such as Women's Equity Action League, National Organization for Women and the American Civil Liberties Union can render assistance or make referrals to excellent lawyers who specialize in similar cases. Some athletic leagues even have funds they can supply for legal purposes. Teacher unions are a good resource in discrimination cases, because they are familiar with the negotiating process and political substructures of the institution, as well as having legal staffs of their own. Women's coaching associations sometimes also have access to practicing lawyers.

LEGISLATIVE CONTACT

Not only do women need to be familiar with laws that affect them, but also pending legislation. Instead of waiting until laws are passed and then protesting them, women must begin to take an active stand for or against relevant prospective laws. Thus, they can prevent much heartache if the legislature heeds their comments. The best way to let a congressman or senator know your feelings on a piece of action is to send a letter to the state capital, Washington, D.C., or the individual's local office.

The California (CAHPER) journal made these suggestions:

Writing Your Legislator

An effective letter to a legislator is not an art form. It is a straightforward, workmanlike exercise in the use of everyday English that follows a few common-sense rules. The following are recommended:

1) Address your legislator correctly: The Honorable (full name), Member of the Assembly (or Senate), State Capitol, Sacramento 95814.

2) The salutation: Dear Assemblyman (or Senator) (last name).

3) Identify yourself—occupation or organization position, state or chapter office held (if any), etc.; put return address on the envelope as well as in the letter.

4) Be courteous, sincere, factual, specific and brief. Don't however, be so brief that you do not substantiate your position.

5) Whenever possible, refer to specific bills by number and author. If an issue is not in bill form, be explicit as possible in explaining what it is.

6) Most important: let the legislator know how the measure you are writing about will affect his/her district.

7) Letters may be hand or typewritten. In either case, be accurate in spelling, punctuation and grammar—

poor use of English may divert the legislator's attention from the points you try to make.

8) When writing as an individual, use plain or personal stationery; use letterhead stationery when writing for your organization.

9) Some "dont's": don't flatter, threaten, exaggerate, generalize, or flaunt the fact that you are a citizen, taxpayer or contributor; don't guess at the spelling of your legislator's name or initials; don't use mimeographed or form letters or printed postal cards.

Note: This is adapted from *Politics and Legislation,* a publication of the California Teachers Association.[3]

STATE AND NATIONAL ASSOCIATIONS

Many times women know they are being discriminated against, but are fearful of making complaints or unsure of action to take. They need the support of other organizations and other women to feel they are taking the right action. This support can be found in state women's coaching associations, state teachers' associations, athletic directors' associations (which admit women), state Health, Physical Education and Recreation (HPER) associations, and other nonathletic women's groups such as NOW chapters, organizations of women educators, etc.

There are a number of national organizations that can be good resources. The following list is a roster of members of the National Coalition for Women and Girls in Education:

American Alliance for Health, Physical Education and Recreation (AAHPER)

American Association of School Administrators (AASA)

American Association of University Professors (AAUP)

American Association of University Women (AAUW)

American Civil Liberties Union (ACLU)

American Council on Education (ACE)

American Psychological Association (APA)

American Sociological Association (ASA)

Association for Intercollegiate Athletics for Women (AIAW)

Association of American Colleges

Center for Law and Social Policy

Council on National Priorities and Resources

D.C. Commission on the Status of Women

Education Commission of the States

Federation of Organizations for Professional Women

Intercollegiate Association of Women Students

Lawyer's Committee for Civil Rights Under Law

League of Women Voters of the United States

National Association for Girls and Women in Sport (NAGWS)

National Association for Women Deans, Administrators and Counselors

National Association of State Universities and Land Grant Colleges

National Council of Jewish Women

National Education Association (NEA)

National Federation of Business and Professional Women's Club, Inc.

National Foundation for Improvement of Education

National Organization for Women (NOW)

National Student Association

National Student Lobby

National Urban League

National Women's Political Caucus

Project on Equal Education Rights (PEER)
Women's Equity Action League (WEAL)
Women's Legal Defense Fund
Women's Lobby

PERSONAL COURAGE,
COMMITMENT AND ACTION

The religious adage "The Lord helps those who help themselves," may well be rephrased secularly to "The Law helps those who help themselves."

The law is an extremely useful tool in bringing about equal opportunity, but it is far from a guarantee. As it has been pointed out, it is virtually impossible to erase the attitudes that created discrimination. In fact, the law may well have a backlash with men who have been flouting it for many years. Note Hennig and Jardim:

> In fact, we can begin to understand why, if threatened by law that either they (men) welcome the outsiders into their midst or be punished for failure to do so, the insiders can make their system work so as to avoid either outcome entirely.

> What makes this particularly threatening to the future of women in management is that the informal system is at the heart of the middle management function and grows still more critical with every step upward. Few women are a part of this system and most women don't even recognize it exists. Thus a picture emerges in which those people whom we have called the insiders operate knowledgeably and carefully within a system whose membership typically excludes women; a system about which few women know anything very useful; and because it is a system, which reacts to threat to its members by functioning in such a way as to make it even more difficult for women to become a part of it.

Another way of grasping this complex issue is to consider the often quoted statement about the Black movement: "You can legislate against segregation but you cannot legislate integration." In other words, saying a person cannot be kept out doesn't ensure that that person can get in, and more important, stay in. Beliefs, attitudes and assumptions which people have about themselves and each other and their resulting willingness or unwillingness to accept each other are untouched by law.[4]

Equal opportunity cannot be legislated; it must be made. Effecting change has been simplified by Title IX and other equal opportunity laws, but women must learn not to rely exclusively on the nation's legal machinery to provide their opportunities. They must seize the opportunity through courage, conviction, shrewd calculations, and dynamic action.

Women are discriminated against by omission; men omit them from decision-making and women themselves withdraw from the battle-lines for fear of losing their jobs. The rate of attrition for women in athletics is frightening. Since Title IX, women in state high school associations and athletic director associations have observed a distinct trend of *decreasing* numbers of women in athletic administration. Some of this comes, of course, from institutions' attempts to merge male and female departments, thereby eliminating women administrators, but it also comes from a reluctance of women to fight for their jobs and to get involved in the issues.

Where Do Women Go Wrong?

1. Women have frequently not shown the courage to stand behind their beliefs. They are afraid to be labeled troublemakers. Instead of fighting, they throw

in the towel. Willingly they become martyrs. It takes assertiveness and even some aggressiveness—certainly qualities contrary to the usual role of women in society—to hold out in the face of great pressure. Says Ruth Berkey, athletic director at Occidental College in Los Angeles, "If you have strong feelings and you can verbalize them, you must talk to the administration—especially if you have a difference of opinion. If you are afraid to stand up for your opinions, you give in for a long period of time and then it's much, much more difficult to protest at a later time." Women need to be buoyed up by knowing they are legally and morally right in what they demand. Additionally, women who do voice their beliefs often give in too easily. Women are so used to being told "no," that they start cutting down their requests instead of being persistent and pesty until they get what they need. Men see women coaches and administrators as unable to withstand pressure on or off the court. They will begin to grant women respect when they see women *can* hold up under duress. There is no question it is a rough uphill battle, but giving in only means that women can be trampled easier the next time. Somewhere and somehow, women must break the pattern of being silently led to the slaughter.

2. Women accept what they are told. One woman athletic director comments, "We consistently heard, 'Don't worry, dear. We'll take care of you. We have your best interests at heart.' Then you find out those things they are taking care of are falling apart at the seams. Then you know you've been had." It is economically and administratively feasible for male administrators to play the role of the fatherly protectors. It is a role with which most women are very comfortable because they and their forebears have related to men in that way for centuries. But women must begin to

think on their own. For too long they have illustrated
they cannot function unless they are told what to do.
Women need to question what they are told and to question tradition. Athletic tradition has women sewing up
old uniforms while men throw them away and buy
new ones. Women begin to create equality when they,
too, refuse to patch up used merchandise. Administrators often express a feeling that there is plenty of time
to comply with Title IX, thus, women are passively
accepting delays instead of pursuing it with a sense
of urgency. They must realize they are being lulled
into complacency and put an immediate halt to such
delay tactics.

Part of this problem is the manner in which
women accept the limitations that administrators put
on their jobs. Complains one woman, "I'm just a glorified paperpusher. I just make sure the paper gets from
here to there." An assertive woman can *make* her job
more than that.

3. Women tend to stay to themselves and act independently of other women. Instead of banning together
with others of their sex, women, true to their accultura-
tion, tend to view other females as competition. As a
result, they are extremely critical. Tutko and Neal note
that it is bad enough when unathletic men scorn
women for their interest in sports, but "as much harm
has been done by the 'feminine' woman who feels more
secure in her self-concept when she can put the 'masculine' woman in her place."[5] A pattern has developed
where women are self-reliant, but in so becoming, they
have weakened their negotiating base. There is power
in numbers. To achieve equality, women must begin
to focus on issues that can unite them, not divide them.
Athletic directors and coaches should begin to share
their experiences and problems, become enlightened,
encouraged and supported by others in similar circum-

stances. When women come together it is too often the case that there are too many chiefs and not enough Indians. It is essential that women leaders be selected who are articulate and shrewd but forceful in a subtle way. Some women will have to settle for lesser roles, but those who are most passive can lend moral support to the leaders. Either way, they are making a contribution.

4. Women often select the wrong avenues for change. They rail at the establishment about not having equality instead of getting inside it and creating equality. Write Boslooper and Hayes:

> To win the war—and end the femininity game—women will have to play, for the time being at least, a man's game; they will have to work realistically within (not *for*) the existing system. The rules may change to accommodate women; the structure must yield to reform; but the name of the game is likely to remain the same for generations to come.
>
> This is not to say that women should imitate the more corrupt tactics of the masculinity rite nor conceive of victory in male terms. But they will have to work within the existing establishment until they are in a position to change it. To do so, they must cultivate the positive side of those qualities that have been denied them so long in the name of femininity. And, precisely because women have *not* been conditioned to the distorted values that men embrace, they will have a certain advantage in this endeavor.
>
> "I have nothing but respect," Gloria Steinem has said, "for women who win the game with rules given them by the enemy."[6]

Women need to look at ways to gain access to the channels of power. For example, they can go back to school to obtain administrative credentials qualifying them as principals and vice principals to sit on boards of state athletic associations. Instead of being *given* the right to a vote, they *earn* the right. Some women feel they can work to achieve equality in positions of physical education, yet many times women who are not athletic directors are shuffled aside. Thus, they must push for jobs in athletics, not physical education, so they are forces to be reckoned with.

Another failing of women seeking equality is an inability to look for any but the obvious avenues. If the men can use subtle, almost undetectable, methods to keep women in their place, why cannot women use similar tactics to improve their status? A discussion of these shortcomings is not an attempt to stereotype all women. The authors, of course, recognize that many women do not fall prey to these difficulties. However, a large number will recognize themselves in these pages, and therefore, it is important to examine the problems closely.

To cite the problems without proposing strategies for reform is not productive, therefore, the following chapters deal with non-legal (not illegal) methods of overcoming discrimination and achieving equality. Implementing them just takes a little courage.

CHAPTER 5

Getting Along with the Men's Department

(She's Really Just One of the Boys)

Laurie has a new toy, but Daddy does not like it because it makes too much noise. Mother sees no reason why Laurie should have to give it up because of Daddy. Daddy grabs it out of Laurie's hands and Mother and Daddy begin to argue. Meanwhile, Laurie looks up at them and thinks, "They don't care about me. They just want to fight."

This is precisely the predicament of female athletes today in America. In the midst of the warring and in-fighting over equality and rights, they wonder, "Do they really care about me? Or do they just want to fight?" Male and female administrators alike too often tend to forget that their objectives should be trying to do what is best for kids—not for themselves and their individual egos and power struggles. Males in particular fail to see the contradiction in their philosophies that females should not compete on a high level because they are not good enough, and males should because athletics are good for every boy. Many boys' junior varsity teams would be eliminated if the same standard that is applied to girls' sports was applied to boys' sports.

There really are not two separate factions; males and females in athletics are fighting many of the same battles against the administration, the student registration fee boards, the public, etc. An old story illustrates the point. Three people are in a boat in the middle of the lake. One of them begins to saw a hole in the bottom. The other two become quite panicked. Their companion responds, "Be quiet. I'm cutting a hole under my seat, not yours." Horrified, the two protest, "But we're in the same boat, too."

It is neither person's problem—not HERS or HIS—its OURS. Agreement, compromise and negotiation should be the modes of problem solving, not fighting. All administrators must first come to the conclusion that sports are for kids. Barbara Tschida, former president of the Minnesota High School Women's Coaches Association, reflects:

1. Can we assume that all of us agree participation in athletics is or should be an educationally sound experience for KIDS regardless of sex?
2. If we agree with that first statement—can we assume we agree that girls' sports has a place in our school, has merit and should be funded?
3. Could we agree with that statement if we were to say girls' programs may be run concurrently in the same season as the boys'?
4. Can we assume the issue before us today is not "equality" and WHY? But rather of "cooperative planning" and HOW?[1]

Tom Byrnes, the Commissioner of the CIF-Southern Section, pleads:

You cannot let the lunatic fringe get in the way of what we're trying to do for both boys and girls. At one end of the spectrum is the man who says, "No way. We won't give an inch." On the other hand you have the women who want to tear down everything because, "We don't have it right now and we want it." We all have to survive. It doesn't behoove us to polarize ourselves. The more we can work together and give and take, the better off we'll all be. To throw the baby out with the bath water is short sighted.

There is no place for the Ultra-Lib Female or the Chauvinistic Male in the mainstream of intercollegiate and interscholastic athletics; WHAT is right should be the premise, not WHO is right. Women are asking, "How do we get along with *those* men?" Men wonder, "What do those women really want?" The problem is that neither has made an effort to really listen to the other and consider the problem from their point of view. The men are defensively protecting their program from the financial raids on it that they expect, and women are defensively protecting their image from charges of "women's libber," or "the girl that should be home in the kitchen." Men have got to realize that not all women are their wives, their sisters, or their daughters.

The burning question is how men and women in athletic programs can learn to work together? How can they resolve their differences and establish a compatible, cooperative working relationship? No one is wrong or right. There are just different sides to the issues. The rest of this chapter is geared to getting away from the concept of individuals winning. If everyone works together, everyone wins. Sharing, trusting, communicating and respecting—these are the answers to the problems that plague athletics.

OPENING THE DOORS

It seems amazing how much misunderstanding there is between the men and women in athletic administration. The men seem to feel the women want to come in and destroy their programs for the benefit of the girls. The women, on the other hand, perceive the men as villainous oppressors who only want to see women kept in their place. One sensitive and enlightened male athletic director protests to his staff, "Don't stereotype me. I've made my decision based on reason, not discrimination."

The beginning of understanding is to put yourself in the other person's place. Notes UCLA's Judie Holland, "I ask myself: What if there was another sex, called 'X'? Now I've worked for and built women's athletics for 25 years and then X comes along and says, Hey, I want half of what you've got.

"Despite the fact that X had been discriminated against for all those years, I'd feel pretty threatened."

It is not the women so much that the men resent as it is Title IX and the potential damage to what they have strived to build. They do not object to women athletes being treated equally *so long as it does not jeopardize the program for males in any way.* But with finances as they exist, the money can only come from a few sources, most of which are already strained. The men assume that the women want to see the males' program cut back, and the only way to overcome their fear is to constantly reassure them that is not what you want. Demonstrate an unwillingness to accept monies if it too strongly affects the quality of the boys' program. Women must begin to show that they have the interest of male students at heart also.

For men the issue is not rights, but money. Men do not care if women get their rights—it does not affect them directly. But they worry the minute women begin to get money. Title IX is a financial measure, not a political one. Thus, it causes tremendous anxiety to a male athletic administrator. A wise woman will never mention Title IX to a man, but instead will discuss what is good for *all* kids. He is less likely to go into orbit and more likely to respond positively.

In communicating with men and overcoming these barriers there is another lesson women must learn. Men do not like to be told what to do. Margaret Davis, administrative assistant at the CIF-Southern Section, recalled how she came to understand:

"I would say to my principal, 'The volleyball coach wants . . .' and he would say, 'You mean recommend.' That is something many women find hard to do. We have locked heads over it. Some of them have been in charge of their leagues for years and have done the same thing I did, but when it came time to say 'recommend,' they balked."

In another situation, male and female athletic staffs were being combined in one office. Instead of *asking* the men not to smoke, the women *told* them not to smoke. All hell broke loose.

Ironically, these are the same courtesies women wish men would give to them. Once they set the example, the men may well follow.

Both men and women coaches and athletic directors have a great deal to learn about communicating with and relating to each other. One of the ways to improve these abilities is to participate in communication seminars and sensitivity training. One woman athletic director in the Midwest noticed that her basketball coach seemed to rub her male peers the wrong way. She sent her off to a sensitivity training course, and shortly thereafter began receiving comments on how much easier it was to get along with the basketball

" I LIKE YOUR ACT, BUT WILL IT SELL ?.. "

By permission of John Huehnergarth.

coach. The ideal situation, of course, would be to have
the district conduct an in-service program of this type
or pay to send the entire staff to such courses, but this
is seldom feasible. In lieu of it, administrators and
coaches will need to explore these possibilities and the
numerous books on communication independently.
Additionally, women can begin practicing the strategies recommended in the following pages to gain the
respect, trust and honest communication that will create a positive climate for solving problems together
with men. These suggestions were gathered from doz-
ens of women in the field.

  1. Get men's respect by being knowledgeable. Men
assume women are incompetent when it comes to athletics. They are usually quite stunned when a woman
proves she is totally capable—without their help. Take
pride in putting on an extremely efficient, profession-

ally run tournament, one that any male athletic director would envy. The disdain for a woman in athletics
will disappear with proven competency. A woman
principal in a nearly all-male board encountered the
attitude, "What could she know; she hasn't been at it
long enough." As her tenure on the board increased,
her reports were received with enthusiasm, unlike in
her beginning year. Putting together a quality program
will impress male co-workers. Winning a championship is a measure of quality that men understand well.
It does no good to tell a man you can do the job—you
must show him. When male coaches avoid the female
assistant athletic director who is their superior simply
because she is a woman, she must show them she can
authorize their expenditures or get them a salary increase, just as the male athletic director can. The day
a woman is treated "just like one of the boys" is the
day she has overcome the "handicap" of being a
woman. Treating her with kid gloves is chivalrous and
patronizing.

2. Work hard. Men respect hard work more than
any other virtue. Says one male athletic director, "In
11 years as a head coach, I've bought all my uniforms,
so when I hear the girls say, 'We want uniforms like
the boys,' I say, 'Fine, go out and sell fireworks, fruit
cakes, lightbulbs and a lot of other stuff, just like we
did.' " The woman who puts in more hours than are
asked of her, or volunteers to help out the men's department if she finishes her game early, is the one who
wins their praise.

3. Do not ask for more than is needed from the
budget. Do not expect to get something for nothing.
Women must put out the *time* and *effort* to earn what
their departments deserve. It is imperative to remove
the image of women in athletics as money-grubbing
opportunists, and the only way to do that is not to be
one. Try to get the district to pay for some part of the

girls' program. Remarks one woman who did just that, "We'd rather let the boys use the booster club monies, because they are unable to tap the district as a source. So we're not taking from them, therefore, they're more willing to give us a lot."

4. Flatter the men by using them as a resource. Ask them for advice, go to their games, attend men's coaching conferences, join men's coaching and athletic director associations, drive with them to conference meetings and pick their brains. They have been in the business far longer, and there is no reason women should be ashamed to ask advice. In fact, Tom Tutko notes that although men are quick to criticize women, women are still in a stage where they can afford to ask questions or make a few mistakes—but make sure it's only a few. Rather than start from scratch take advantage of 60 years of experience. Build on the positive things men have to offer. Ask for the male athletic director's opinion on a matter. It bolsters his ego. Invite the male athletic director to do the invocation at the women's sports banquet.

5. Get involved in the men's program. Volunteer to help with supervision. Become knowledgeable about the NCAA or whatever concerns the men, so that they feel they can talk to you about it. Offer to act as a timer at their track meets. Know who the men coaches are and know about them as people. Show an interest in their program. One woman athletic director frequently says to her coaches, "Have you talked to a male coach yet today?" Ask if there is something you can do to help them. Express a pride in the total program, not just women's athletics. When speaking to groups, present an image of solidarity. Marna Bauer of Illinois observes, "Women feel if they get involved in the men's program that they are giving in or relenting. Four years ago I was the first woman asked to join the Illinois

"*I DON'T KNOW... SOMEHOW IT DOESN'T FEEL RIGHT PLAYING OUT OF SEASON...*"

By permission of John Huehnergarth.

Athletic Directors Association. I wear the pin with a great deal of pride and I was the first woman to whom they've ever given an award and they gave it to me because I got in and worked. I know that if you want to learn something, you've got to go to the people who have the expertise."

6. Learn to share. Offer, for example, to have the women's matron sew up the boys' old uniforms, if the men's equipment manager repairs the equipment. Provide golf balls for the boys if they run out, for an exchange of tennis balls. Be quick to volunteer, so that it is a goodwill gesture and not a compliance with a request.

7. Be conscious of communication techniques. Do not put any barriers in the way. Invite male athletic directors to women coaches meetings. Place your desk in a position near the only pencil sharpener in the department, so you have a chance to chat with men

coaches as they come by. Discuss decisions with the male athletic director. Never withhold information from him. Let him know what you're doing at all times. Always explain everything carefully and thoroughly, so that he cannot misconstrue motives. Make sure that everyone has the proper information. Breakdowns can occur when a male athletic director does not receive the women's schedule and accidentally plans a men's event in the gym on the same night as a women's event. Be a good listener and do as much business face to face as possible. If the athletic director holds a differing opinion on a matter, discuss it, fight for your point, but realize that he expects you to have a certain amount of courage to stand up for your beliefs. Nevertheless, differences of opinion do not mean he does not like you. It just means there is a difference of opinion. Do not tell him, "You're wrong. I don't like this." Tell him instead, "I think we're wasting money here. I need some suggestions to solve this problem." Don't gripe—communicate.

8. Do not overreact. Remember that fire only makes fire. Calmly assess a situation and then carry out a thoughtful decision. Never act in haste. Try not to be overly forceful. Present the point in a factual, businesslike manner (men can relate to carefully planned factual campaigns). Do not yell discrimination unless it is a very last resort. A chip on the shoulder is sure to be knocked off. One can be assertive without being aggressive by simply stating how one feels and not attacking the other person. Women must avoid being sensitive to jokes about women. Says one woman athletic director, "Because I don't feel resentment toward the men, I don't look for them to put me down. Whereas they might make a joke about girls or women, some women might feel put down and react. I trust them and respect them, even though I may not appreciate the remarks. I have seen women cut their own

"EQUAL OPPORTUNITY IS A RIGHT NOT A FAVOR"

By permission of John Huehnergarth.

throats in meetings by the way they react, probably feeling it was necessary to defend something, but by trying to regain a foot, they lost a mile." One male athletic director spoke of Barbara Twardus, a woman administrator in Seattle, thus, "She's a good guy. She knows how to laugh *at* herself and *with* us." Maintain a sense of humor. The best way to respond to a putdown or an inadvertent slight is with humor. It is an excellent tool for consciousness raising.

9. Be professional. Hold practices regularly. Do things in the manner to which men are accustomed. They become critical when women fall back into the rut of treating athletics as if they were intramurals. This destroys the image of the competent woman, because competency is judged by *their* standards.

10. Do not be afraid to socialize with the men. Much can be resolved over a drink or a casual dinner party of all staff people. A great deal of education and camaraderie can occur under those circumstances. Hold a few social functions with staff members with

or without their spouses throughout the year. Have the women in the department make a spaghetti dinner for the men's department. Invite the men over for coffee and donuts after school, at the snack period, or for breakfast. Do things to get to know each other better—sailing excursions, retreats—anything where people can begin to gauge each other's personalities instead of images.

11. Try to analyze your own prejudices and then try to measure the real people up against the stereotypes. Women frequently make excuses:

> Men are lazy (we teach, they throw the ball out).
>
> Men do not *give* us time and facilities (who owns them, the men or the taxpayers?).
>
> Men do not take care of the equipment.

Look at what is really happening, not what you perceive is occurring.

12. Educate! Take the time to help the men become more accustomed to the philosophies and practices employed in women's athletics. Men become very frustrated with things they do not understand and with which they are not familiar. For example, the men might be unaccustomed to the affidavit of eligibility that women administrators must sign when their teams enter regional championships. There is solid logic behind such a document, but the men are not likely to understand why it is necessary unless it is explained to them. Male school administrators and some athletic directors may be very out of touch with what is occurring in women's athletics. Until recently many men in the institutional administration have had little knowledge of the ongoing women's athletic substructures—leagues, conferences, organizations, that for a long time conducted competition without recogni-

tion. Many of these men think they are just now bestow-
ing on women this opportunity to compete. It may well
be prudent to acquaint them with this "hidden" history,
so they may better understand the women's reluctance
to give up power and decision-making abilities.

13. Former HEW secretary Caspar Weinberger
once observed that much of the discrimination against
women in education exists unconsciously and through
practices long enshrined in tradition. Many men do
not realize that they are being discriminatory. They
must be convinced that discrimination exists before
they will take action to eradicate it. Therefore, men
must be made consciously aware of their discriminatory actions. Again, this can be done with a light touch.
Few people have to be bludgeoned to death with a point
before they can see the logic.

14. Unfortunately, the extremist element of the
women's movement is likely to have a negative effect
on an athletic program. Many men—as well as
women—are turned off by the Gloria Steinems and
Betty Friedans. They associate feminism with "bra
burning" and "cigarette lighting," issues which are so
superficial and very unimportant in the fight for wom-
en's rights. The best way around this is to strongly
avoid the term "women's liberation" and focus on the
right of every *woman* to do as she chooses, or the right
of every *person* to do as he or she chooses. Many independent women who claim, "I'm not a women's libera-
tionist, but . . ." often come to understand that they
actually are feminists when given that definition.

15. Perhaps one of the most difficult tasks of all
is erasing the erroneous impressions that men hold
of a women's program. Take for example the following
paragraphs taken from an article in a suburban paper
in Southern California:

Would you like your son to have a chance to play college basketball?

That chance may be slipping away! The CIF Council will take a vote Thursday that could ruin high school basketball in Southern California.

The proposal is actually designed to give girls sports an equal footing with boys sports, which sounds harmless enough, but the means is a severe cutback primarily in basketball and volleyball.

The proposal would do away with class-level competition (the freshman and sophomore programs), shorten the seasons and place girls basketball with boys basketball in concurrent seasons.

This proposal would not bring girls basketball up to the level of boys basketball, but it would bring boys basketball down to the level of girls basketball by eliminating the important training grounds, the class-level teams.

We strongly urge our local administrators to oppose this measure, but we would like to see them go one step further. We oppose the present structure of all girls athletics. We feel the CIF should eliminate the so-called girls "varsity" programs.

Girls sports are a frivolous waste of the taxpayers money. There is no intensity of competition, there is little in the way of coaching and there is no interest from the general public. What there is is a great deal of expense, and none of these sports are self-supporting.

What we taxpayers are financing is nothing more than a glorified recreation program. What we should be financing then is recreation, in the form of better girls intramurals and a rejuvenated GAA (Girls Athletic Association).[2]

The reporter probably got these wonderfully insightful views from a male coach who has not bothered to look closely at the girls' program in quite some time. He went on to say that few females were willing to make the sacrifices necessary to raise the level of competition to the point where girls' sports would be "entertaining, meaningful or self-sustaining." He also maintained that what made male sports worthwhile was public interest.

First of all, the way to correct the interpretation that women's sports have "no intensity of competition" is to invite these gentlemen down to the games or a tough practice. Many men who complain about the poor quality of women's sports have never seen a game! Secondly, complaints that women's sports is not marketable can be halted with some statistics illustrating the thousands that attend regionals and state high school girls championships. Last, it should be pointed out that "public interest" is not an educationally sound reason for sports for boys or for girls. What justifies athletics is giving young people a chance to experience the excitement of competition and learn about some abstract values such as teamwork and coping with disappointment (losing).

16. Do not be afraid to admit mistakes. It is unwise to defend an action which does not work just because you introduced it. More respect is given to the person who can say, "Sorry, I misjudged the situation," than the person who says, "It's not my mistake. It's his."

17. Spend time cultivating a little public relations. The worst kind of relationship is a "crisis relationship," where the men only see you when something is wrong. Make a point of finding out about them as people—their wives, their kids, their favorite cookies—and show you care. One woman tells the story about the male wrestling coach who cut up her gymnastics mats to use for wrestling. The moral is do not wait till he cuts up the mats. Develop a rapport long before that happens.

18. Cultivate a sense of patience. Do not expect

the moon right away. Tom Tutko remarks, "If a woman athletic director makes very sudden, abrupt moves, she will not be taken seriously. They will think she is playing a role—that she has a little power now and she's taking advantage of it. She instead must start by making slow but sure steps."

19. Publicly praise the men's department for their cooperation. That is a classy thing to do, and a smart tactic. It is positive reinforcement and encourages further cooperation because the men feel appreciated, not taken for granted.

20. Be fair. When the matter requires judgment, consider both the male and female coaches, students and athletic directors. Use discretion and objectivity, instead of looking after *your* best interests. The men will begin to trust your judgment.

21. Take pride in the total program. Begin to speak of it as OUR program, OUR problems, OUR victories and defeats. It makes the men feel as if you view them as allies instead of enemies.

22. Be honest and forthright. This anecdote tells exactly what not to do:

At a major university, the new track stadium was in the last stages of preparation. The men who wanted to hold the last big double dual meet of the year in it, but so did the women. The men, who were paying for the building of the stadium, said it would not be ready by the day of the women's meet, but agreed to pay for their expenses at another nearby track if the women would accept that agreement. The women's athletic director concurred. The men's department subsequently called around to other schools until it located a place to hold the women's meet, made arrangements for the public address system, an announcer, ticket operations, all of the pre-event details, including transportation. As all this was being accomplished, the woman athletic director reported to the campus paper that the men were being selfish with their track and had refused to help them. As a result, the student body was furious with the men's department, the department got stuck for the bills at another school, and the women went back on their word by flatly refusing to compete anywhere but the track stadium. The workers were still painting the lanes while the meet was beginning. The men did not even get a chance to inaugurate their own stadium.

This is not the way to make friends and influence people. Underhanded dealings like the previous one only serve to inflame ill feelings. By and large, men in athletics are up front about their disagreements. These types of actions reinforce the stereotype of the catty, subversive woman. Learn to deal with men the way they deal with each other, and thus, remove their discomfort. If they feel "you're one of the boys," they can relax with you and forget "you're just a woman."

23. Pick specific projects where the whole staff works together—planning a tournament, a curriculum, redesigning the program, Title IX compliance. Getting coaches involved in the problem-solving together gives them common goals to work toward, places them solidly behind common solutions, and gives them a feeling of participating in their own destiny. Present it as a challenge, a problem that nobody particularly sought, but which can be made to work for the good of all, provided everyone puts forth their best effort.

MALE CHAUVINISM

Some classic quotes:

"There is a possibility that a boy would be beaten by a girl and as a result be ashamed to face his family and friends. I wonder if anybody has stopped to think what that could do to a young boy."—Charles Maas, Indiana coach.

". . . historically and traditionally a woman will be a professional person for three or four years; then she gets married, has a family, and abandons professional life as a coach. . . . I hope that'll never change. We've got to have some housewives and some mothers or something's going to happen to this society."—E. Wayne Cooley, secretary of the Iowa Girls' High School Athletic Union.[3]

What should be done about long lines in women's restrooms in stadiums across the country? "Take out the mirrors."—Don Canham, Michigan athletic director.

"To play football you need a bullneck, and I don't like girls with bullnecks."—Woody Hayes, former Ohio State football coach.

On Title IX: "The end result very well could be that we have to give up all athletic programs."—Darrell Royal, Texas athletic director.

"I think we may see the day. Can't you hear it . . . kill the umpress."—Dick Butler, American League supervisor of umpires.

Unfortunately, chauvinism exists and we are stuck with it. How do you combat thousands of years of belief that women are inferior? It is by no means easy. It takes a cool, analytical head, extreme competency and a sense of humor.

The first concept to learn is not to constantly search for discrimination or dwell on it when it is discovered, because that can drain a woman emotionally. To dwell on it is to become like many radical feminists, bitter and defensive, unable to deal with men at any level. The result causes a woman to become too emotionally caught up in the search for discrimination, which in turn makes her unable to discern the real obstacles in her path. Instead of bettering her own skills, she uses chauvinism as an excuse for failure.

Men and women alike are subject to smatterings of chauvinism simply because of years of indoctrination. Think back to possible times when you assumed a woman who answered a phone at a company was a secretary and not an executive. Many men are just not aware of their prejudices and thus, they must be subtly and tactfully pointed out.

The following are some male chauvinist misconceptions about business women compiled by Marcille Gray Williams in her book, *The New Executive Woman:*

1. You really don't want an executive job or a promotion. In 1965 Harvard Business Review concluded from a study that top corporate executives believed that women really don't want more than just a mediocre job, that we really don't want responsibility.

2. There must be something wrong with you. They believe that most successful women are neurotics, or bitches, or both. The more successful you become, the more aberrant the male deems your personality.

3. Men are forced to behave differently around you. Men love the jungle aspects of corporation life (VERY TRUE OF COACHES). They like the real he-man fighting for survival amidst a hostile environment. The intrusion of women threatens them. They believe we will require them to behave differently. They believe that we will deny them some of their male rituals.

4. He can't take you to lunch (what will everyone else think?).

5. You're too emotional. They fear that during times of stress, we'll fold under the pressure. (It's been

known to happen.) The only way to combat this mis-
conception is to demonstrate an icy stability during
times of stress.

6. You need protection. They feel the need to fa-
ther you and protect you from the harsh realities of
life (especially their sex hungry male colleagues). Deal
with this male chauvinist tenderly because he could
become your mentor. He's the kind that will.

7. You'll accept less salary or benefits. Just for the
opportunity to get the job. You may try this approach
(when getting started) to get your foot in the door. But
never accept less pay once established.

8. You're out to usurp his masculinity and/or his
job. He automatically assumes that a woman is a feminist, and that means she is out to usurp his masculinity, piquing his feelings of inadequacy.

9. You have no authority. Men may treat a woman
as though she is an executive, but when it comes to
business he will go over her head because he truly
believes the authority lies in some male above her.

10. Your home responsibilities take precedence
over your career.[4]

Men have some very creative methods of putting
women in their place. A smart, successful woman has
to be equally creative to parry them. The following
are some attacks and counterattacks:

"While it may never be easy for a man to lose his
job to a woman," maintains Dr. Joyce Brothers, "it becomes less painful if he feels that woman is not his
equal, but is a rare creature with whom it would be
almost impossible to compete. This fear of competition
with a near-equal may be a significant factor on why
insecure men and woman are often particularly eager
to maximize the differences between male and female.

The greater the differences are made to appear between the sexes, the more secure both male and female can be in winning and losing."[5] In this type of situation, it may well be to the woman's advantage to allow him to perceive the differences as notable. In other circumstances, however, such as when she is being discriminated against, it is prudent to point out the similarities between herself and men who are treated with more respect or given more credit.

Men exploit women's emotional vulnerability. They attempt to control women through intimidation, because extreme pressure can result in tears or other emotional displays that clearly mark a woman as incompetent to be a manager. The way to avoid this tactic is to never cry before male co-workers and show a cold emotionless side when pressured. Save the breakdowns for a private scene. Scream at the guy who runs a red light ahead of you—but not at the administrator who demanded next week's report today.

Men will protect you as they would their wives or daughters. This is a form of chivalry that can be just as degrading as an out-and-out putdown. It is very deceptive. Women can think they are getting ahead because they interpret chivalry as respect, when, in truth, it is far from it. Chivalry is unnatural; it keeps a man on edge. He cannot accept a woman as long as he has to look out for her. It places her in an inferior position. This manifestation usually occurs when there is only one token women in a department, but it signals that the men will not let any more women into the department simply because they cannot afford to treat colleagues with chivalry; they have to be taken out of the context of wife or daughter.

Wives can also be a threat to a woman in an office dominated by men. It behooves the woman administrator to get acquainted with the wives of the men, so that they do not view her as trying to "take away" their husbands. A woman can tell a great deal about how a man will treat her by (1) whether his wife works and what she does, (2) whether he has all daughters. Dr. Judith Stiehm, a specialist in the field of sexual politics, says, "If a man is married and his wife does not work, then he has a 'two-person career.' He and his wife together are making his career possible and he obviously is not in a position where he is going to be very accepting of a woman in a similar position, because if it takes two of them to do the job, he'll never believe just one woman alone can do it. In that situation you'd better start walking on water." Stiehm holds that a man with a professional wife and/or all daughters relates far better with women. She comments, "If a man has boys and girls or just boys, you can forget it. Boys are raised to be boys and girls are raised to be girls in a mixed family. But in a family where it is just girls, they are raised very differently. The men's hopes for their expectations are not like those for girls in families where there are boys." Jardim and Hennig's study bears Stiehm out. Of the 25 women top executives surveyed, nearly all were only children.

Men have a way of reminding women of their roles as females by performing certain courtesies such as opening doors and lighting cigarettes. Usually, the slight is unintentional. It results from many years of habit. If a man offers the courtesies of the "old school," accept them graciously without making a fuss, but at some opportune time drop the hint that you prefer to be treated otherwise. Save your energy for the important issues.

Though you may perceive you are being accepted by men, that may not be the case at all. Stiehm's research on women in the military academies revealed that the females felt they were being accepted, while the males felt the women were not accepted at all. They were still considered outsiders. Here a male confidant on the staff is very helpful to elucidate precisely what your status is.

However, be suspicious of young male colleagues who are in competition with your job. They may seem to be allies, but they are likely to cut your throat. Despite the image that older men are mostly diehard chauvinists, some are inclined to be mentors, and somewhat more trustworthy than competitors who have something to lose by supporting you. It is wise to be very competent and a touch aloof, so that they hold a bit of awe for you.

Subverting a woman's work is another male technique to keep a woman from feeling or appearing equal. According to Dr. Marythea Grebner of Southern Oregon College, the best way to deal with that, as well as some of the sneering insults behind her back, is to have patience and occasionally blow off steam to a sympathetic colleague, co-worker, boss or friend. Although it is unlikely that a man would betray another member of the old boys' club, if he thinks enough of the woman, he might carry her defense to the boss, requesting he look into the sabotage.

One of the most degrading things a man can do to a woman is to proposition her. This takes their relationship out of the context of business person-business person and puts it on the male-female level. It is probably the most difficult problem a woman in a chauvinistic environment faces, especially when the perpetrator is her boss. Hennig and Jardim suggest a woman should not "play the game." She should act as if she did not hear the pass, did not see it or understand it.

Instead she should immediately revert to business matters, such as responding, "What time do you need the
gym tomorrow?" Tom Tutko says:

> The first thing a woman must realize in that situation
> is that person carries some degree of threat. She must
> keep that in mind. However, if she is insulted or hurt,
> that is the purpose of it and she is already playing into
> it. Ignoring it is the best tool. But if it gets so offensive
> she can't ignore it, then she should tell the person in
> private that it is really insulting. Say something like,
> "It may seem like a small thing to you, but it doesn't
> help you, it doesn't help the program and it doesn't help
> our working relationship." The third action I would
> take if the person does it, particularly in public, is to
> say, "You know, Hank, we have talked about this pri-
> vately that I think it's demeaning and degrading. And
> I'm telling you now in public that I would really appre-
> ciate your not doing it." Lastly, if he did not refrain, I
> would write to the president of the university and ask
> him to do something about it.

Hennig and Jardim further suggest keeping a di-
ary of remarks and circumstances, including witness's
accounts or proof, that can be presented to superiors
in the event it becomes necessary. This is particularly
important when a woman makes allegations that a
man is giving her an ultimatum of submitting or losing
her job. One more thing a woman should do is examine
her own dress or behavior to make sure she is doing
nothing that might be the slightest bit inviting. A very
businesslike manner—and that is not to say un-
friendly—will often curtail such acts.

A related means to put a woman in her place is
to challenge her right to hold her position, to constantly
make insulting remarks about her and her capabilities.
The way to handle that is to ignore it and to once again
refer back to business matters. Hurt, hostility, hysteria

are the reactions he wants. If you don't play the game his way, he will eventually come around to playing the game yours. Anticipate such remarks and prepare some answers so you are not caught off guard. Humor goes a long way in dealing with these types. A group called the Feminist Invention Group, Inc. (333 E. 49th Street, New York, New York 10017) puts out small booklets, *Here Are the Answers to Those Male Chauvinist Putdowns.* A few samples:

> Man: What do women want?
> Woman: Power!
> Man: How come you're not married?
> Woman: Sheer luck!
> Man: A woman's place is in the home.
> Woman: We've got a place for you, too.
> Man: If you're so liberated when are you going to take me out?
> Woman: When I take home your paycheck.

Working with chauvinistic men is hard even when they do not use typical putdowns, but are merely resistant and unresponsive to women. Sometimes this requires an out-and-out confrontation to bring the issues to a head. In one instance, for example, the male athletic director was hoarding the money, and the woman assistant put it very bluntly to him, "You're telling me kids have to have a certain kind of anatomy to be entitled to some of the budget?" In another case, a woman went before the high school association's male-dominated committee to work out an equitable season of sport. She read a very biased article that stated girls' sports had no value, and accused them of agreeing with it. In a third incident, the male vice-principal allowed the male athletic director to report directly to him but refused to talk to the woman athletic director, forcing her to go through the physical education chair. The

woman director pointed out the inconsistency and refused to work through the physical education chair.
She explained that much could be simplified and
speeded up through direct communication. He eventually saw her point and relented.

Says Tutko:

> It takes a very strong, courageous, but obviously
> very mature female to deal with the old diehard football
> coach-type of man whose mentality is that women do
> not belong. Why? She's got to be able to understand
> where he is coming from, listen to the tack he takes
> and then stick to her guns. It's so easy when she gets
> in the position of power of being inclined to retaliate,
> but fire only makes fire. The ones I know who have
> been successful have stuck to their guns, remained
> strong and not attacked in return because that is child-
> ish. They formed policies and made it clear where they
> stood. They were not going to back down, implying that
> they were entitled to what they were getting. I hate to
> say, but where you have domineering men like a Woody
> Hayes or Darrell Royal, it is simply a matter of fact.
> Women must produce pure facts, go strictly by the book.
> Everything is written on paper. There are no gentle-
> men's agreements because so much of it can be pur-
> posely misinterpreted. Any attempts to get him to be
> humanistic, to change the man in any way are very
> remote.

Where a woman holds rank over men, there are
potential problems. One of the nation's few women
high school athletic directors for a combined program
recalled the time a male football coach on an opposing
team refused to end the pre-game warmups so the
game could get started on time. She politely asked him
and he refused again. Suddenly he turned on her yell-
ing, "No damn woman is going to tell me what to do!"
Fortunately, as his superior, she sternly responded, "I

don't choose to discuss it on your level of language and you take your team off the field or I will go to your administration." After the game, she reported the scene to his athletic director and it never happened again.

Although it sounds almost sexist to note it, one of the most effective tools a woman has in dealing with chauvinism is her femininity. Remarks Williams, "As long as you're not devious or insincere, using femininity is fighting fair."[6] In the chapter "The Power of Femininity" within Williams' *The New Executive Woman* are a number of excellent strategies for employing one's femininity fairly and effectively.

Male-Female Groups

Dealing with male chauvinism one-on-one is vastly different from encountering it in a group environment. When a woman is the single female in an all-male department, she experiences different behaviors than if there are several women involved. Either way, men react differently to women individually than they do collectively. The man who seems to be your best ally in private may revert to the role of "good old boy" when with his male peers.

Hennig and Jardim have made the following observations:

> A woman's presence will change the group's identity. The group is no longer all-male. The traditions we have grown up with mean that a woman's presence will be seen and felt (not necessarily thought through) as lowering the social and sexual status of the group, thus reducing the identity-affirmation aspects of group membership. Yet this woman may well advance the group's intellectual status. She will in effect be a test of the group's orientation to task achievement. To what

extent will they give priority to the task to be done? To what extent will they instead concern themselves with a sensed diminution of the other aspects of their former status? The chances are they won't know—and remember these are not issues which present themselves in a conscious, clearly thought-through form. They are for the most part emotional, self-esteem issues rather than rational ones. So they will test her, and they will test her on all three dimensions—intellectual, social and the explicitly sexual.

. . . .

If these incidents occur in a group in which you are the only woman (and they often do) it is even more important not to respond. If you do, hoping for support from the other men in the group, typically you won't get it. At best you will get silence from the others, and that won't help how you feel. At worst one or two will actively support your attacker, particularly if you respond in a way that seeks to put him down.

So don't respond. By not responding, by ignoring the incident, you relieve the others of a burden they don't want and typically won't accept—which is to support your own necessarily defensive challenge to their concept of themselves as men. They will leave you to fight this battle alone because, in front of you, a woman, they're not going to do each other in. If you want support from men on this issue you will find you get it not by asking for it, but by proving you can weather the strain.[7]

Williams further notes that the best way to unbond a male group is to find a common denominator between yourself and the men. "Bonds exist between people who attended the same school, are close in age, share same religious or political beliefs, same kind of food, etc. . . . (sports). However, if men have bonded in a group to reinforce a sense of masculinity, you are in trouble."[8]

Two fascinating studies have explored the male-

female group dynamics. The first was conducted by
Robert W. Shomer and Richard Centers.[9] They measured the degree of feminism on the part of males involved in six different groups. They discovered that
when one woman was present in an all-male group
where the leader or "experimenter" was a man, there
was an extreme amount of chivalry, a feeling of protection for the poor helpless female. Conversely, in a
group that was all male, the maximum amount of male
chauvinism existed. When the group was half male-
half female with a male leader, there was a balance
of chauvinism and chivalry. Yet, when all of the group
was male with a woman leader, there was a slight re-
duction in chauvinism but still not much chivalry because she was in the dominant role.

The second study was performed by a medical doctor, Carol Wolman, and a Ph.D., Hal Frank. They looked
at six groups consisting of one woman and the rest
men. The result was that four of the women were considered "deviant" by the men, producing a feeling of
depression on the part of the women; one woman selected the role of outsider and made the best of it, and
the sixth woman through her competence and low-key
attitude was accepted as a low status member of the
group. The men tended to ignore assertive actions by
the women, and stereotyped all of their behaviors as
"feminine." Men avoided acting as an associate or ally
of the women because they felt they would also be considered deviant in so doing. The women's sexuality was
either ignored or considered a threat, either way creating a greater distance between the female and male
members. In each group, the women found themselves
caught up in double binds: Trying to become accepted,
a woman increased her interactions with the men,
which caused greater distance; if a woman acted
friendly, she was thought to be flirting; if she seemed

weak, the men protected her; if she was apologetic,
she was considered submissive; if she displayed anger
at what was being done to her, she was seen as competitive and bitchy. When a woman employed a tactic that
was associated with femininity, it emphasized the
differences, but when she used techniques that were
considered masculine she set herself up as a com-
petitor and a threat. Either way, she increased her
deviance.

Wolman and Frank point out that when the men
are faced with losing their "hunting-group" atmosphere they either mourn its loss with resulting hostility or ignore the women in order to maintain its existence. A woman, in their eyes, diminishes the group
because if she acts weak, one of them is responsible
for caring for her, a "soft, non-macho" activity. They
view her as a threat to their masculinity, should she
be more successful than they. Her sexuality might create a sexual rivalry among the men, thereby unhinging
their male-bonding. Lastly, by associating with her, a
man presents himself as being on "her level," thus creating doubts about his masculinity.

The researchers feel that there are ways single
women in a group can overcome some of these problems. One method is to understand that the men will
be hostile for awhile and accept the role of the outsider
or low status member without becoming depressed
over it. A woman then gives the men time to get to
know her instead of forcing interaction. This role
calls for avoiding all flirting and emphasis of sexuality.

Secondly, she can introduce another woman into
the group if she cannot cope with her deviant status.
Another solution is to discuss with the leader in private
her unhappiness and make him see the dynamics of
the situation, pointing out the stereotyping.

"Alternately," state the researchers, "she could share her feelings about being the lone female, and try gently to raise group consciousness. This takes much patience, strength and emotional stability. If she remains silent, the men may eventually notice that their view of her is no longer being reinforced by her and give her another chance to join the regular members. If the men can accept the loss of their all-male group and work through their hostility toward the woman who caused it, then they can see the hostility as a group phenomenon rather than something that she as an individual deserves. Then, they may release her from the deviant role."[10]

MERGING

When is a merger of male and female athletic departments viewed with enthusiasm? About every third leap year. Seriously, mergers meet with least resistance when male and female staff members get along well together and look forward to working closely in the efforts to bring the best possible program to athletes of both genders.

These types of mergers are rare because people usually feel as though they are giving up something—be it power, autonomy, freedom, time, effort, energy, or independence. But that view is destructive. A merger can be a *gaining,* not necessarily a *losing.* Merging is certainly not avoidable when mandated by the institutional hierarchy, but it does not have to be destructive. Instead, it should be looked upon as constructive, an opportunity, and one that is inevitable. Sure, the growing pains are difficult and there will be much unpleasant conflict along the way, but out of that conflict will come a great sense of achievement if everyone is treated fairly.

Title IX recommends against merging if one sex is disadvantaged by it (women are given subservient roles in administration, less number of positions are open to women, etc.). But since the law requires equal opportunity for both sexes, many institutions are viewing merging as a logical step toward equality. In reality, merging is occurring for several reasons—economic and administrative efficiency, "outside" pressure, better utilization of staff expertise and facilities, and more consistency in program goals and policies.

There is no question that merging some departments has significantly curtailed the women's programs at some institutions, but at others it has noticeably increased opportunities. The difference has largely been the personalities involved, their willingness to compromise, and the administration's commitment to women's sports.

Emotional and Philosophical Implications

When two departments are *forced* to merge, there will be conflict. However, Hollmann and Hollmann see that as a positive influence:

> Conflict within an organization provides a mechanism for survival and growth in a changing environment by affording the opportunity for (a) dissent; (b) reassessment of values, norms, goals, and power relationships within and between groups; (c) stimulation of innovation from existing personnel or through personnel changes; and (d) establishment or re-establishment of cohesion and unity—the conflict itself can increase cohesion within each conflicting group, and resolution of the conflict may increase unity between the conflicting groups.[11]

The hostilities, misperceptions, and differences between male and female coaches and administrators can be reshaped and refocused for positive uses with the proper guidance. The following program developed by Parkhouse and Holmen was designed to facilitate the merging of physical education or athletic departments. It has been tested on over 200 men and women and proves to be very successful.

A series of instruments are used to figuratively x-ray the department; assess the climate as it currently exists. Each instrument is designed to evaluate a different aspect of the department as follows:

1. *Athletic-Physical Education Climate Assessment Instrument (APECAI)*—This is an 80-item scale which is administered three times to each male and female member of the athletic department. The participants indicate the extent to which each item describes a) how we see ourselves (females respond to the women in the department and vice versa), b) how we see them ("them" refers to members of the opposite sex in the department), and c) how we *think* they see us. In reality, the APECAI helps members of the department become aware of areas of agreement and it pin-points where the discrepancies exist between the two groups.

2. *School Athletic and Physical Education Environment Questionnaire (SAPEEQ)*—This is a 16-scale diagnostic instrument used as a basis for goal setting (what the department would like to have and what can be done to get there).

3. *Departmental Characteristics Description (DCD)*—This is a 32-item Likert-type scale which describes the department's characteristics rather than its functioning.

4. *Task Influence and Work Interaction Scales*

(TIWIS)—These two scales indicate the degree to which other members of the department and institution influence a person's work and how much interaction exists between individuals.

Based on data generated from the above assessment tools, an action research process (ARP) is used to augment the positive aspects of the department and reduce areas of resistance or conflict.

The next step in the ARP process is to distribute a copy of the male and female average scores per item to each participant. Explore those areas where the males and females disagree. Are there real differences in definition or opinion:

1. Do we agree in describing the same thing or do we actually disagree?
2. How well can we predict what the others say about us?
3. How accurate are our predictions?

Once it is determined where there is a very real disagreement, discuss those items and also where there is an agreement of opinion. When all of the people understand the perceptions of themselves and each other, in addition to the perceived goals, department functions/characteristics, etc., the group should begin to try to reach some agreement on the following questions:

1. The forces which lead to or support merging
2. The forces which prevent or inhibit merging
3. The relative strength of each of the forces
4. Ways to increase the strength or number of positive forces
5. Ways of reducing the strength or number of negative forces.

From that point, the group needs to begin setting specific goals and objectives that can help to attain those goals. The goals can be seen as major changes that must be accomplished for merging to succeed. They should be based on the positive forces which, hopefully, have been strengthened. The objectives consist of two types: First, those which can be accomplished by the participants, generally of the "social exchange" type—giving up this in exchange for that—so both groups realize a net gain from the exchange. Second, the objectives known as distributive justice on which outside assistance is needed to accomplish or to insure fairness to all parties involved.

Lastly, these goals and objectives are set down in contracts between members of one department, members of the department and the institution, or the department and/or others as needed. Deadlines for the accomplishments of the objectives are included within the contracts. Sample objectives might be:

1. The men agree to give up one-half of the athletic facilities during "prime" practice time for improved office facilities and secretarial support, previously dominated by the women.

2. The department members request that the institution appoint one male athletic director and one female assistant athletic director who would operate in that capacity for one year, at which time they would reverse their jobs.

Each contract will require a series of established review dates. This can be done at monthly staff meetings, for example. In addition, the contract must have a final agreement date by which time the project should be completed. Progress reports and modification of contracts, as needed, should involve all the original participants or their selected representatives.

It is vital that all of the real and perceived problems are out in the open before a merger is attempted.

That may mean some unpleasant scenes, but both genders must come face-to-face with the others' feelings.

These conciliatory actions can be continued through summer workshops at which time the practical aspects are worked out by all concerned.* Additional help can be sought from facilitating agencies like Project Equity in California. The regular staff meetings, which members of both sexes should be required to attend, are an ongoing attempt to compromise with each other and confront the issues. These can be very formalized with agendas and operating rules (Robert's Rules of Order) where the women feel insecure and the men feel threatened because they fear women will introduce topics which they did not know were coming; or they can be very informal in departments where the staff is building a good rapport. The benefit of such joint meetings is that each member is fully informed and involved in activities in both ends of the program. Another method of creating a better climate is putting men and women on committees together, working toward a common goal. This gives them a feeling of shared purpose and a chance to see each other as allies instead of adversaries. A very important factor is the administrator's anticipation of problems between staff members. If these can be spotted, they should be ironed out before they affect the rest of the staff.

These procedures *should* bring about a peaceful and successful merging of departments, but they are no guarantee. In rare circumstances, the men are just plain uncooperative and domineering. Although no

---

* A detailed description of the action research process (ARP) is presented in the following source: Parkhouse, Bonnie L. and Holmen, Milton G. "Action Research Paradigm to Facilitate Merging Male and Female Athletic or Physical Education Departments." *Research Quarterly,* Volume 49, Number 2, May, 1978, pp. 228–236.

one should go into a merger with this thought, it bears noting that nothing is irrevocable. Should the women discover that the men are taking more than their share of the funds, or that the men are literally destroying the women's program, there is the option to seek a separation of departments from the administration. This should not, however, be done until the merger is given a year or two on a trial basis.

Practical Implications

A merger cannot be just a handshake and then a helter-skelter attempt to consolidate offices and services. It must be a well-planned and documented coalescence, complete with a timetable and a reevaluation of every person's job.

It is extremely important that the order for merging comes from the top in an administration, so that those involved in the merger are aware of the administration's strong support of the idea. That optimism may filter down to some of the staff. The administration, if not bound by prior commitments, should attempt to select male and female athletic administrators who can work together without animosity. Choosing the personalities is a key to making it work. One problem that dooms many mergers is the selection of a biased person as the athletic director. This person cannot be discriminatory—either in favor of a sport (football or basketball) or a sex. (This fear is also present when women are given jobs as athletic directors over combined programs.) Either one must go out of his or her way to show that he or she will be fair.

The plan for a merger, which should be drawn up with the input from those who will be affected, must be put on paper. The first task is to come up with a common philosophy and goals. It may be difficult, but it is not impossible. Secondly, evaluate the staff positions, look at what jobs can be consolidated, where duplication can be eliminated, where paperwork and tasks can be simplified. One important thing to note is that giving women and men crossover duties (responsibilities for athletes of the other sex) encourages trust, competence, and understanding. All of the lines of communication and authority must be clearly defined for members of the staff. Women coaches may have to discover that they report to a male assistant, and some male coaches must learn to report to a female assistant. Coaches need to understand that they do not go to the man simply because he is a man. Similarly, coaches must realize that they have to go through administrators of another sex for approval of budgets, etc.

Thirdly, the relocating of the staff is important. Where are the tasks most effectively carried out? Does the secretary need to be near both the male athletic director and female assistant athletic director? Should the male and female basketball coach be in the same office? Should there be coed training facilities? How can communication best be facilitated? If there are two buildings (formerly girls' education and men's athletics) how can people be rearranged without regard to sex? If that is the case, is another satellite training area required to be put in what was formerly the girls' physical education gym? Beware of simply crowding the women's sports staff into an already crowded men's sports office. An answer to avoiding that is perhaps the addition of an inexpensive used house trailer. If it is not possible to relocate the staff in an integrated fashion (because of boys' and girls' locker rooms surrounding the offices) then a joint lounge or meeting room must be established where coaches and administrators spend their lunch periods, hold meetings and discuss common issues. That is where the coffee pot should be; where both sexes can convene.

Fourth, the planning will entail whether to join two budgets or leave them separate. Will like sports get like budgets? What will be the financial priorities? If both male and female basketball coaches have one joint budget, is each given $250 to spend or are they jointly given $500? The latter is unwise because one is likely to assume the other is spending too much. It is important that more than one person have control over the budget in a high school, or one *objective* business manager in a college. Money is power. In a high school, a shrewd female athletic director will volunteer to handle the books in exchange for the men handling the politics (negotiating with the male administrators for additional funds). Keeping an excellent set of books—or if the men keep them—an extra set of books, protects both the male and female athletic director. He cannot be charged with cheating if both of their books concur, or if his books check out. The books may also be a good tool for the woman athletic director. She can go to him and say, "I see here where we've bought two sets of uniforms for the boys' volleyball team in the last two years, but none for the girls. I have to explain to them why. Can you help me?"

The next task is to look at the policies—hiring, firing, promotion, seniority system, student discipline, uniforms, scholarships, inventories, facilities, supervision, salaries, support services, etc. How can they all be made uniform? What are the priorities? Do the women get use of the Sports Information Director 25 percent of the time, or 50 percent? Will the women have access to a computer printout on students' grades now that they are part of the men's department?

Facilities are a major factor. How are they to be divided and utilized to their best advantage? Will there

be a coed training room? Is there to be one or two equipment rooms? By whom and how are the locker rooms
to be supervised? Who pays for the added cost for lighting and maintenance? Where will the equipment for
coed teams be stored? Men's gym? Women's? Neutral
location? Paperwork and mundane routines must be
made consistent. Are all the same forms used for male
and female athletes? Are all insurance contracts col-
lected and issued in the same manner? Do both the
men and women coaches use the game contract?
(Women are just now employing them.) There are
some very subtle changes that must occur in a merger.
For example, the male athletic director has the authority to call for a bus himself, but a woman athletic director is required to go through the administration. These
kinds of inconsistencies are easily spotted in a combined program and must be eliminated.

CHAPTER 6

Manage Men(t)

Men are not going to hand over the keys to the vault or open the doors to the facilities without some coercion. But it does not mean women must instantly resort to heavy-handed tactics of invoking the law. Going through established administrative channels or finding new ways to create change are strongly preferred. Alternative procedures must take the path of *least* resistance.

All the previous skills and strategies may be useless in an environment where the men can discount or belittle a single woman. Says one woman, "There are times when you are alone and can get no support that you have to keep your mouth shut. The odds get to be 2,000 against one. Those times are just not worth it. You must have a lot of belief in yourself and know the limit of pressure you can take to hang in there."

What is the alternative? Group action. Notes Ruth Halsey, founder of the California Women Coaches Academy, "You can make waves, but they won't listen unless you have numbers behind you. You need an organization." There are countless advantages to aligning with others, among them:

It is safer. A school cannot fire all of its coaching staff or women faculty members without creating a dramatic media sensation.

Women can draw support from each other in times of stress.

There are more people to do the work.

Numbers are impressive to administrations. They make schools face the fact that there are more than a few dissidents.

The wider the expertise of the group, the more knowledge can be assembled.

There is greater visibility for the cause when a group of people assemble to address it.

There is power in numbers. Such a group can act as a voting bloc or a lobbying organization.

Women need other women to bounce ideas off and to share problems.

Women can use each other as resources, boosting each others' reputations.

Women can exchange information about sympathetic male sources and pool their influences with them.

Much of the subsequent information comes from the American Civil Liberties Union's *Sex Discrimination in Athletics and Physical Education* and AAHPER's *Equality for Women in Sport.*

THE "INSIDE GROUP" EFFECT

It is vital for women to develop formal and informal organizations and networks that can help them advance. These groups can be of several types:

Branches of National Organizations. Although many times women in athletics and physical education fear association with "radical" feminist groups, membership in these organizations is becoming increasingly less radical and more middle-of-the-road.

Departmental. All of the women in the department act as a unified force.

Interdepartmental. All women on the faculty of the institution.

Task Force. With student, faculty, coach, administration and Title IX officers represented. (Student groups will be discussed later.)

Interorganizational. Women coaches from many schools, women athletic directors, women educators, women in the league. Select and recruit a number of women who are enthusiastic *doers,* who are action-oriented and do not mind taking on additional work for the cause. Utilize these people as a core—organizing, seeking new members, planning meetings. Compile a mailing list of potential members and arrange a meeting time and place. The initial notice, which may be placed in newspapers, newsletters, sent out in letters to prospects and read at women's organizations, should include:

1. Announcement of formation of the group
2. Purpose
3. General goals and objectives
4. Date and place of first meeting
5. An RSVP number.

Before the first meeting, the core group should develop an agenda. It is important to be organized in the initial presentation so that people will want to be part of the group. In order to keep down the amount of "busy work," it may also be a good idea to write a constitution (see Robert's Rules of Order), which can be presented for ratification at the meeting. Establishing some minimal dues to pay for operating expenses may be necessary.

Undoubtedly, at the first meetings there will be a large turnover of people; therefore, the core group should be prepared to hand out weekly updates on accomplishments by the group as a whole and committees individually. The following tasks should be accomplished in the initial meetings:

1. Keep attendance list.
2. Ratify constitution and elect officers.
3. Spend the major part of the time discussing the issues. Summarize what has been learned through initial research.
4. Establish work groups and assign specific tasks:
   a. Correspondence/Communication
   b. Research
   c. Etc.
5. Establish a list of priorities.
6. Set goals and determine deadlines.
7. Decide on a next meeting date and place.
8. Determine a way in which members will be notified of developments.

Much of the work will fall on the shoulders of the core workers; however, for the organization to operate at maximum efficiency, it is best to delegate a large part of the work.

Goals

This is where the long-term plan produced by an athletic program can be of tremendous assistance. It gives the organization a guide for determining what should be the immediate, intermediate and long-range goals. The plan can be expanded as needed to include those factors not normally included in the dollars and cents of a multi-year plan, such as more women from the athletic department on the faculty boards, or other ways in which women can achieve equality. Along with goals must be planned actions that can accomplish those goals. A timetable should be established in order to maintain a rapid rate of progress, since organizations have a tendency to get bogged down. Set realistic deadlines based on both the organization's capacity and the administration's willingness to act. Its inertia can slow down the timetable and discourage many participants.

Communication

Communication within such an organization is a must. If the group does not know what the leadership is doing, then the organization is sunk, because only a few people will be supportive. Either the people begin to drift apart or there is a rebellion in the ranks. For example, if the organization consists of the women on the athletic and physical education staff, everyone must understand what the athletic director and/or leaders are trying to accomplish, so that they can act as disciples, spreading the word, so to speak. The communiques with the members can be verbal, written in letters, a newsletter or distributed in handouts at meetings.

Evaluation

A step that is frequently overlooked is evaluation, but for an organization to maintain its effectiveness it must be able to ascertain its strengths and weaknesses and

those of the opposition. The ACLU suggests examining
the following questions:

1) How has/will movement toward your organization's
   goal been/be effected?
2) What are the major weaknesses of your group—problem
   analysis, determining strategies, recruiting members
   and/or public support, follow-through? What can you
   do to correct these weaknesses? How long will it take
   to correct them?
3) What was/will be the response of your opponents to
   your action or position?
4) What are the barriers to settlement of differences between you and the opposition?
5) What are the forces which are shaping your opponents'
   position—monetary, alumni, male students and
   coaches? Are these forces real or are they the result
   of presumptions made by your opponents? What can
   you do to counter the real forces and disprove the imag-
   ined forces?[1]

STRATEGIES

Research

No action can be taken until the current climate can
be assessed thoroughly. It is vital that women look at
three major areas: the administrative and male power
structure (overt and covert), the state of the women's
program, and the institution's stated policy on women's
athletics as opposed to its practiced policy. One special
committee should be established to collect information
on what other women have done to achieve equality
in the same circumstances and whether those techniques are viable.

In examining the administrative and male power
structure, *Equality in Sport for Women* makes these
suggestions:

Obtain and study the institution's organizational chart (generally available in the operations manual of the institution). Most public schools have equivalent manuals and only where they are not available will it be necessary for the core group to create an organizational chart.

Put names to key positions.

Learn as much as possible about key people.

Determine who primarily holds the power in the institution (not always the person in the top position).

Determine who holds the purse strings.

Establish the lines of communication up to the key people.

Determine to whom these key people are responsible.

Know where positive support can be expected.

Anticipate who is likely to be a roadblock and establish possible detours.

Determine which are the key committees on campus.[2]

The women need to look at where they fit into the power structure. Where are the weaknesses that women might exploit to gain admittance to it? For what key committees can women volunteer?

As for the institution and/or district's stated support of women's athletics:

Obtain a copy of the school and/or district's written policy on men's and women's athletics.

Obtain a copy of its stated objectives for the men's and women's athletics.

Determine the institution's existing priorities and stated priorities.

Collect specific examples of the failure to uphold these policies, objectives and priorities.

Make a list of rationales used by the institution to avoid fulfilling its obligations to the women's programs.

© 1979 United Features Syndicate, Inc.

Perhaps the easiest task of all is compiling the information on the state of the program. This can be done by:

Getting a copy of the budget for the women's program.

Ascertaining what the sources of funding are.

Who controls the money?

Looking at the inventories, administrative structure, number of female coaches and administrators, schedules, travel records, number and levels of teams, support services and the rest of the Title IX laundry list.

Obtaining any annual reports, brochures, catalogues, alumni newsletters, affirmative action plans, minutes from athletic board meetings, copies of directives on athletics from the president's office or the trustees'.

Seeking unpublished information through "insiders" or well-meaning clerks in key offices.

Reviewing any student surveys completed to see if the program reflects the students' interests.

Checking out any available records on salaries and benefits received by coaches and administrators.

All of the corresponding information for the men's program should also be compiled to use as a comparison.

National organizations, such as NOW, NCAA, AIAW, may be helpful with fact gathering, as well as local task forces. The Office of Federal Contract Compliance and HEW also maintain records from all large grant receivers indicating the sexual composition of the employees.

Out of the research material a report should be prepared which will be used to illustrate to the administration the inequities of the program. Well written and well documented, this report should include all of the pertinent information discovered in the researching, plus proposals on methods to improve the current situation. Again, this can be in the form of immediate, intermediate and long-term goals. It must also include methods to measure the progress of the plan and a means of regular communication between those carrying out the plan and the organization. *Equality in Sport for Women* makes the following recommendations:

> Establish the purpose of the report, e.g. exposure of inequitable situation to administration and/or concerned public, media and government agencies.
>
> Be accurate, frank and objective with regard to the current situation and to proposed changes. Be positive, when possible, and have concrete suggestions (possibly several alternatives) to remedy each problem area. Be imaginative, creative and receptive to new ideas when dealing with the future of the program. Create a thorough yet concise and readable document which is well organized and well thought-out. Present a professional-looking report.
>
> When dealing with the area of recommendations which also determine the desired direction for the program, it would be wise to use the entire group for a brainstorming session to ensure agreement regarding the program's basic characteristics.
>
> Have two or three of the best writers in the group actually write the report, which can then be resubmitted to the group for suggestions and comments.

Set realistic deadlines for completion of the various research units and attempt to hold to these deadlines.

When the first draft is completed, the group may wish
to solicit suggestions/comments from influential people
who are likely to be supportive. Input from outside departments which do or could contribute to the program
might also be sought.[3]

The report's effectiveness is largely dependent on
the method of presentation (whether the spokesperson
is respected, whether it is presented with hostility or
in the spirit of cooperation, whether it is boring, etc.),
but it will also be judged on the organization, documentation, clarity and approach (accusatory or conciliatory) and ability to portray the discrimination in a way
the men can comprehend. The initial copies must be
distributed to the targeted people in the administration
for their reading before it is discussed in a meeting.
A resource person should be listed on the document
whom administrators can call to clear up questions
they might have. At later times, the same report can
be presented to the school board, trustees, state and
local officials, parents, students, and the media. However, it is unwise to approach the media in the bginning
because it only creates bad feelings among administrators who do not like seeing "dirty laundry aired in public." That could only make them more resistant. Nevertheless, in the event the administration fails to move
on the recommendations, the media is an excellent alternative to force some action.

Negotiations

It is essential that in making requests for change in
an institution that the individual or group follow the
chain of command. If you start at the top, inevitably

someone will say, "Go back and start at the bottom—
exhaust all the other possibilities before you come to
me."

The first people who should be presented with the
report are the immediate administrators, be they the
president, vice-president and faculty senate, or principal and superintendent. After that comes the Board
of Trustees or the Board of Education and Title IX committee. Request the meeting in writing.

The organization may present itself as a representative of the athletic program seeking equality, or it
may ask to be designated part of the affirmative action-
self evaluation committee. Either way, it must portray
itself as willing to work *with* the administration, as
opposed to *against* it. Two or three people should be
selected to make the presentation because more than
that makes a meeting less structured and the group
must be well organized in order to make a good impression. Those making the presentation should practice
beforehand. This is an excellent technique for any
woman making a proposal to an administrator, especially one who intimidates her. Have a friend or colleague (preferably a man) play the role of the administrator, being the devil's advocate. By applying the
pressure in a mock situation and asking the questions
the administrator might ask, the man allows the
woman to become confident in her ability to handle
the pressure and answer the difficult questions. Anticipate arguments that might occur, and consider the
compromises you are willing to make. Know just how
much you are willing to give up, but fight for more.

Remarks Pat Joe, a junior high school administrator in Southern California, "What has worked best for
me has been trying to anticipate all possible reactions
and trying to be ready for them. I do not present something unless I've covered as many avenues as I can

think of in terms of getting my facts and information.
I go through a dialogue with myself, countering with
all the positive aspects to any criticism they might
bring up."

Plan the program so that it runs smoothly. Provide
an agenda if necessary to the administrators so they
may see what direction the group wishes to go.

Administrators, men in particular, are evidence
oriented. They want to see an impressive track record;
therefore it is crucial to cite specific examples when
dealing with them. The best presentation is one that
keeps the men alert and this can be done with charts,
visual aids, or student presentations, but all must be
based on fact. Emotional pleas merely turn them off.
Boards of education are sometimes swayed by passion-
ate pleas (especially from students), because they are
aware that young people have a profound effect on public sentiment. Other times they may be annoyed with
such tactics, feeling the women are attempting to prey
on their emotions. These types of displays should be
reserved for public hearings or other open meetings.
Nevertheless, when you have something to sell, make
it interesting. Assuming the women are familiar with
the administrators involved in the meeting, they can
go in without further investigation. They should know
enough about the members of the board to ascertain
how they feel about the issues, where each person's
weakness lies (his wife is a tennis player) and where
he will lend support. Know who will represent the
greatest opposition and try to prepare ways to handle
him. Speak to male colleagues who know him and have
dealt with him in the past. If the body is a Board of
Education whose members are unfamiliar to the
women, they should attempt to make appointments
with each member leading up to the meeting. Discuss
with them the issues and let them get to know you.

This will knock down the added barriers of meeting a stranger. Find the person who carries the most power among the board and try to convince him with logic that he should support the proposal.

During the presentation, never allow it to degenerate into a shouting match. Keep cool and logical. Never allow the administration to select one person as *the* person to negotiate with. Each person merits the same respect to be heard. People on the team must always take the same side on an issue. If one party does not agree, that should be stated in private, not before the administration. Divisions in the ranks make it easy to write off the group as "just another bunch of women who can't make up their minds."

If presented with a question that cannot be answered immediately, do not try to make an excuse. Simply state that it requires further research and you will get back to them. Permitting them to play games or manipulate the negotiating team will only make the meeting meaningless. Being direct and honest and refusing to be party to manipulations forces the men to be direct and honest. Never accept the old standard refusal, "It's board policy." Ask to see it in writing and then seek ways to change board policy.

One factor that women must be cognizant of is when to stop pushing. Too many times people push beyond the point where the captive audience is willing to listen. Be aware of becoming so emotionally involved in a presentation that you cannot observe the reactions of the other people. Oftentimes people get to the point of crusading, where they are not open to logic or sensitive to those around them. Watch for telltale signs that the presentation is too long—fidgeting in the seat, daydreaming, pencil tapping and other forms of body language. At that point, cut it short.

Have one person from the group keep excellent

notes. In the days following the meeting, these should
be sent to the people who attended.

Media

Many administrators can ignore equality issues on
their own campuses if the women coaches and administrators only are concerned. Women physical educators in particular are known for being fairly close-
mouthed, so these men figure they have nothing to fear.
However, in recent years women are learning to take
their fight to the public through the media. They saw
how effective a tool the media was for the Civil Rights
and Anti-War movements and are beginning to realize
the potential for getting equality for women in sports.
Coupled with this new awareness is the media's em-
bracing of women's athletics. Issues that never made
page 16 are now on page one. In fact, many times Title
IX is bigger news than a league championship. Take
advantage of it!

An excellent guide to handling the media is *How
to Make the Media Work for You,* published by the
Women's Action Alliance ($1.50), 370 Lexington Ave-
nue, New York, New York 10017.

Certainly the sports editor in a town should be the
first notified of your displeasure with discriminatory
practices and any intention to pursue the issue, in order
to give him the initial choice and not alienate him.
But if he turns it down, it should be offered to the news
editor, the women's or family section editor and lastly
to the editorial page editor. A well-written press release
should be available to any of these editors in the event
they are interested. (On issues not as vital as a call
for a total revamping of a program, it may be best to
send the release first and then call papers, radio and
TV stations after they have received it.)

Keep the people who normally cover the beat informed of any developments, because these people have displayed the most interest. Let them know what steps you are taking and then suggest they speak with the administrators for their side of the issue. No one in your group should attempt to explain the administration's actions. Put the ball in its court.

The ACLU makes some very valuable suggestions in presenting a women's campaign for equality to the media:

1) Establish your group as a reliable and accurate source of information. Most reporters and newscasters have responsibility for a broad area of news coverage. As a result, they probably will not have extensive knowledge of your issue and will depend on the information they obtain from you and from your opponents in writing their story. You should have a fact sheet available and be prepared to spend time explaining your issue in detail and answering the queries of the press. . . .

   a) You don't want all your news stories limited to the sports pages.
   b) You may encounter initial hostility from male sportswriters who see "their" turf being invaded by "women libbers."

   You can offset both of these situations by:

   a) Using your sportswriter contacts to introduce you to the newswriters and
   b) Wearing down the fears of sportswriters with intelligent and factual arguments for the participation of women in sport. When sportswriters understand that women are truly interested and knowledgeable about athletics, they may become valuable supporters.

2) Use the media judiciously. The reporter who has been led to believe s/he is covering a major event and then learns that it is your group's weekly demonstration, may not cover future actions that *are* major. Badgering re-

porters into covering your actions is not a useful tactic. The media will cover those events that it believes are newsworthy and in the public interest. A clear and accurate presentation on why your issue is such will be more effective in gaining coverage than harrassment. Finally, an issue is only considered "hot" by the media for a limited amount of time. Regardless of how dramatic your actions or news, if the media does not perceive that its audience will be interested, you will not get coverage.

Before seeking coverage, you should evaluate when, where and why you want coverage:

When—your facts are well documented;
　　　—your action is well organized;
　　　—your issue or action is "newsworthy";
　　　—you can make a sound case against your opponent.

Where—at events where breakthroughs or wins might happen;
　　　—at events where leading members of both sides are present;
　　　—at creative or public interest happenings.

Why—to further public education on the issue;
　　　—to exert public pressure on your opponents;
　　　—to expedite your campaign;
　　　—to solidify public and intra-organizational support.

Media coverage does not depend on your planning. Once your issue has evoked enough public interest, the press will closely watch your activities for events they think will be of general interest. Therefore, your pressperson must be accessible to the press and must be kept aware of all developments on the issue so that s/he is prepared to respond to the inquiries of the press.[4]

Good times to hold press conferences and/or contact the media are:

When the administration has failed to act on the recommendations

When the administration refuses to meet with the organization

When the organization has filed a complaint with HEW.

CHAPTER 7

Persuasion: Getting It from the Administration

In the previous sections we have looked at methods to achieve change on a grand scale. But every day the woman athletic director interacts with the institutional administration on a small scale, trying to improve her program. In Getting Along with the Men's Department, we discussed strategies for peaceful coexistence with male counterparts. Herein we examine ways to influence male administrators. On page 148, specific approaches to group negotiations are cited, however, many of these techniques are also applicable on a one-on-one basis.

There is little doubt that the old saying, "You catch more flies with honey than with vinegar" is true. Demands and hostility only result in anger and frustration. Administrators respond to reason and civility. But there are ways to insure a more positive reception for your recommendations and requests.

SCOUTING THE ADMINISTRATION

Probably the most difficult task in many large institutions is finding out who the key people are that make the decisions, and then getting to see them face to face. *Ask questions.* There is a way to do it conversationally so that people are not aware you are garnering information. Although you might feel a bit like a pest, keep at it until you find out everything you want to know. Seldom will people shortstop you by saying they do not want to answer the question; usually, they will respond with at least a partial answer. Sometimes the answers will not come from within your institution. It may be necessary to ask questions at the district office or of neighboring schools. For example, say you need to know who has the final say on the budget within the schools in your district. You meet the vice-principal of a nearby school at a conference. Instead of asking your own administrators who might get suspicious of your motives, ask him. Volunteer for a week-long internship with the district athletic coordinator. Follow him or her around for that week and pick up new information that may be helpful in your job.

OPENING THE DOOR

Establishing a face-to-face communication is paramount. It is far too easy for someone to say "no" in a memo or over the phone. Make them say it to your face. An especially easy way for administrators to push aside your request is just lose the memo somewhere on their desks. In watching someone's response to your request, you can assess their thinking and then modify or proceed with the request based on that evaluation. It is not that much of an effort to walk across campus or pick up the phone and make an appointment to talk

with the administrator. Personal contact opens doors.
Never hesitate to use your title. Evaluate the office you
are calling and decide what title might be most useful—director of women's athletics, associate athletic
director, league commissioner, president of the state
coaches' association, etc. Instead of getting shuffled
around and put on "hold," call the head of the department (avoid dealing with underlings) and leave a title
and phone number.

If personal contact has previously been established and the issue is not a matter of grave importance, it is acceptable to use the phone. Never send a
letter and wait for an answer. Instead, pick up the
phone—ask, negotiate, talk it over—and then back up
the verbal agreement with a written follow-up. Says
Fran Schaafsma, associate athletic director at Cal State
Long Beach, "I've found I get more done in one day
on the phone and through appointments than waiting
three months for a letter to surface on that person's
desk."

It is not wrong for a woman to throw her weight
around. If you and the male athletic director generally
report to the vice-president, but you know the president
socially, call for an appointment with the president.
Be able to assess the type of individual you are dealing
with. Does he have money power, position power or
power built around success? For instance, the chairman of the faculty senate is a person who has tremendous influence on both faculty members and the vice-
president. His is power developed from his success.
You want the budget increased. He does not hold the
purse strings, but the vice-president does. Know how
best to utilize the chairman's influence. Going to him
may well have better results than going directly to the
vice-president. Always keep in mind a person's title,
job and influence when talking with him or her. Find

out how the person likes to be addressed. Show defer-
ence to superiors, even if you are on a first name basis.

Get to know the administrators on a social, as well
as a business level. Search for what makes them tick.
Men have traditionally done business over a round of
golf. There is no reason women cannot do business
over a game of tennis. Says Linda Estes, women's athletic director at the University of New Mexico, "I almost never play tennis anymore for fun. Tennis for
me is like taking somebody to lunch. It's a great way
to meet people." Other people close to the administrators can be helpful in telling about their personalities.
Does the president need his ego stroked (most powerful men do)? Or would he rather be treated as an
equal?

Another major factor is involvement. The woman
who becomes involved in faculty affairs allows administrators and influential faculty members to become
familiar with her. They do not see her only when her
hand is out for money for her program. Instead of resentment at her isolation from faculty matters, they
have respect for her and grow to like her. Those who
would never have any interest in women's athletics
take an interest because they can respect her judgment
and because she shows an interest in their pet project.
Volunteering or getting herself appointed to key committees is a crucial plus. Thus, for example, if she sits
on the faculty senate, one of that body's tasks is to select
those people to sit on the athletic board. Through her
involvement, she has a voice in the makeup of the
board. By moving about through the campus machinery, she develops relationships with key people who
can be of assistance in achieving equality. The closer
she comes to them in social settings, meetings, committees, etc., the better she can evaluate how to deal with
them and the better they can get to know her as more

than just another feminist. Faculty involvement also shows an interest and support for the entire school program, which will impress administrators with your good judgment and intentions.

There is a certain amount of give and take in these athletic director-administrator relationships. The vice-president may be very involved in the American Cancer Society or the local cultural association. By getting involved in his charities, you earn his respect and he is more likely to reciprocate when you make a request of him. But be cautious that the personal and social contacts you have with the administrators are not always in preparation of asking for something. Make them light, enjoyable circumstances that serve as foundations for an honest and open communication.

Make a point of getting administrators involved with the program. Invite them to banquets, games, staff meetings. Some coaches are amazed to see principals and superintendents serving as timers and scorers at track meets, but that only shows that the staff and administration have a healthy, cooperative relationship.

Making requests is one aspect of the partnership of administrator-athletic director, but it should also include getting administrator's input. It is a wise step to encourage input from administrators because that makes them feel as though they have a vested interest in the program.

CREATING THE RIGHT CLIMATE

Administrators often lack knowledge of the intricacies of women's sports and they make pronouncements and decisions from a position of ignorance. It is up to the women's athletic director to give them a grounding in the philosophies, objectives, and facts that have a bearing on women's programs. This can be accomplished through personal interviews, position papers, memos, and bringing to their attention specific readings. In order to make educated decisions, they must acknowledge the needs of the women's programs. Sometimes it's just a matter of pointing needs out. As one woman says, "I know the men I'm working with really believe they want what's best for the athletes, yet little things happen that rile me up. I can stew about it, or I can ask them where their head is, what they are thinking and then explain my point of view. Being factual and open has been eye-opening to them. We must take some responsibility for their unconscious discrimination. Once you've gotten their support and respect, you can't find anyone who will back you more fervently."

Respect and credibility are the two most important ingredients in establishing a rapport with administrators. A woman must show she is worthy of their time and effort, and to do this she must have a positive, confident attitude of self-worth—she must respect herself. Credibility comes from demonstrating an expertise. Establish your credentials as an expert. People respect your opinions with more conviction if you demonstrate that you have the ability and talent you say you have. You must be regarded as being worthy of their trust.

Ways that a woman can develop her credibility, a process that takes much time, are:

1. Always meet deadlines of projects.
2. Make sure reports are thorough and professional looking.
3. Be well prepared.
4. Be willing to put in extra time on a project if it requires it.

5. Always fulfill obligations.

6. Be full of good ideas (practical ones) that bring the department and yourself visibility. Do something "splashy" such as hiring six Olympic medalists for a summer workshop.

7. Show a good track record where financial investments in the program brought results, where catering to the media resulted in an entire scrapbook of stories, where testimonies of key people bear out that your recommendations are solidly based on fact.

8. Always make sure that your suggestions are not idealistic, but practical and applicable. Nothing has the sobering effect on men that "flighty, unrealistic" women do.

9. Establish yourself on a national level, so that you are respected and seen as an authority outside the school. This forces administrators to evaluate you through the eyes of other respected authorities in the field.

10. Never be vague about what you want. Provide specifics—number, cost, size, space, students served, etc. Men know you've done your homework.

11. Demonstrate that you think ahead by showing contingency plans.

12. Run a "classy" operation. This may mean spending a little of your own money, or especially active fund-raising to get the little extras: a cocktail party for alumni and administrators, Support Women's Athletics buttons, small gifts for those people who work hard for the program, etc.

13. Show a total pride in the entire institution. Take into consideration what is best for all students. Do not be overly biased for your own program.

14. Return unused monies.

15. Admit you're wrong or have used poor judgment.

16. Do not play games, be direct, honest and forthright. Never try to justify something that cannot be justified. Do not lie just to get something you want. Never hit them with something unexpected and overwhelming. If you want to add a new sport, give them six months' or a year's warning. Administrators do not like to be surprised with bad news. Handle a problem as best you can when it arises and apprise administrators that it could get worse. If problems are foreseeable, keep them informed of the possible difficulties before the problems demand attention.

17. Display loyalty. Walk the tightrope between representing the students and representing the administration. It is best to take stands on issues that are not all pro one group or the other. By varying your positions based on your conscience instead of an allegiance, neither group can accuse you of being biased. However, loyalty to the administration can be illustrated in other ways. Publicly show your gratitude and approval of the administration in exchange for the right to privately express your displeasure. One woman administrator comments, "If I could be very frank internally in the meetings, I told them, I would not go to the media and publicize the inadequacies of the program. I wanted to be able to talk openly without harassment. This bargain gave the administration room for comfort. They knew they could trust me."

18. Be willing to listen as well as to talk.

These practices will pay off in jackpots. Administrators will begin to consult you on important matters. You will be forewarned of impending decisions which may affect the program. Opinions you voice will be weighed instead of ignored.

It is crucial that you express a belief in the program and state your feelings on issues clearly and concisely. As a woman assumes an important stature in the administration, she will be expected to comment on her area of expertise and to participate in the decision making. Any attempt to "pass the buck" will result in a lowering of esteem. Decisiveness is a trait that is highly prized.

PREPARING FOR THE MEETING

Get your own department behind you. If the women coaches cannot agree, then they cannot sell it to the administration. The most damaging thing that can happen to a proposal is to have someone in your own ranks arguing against it. It is essential that the department take a stand as a unit. Then, if the needs are not met, and it becomes necessary to threaten to strike or not run the athletic program, you can back it up. Never make a threat without total knowledge that you can carry it out.

It is a major plus for a proposal when the male and female athletic staffs make a pitch for it together. Seek the support of the male athletic director before submitting a proposal, and either include his statement of support or ask him to attend the meeting with you.

Although it is not something that should be done only when leading up to a proposal presentation, it is wise to become involved with the wives of the administrators through faculty associations or other bodies. These women can be a tremendous asset. Dropping a hint to the wives prior to a proposal presentation and getting their support means they will lobby for you at home.

Sometimes it is best to do some of the preliminary work yourself. Instead of waiting for the go-ahead, begin drawing up the architectural plans for the softball diamond. Talk to the draftsman on campus or the

drafting teacher and be prepared to present a completed plan for the administration. This is an impressive move and leaves few questions unanswered. All the administration has to decide then is whether there is enough money. You have done the rest.

THE MEETING

One of the most effective strategies is to *show* the administrators why you want what you have requested. Take them out to the handball courts where the walls have holes in them. Let them see the overcrowded storage room, etc.

Find out what type of presentation best appeals to the administrators and do it that way. Do they like a summary first and then details, or the reverse? Do they prefer a folksy, informal style of presentation or a sophisticated formal approach?

The key to success is the ability to make other people see things your way—effective persuasion without persuading. Harry Turman once said, "Bring people in and try to persuade them to do what they ought to be doing anyway, without persuasion. That's what I spent most of my time doing." The task is to make people agree without having to argue with them. The person who agrees against his instincts will not be supportive in a time of crisis. Men as well as women must be made to see why something is advantageous to them.

They must support it because it is a good idea. Ironically, one of the most effective techniques, and one that is used mostly by women, is to make a man think it is his own idea. Lead him up to the door and then let him open it. If a man thinks it is his idea, he will support it with a vengeance. There is nothing wrong with letting a man take the credit if the women get the benefit. Thus, it is key for women in athletics to know the men with whom they deal—know their weaknesses, strengths, pet projects, prejudices, patterns of behavior, anxieties, likes and dislikes. Knowledge of the man will strongly influence how he can be influenced.

Encourage administrators to consider you as a resource and *always* be available should they want to talk. If you turn them down even once, they may never ask again. Request to be consulted on all matters pertaining to the key aspects of the program—budget, capital improvements, reorganization—and ask for permission to initial all documents. In so doing, attach constructive suggestions and comments to them upon returning the documents to the administrator's office. It is also wise to occasionally submit unsolicited opinions in writing so that the administrators recognize your concern and begin consulting you. Keep them informed on developments and issues. Let them know, for example, that there is a limit below which the program cannot operate. Give them some alternatives and parameters for decision making. Should they seek you out on an issue on which you are not knowledgeable, admit it and say either, "I'm not an expert in this area, but I have talked with experts. Here's what they advise and I agree . . .," "I cannot answer that for you, but I have a colleague who can. Her name is . . ." or "I cannot answer that without some research. I will get back to you tomorrow."

THE APPROACHES

An excellent guideline for dealing with administrators can be found in Mortimer R. Feinberg's *Effective Psychology for Managers*.[1] Research shows that the most effective persuaders are those who appeal to both the intellect and emotions of their listeners. The more intelligent a person, the more effective an argument based primarily on fact and logic. The less intelligent an individual, the more effective an argument based primarily on emotional appeal. The more intelligent person can draw his own conclusions and doesn't require that implications be pointed out, as in the case with less intelligent people. However, if the issue is complex, it doesn't hurt to draw the conclusions and implications clearly, no matter how intelligent your audience.

The more logical you are with men, the more likely you are to win because men are trained to be logical. If they turn you away, come back with more facts. Make sure they know more than they ever wanted to know on the subject.

THE PROPOSAL

A good proposal is much like a dissertation. It contains:

1) background
2) statement of the problem
3) financial statement
4) cost prediction
5) expense and income
6) fact sheet

This format can be adapted for any need—proposing an expansion of the program, added facilities, additional scholarships, staffing, etc. Confine a proposal to no more than five pages (be brief, but complete). Out-

line the need, including any information necessary,
so they know exactly what you want them to do in
order to help. The precise outline of the proposal
should be as follows:

1. Why it is needed (list objectives of the proposed
project and include a section on the advantages, contributions, benefits)
2. Description of current status (present conditions)
3. Survey results (parents, athletes, support
groups, etc.).
4. Additional pertinent facts (a fact sheet perhaps)
5. Methods of implementation (programming)
6. Cost/revenue projections (itemized budget of
cost)
7. Completion date (project time-line for implementation).

Determine the purpose of the proposal. What do
you want to achieve? What do you need? This entails
looking at what is currently being spent, how much
is within the school's or district's budgets, and seeing
whether your proposal is out of line. Then decide what
must be included within the proposal to support the
idea.

Talk to a number of people to get their opinion;
they may have a different perspective of the purpose.
"Tunnel vision" (not looking at the total picture), may
result in an inaccurate or biased position. Seek out
deans and other administrators to ascertain what their
positions on such a proposal might be. Once you have
gotten feedback on all views of the issue, develop your
position statement carefully. Be prepared to take a logical, feasible stand and be able to realistically defend

your position against all contrary opinions. Those individuals to whom you will be submitting your proposal generally do not have a lot of information at their disposal regarding women's athletics, and unless they have the exact answers before them, they may rely on the counsel of others who are also not as knowledgeable (i.e., male athletic director). Allowing individuals to gain their information by hearsay or from other people's biased opinions makes your case difficult. Be able to give evidence which shows that your position is better than opposing views. Cite facts (statistics), positions of authority such as the President's Council on Physical Fitness, quotes from prominent people in the field, student surveys, testimonials from athletes in the program. Marshal the supportive evidence to show that:

1. It is safer (state the percentage of swimming-pool drownings which occur annually due to an inability to swim).
2. It provides physiological benefits (provide doctor's statement).
3. It has lifetime carry-over values (quote number of people playing racquetball in the United States, rate of growth of the sport).
4. Parents and other community members can also use the facility (draw up a prospective schedule for facility use).
5. It is cheaper to do it now than in five or six years (cite increased building costs over the last five years).
6. It is less expensive to build than to rent facilities (show the cost differential).
7. Additional facilities are necessary because current tennis courts are overused (illustrate that they are in use by classes and teams until 11 P.M., and use a

comparative schedule for the proposed courts to show a better usage).

Make sure that all figures are current. Never give "ballpark" figures, because if they are low, you will never get the administration to consent to additional monies. Break down every dollar and state for what it will be used.

Your position should be carefully written in order to target it to their specific interests. Do not compromise the integrity of what you are trying to accomplish, but make it appear that you have the same interests that they have. Look at sample proposals to see which ones were successful and why. Submit the finished product well in advance of the deadline, at least two weeks prior to the meeting on the topic.

In the event you have teamed with the male athletic director, it might be best to allow him to make the presentation. Many men relate better to other men. That might be difficult, but the odds are better with a very chauvinistic administration.

Here are some additional tips:

1. Do not communicate your fears. Keep them to yourself. Otherwise you can destroy people's confidence in you and your proposal.

2. Everyone has defense mechanisms, an automatic way of responding to anything that presents a threat. Criticize the act and not the person when debating an issue.

3. Play down the fear theme. When men become afraid, they acquire a "denial" attitude.

4. Avoid pushing for immediate compliance. Give them a chance to think it over. If you push, they may later think they have been hoodwinked, tricked and conned.

5. Minimize their fear of change by likening the

situation to one they've encountered before—a successful one.

6. Be sincere. Show that you have a real interest in the administrator's concerns. Make sure they realize there is nothing in it for you—only for the students.

7. Feinberg offers these suggestions:

> First, in a situation where you want to persuade a group to follow your lead, never attack the group. Single out the leader, if you can identify him, and concentrate on his attitude. If you win him, he will help you influence the others. And winning this one man will be far easier for you than trying to win a dozen men, who, in their unity, find strength.
>
> Second, keep in mind that you can use the rest of the group to your advantage in working on the leader. Collect opinions and ideas from the group. Perhaps the individuals never had a chance to express themselves. You might suggest that the leader collect opinions or facts from individuals, then funnel them to you. This accomplishes two things. It preserves the leader's dignity, and it alerts the group to the fact that a change may be forthcoming. . . .
>
> You "use the competition" by anticipating opinions and reactions that are contrary to yours. Typically, you would anticipate a negative reaction to your proposal, then answer it fast and proceed to make a strong case for yourself.
>
> Studies show that if you present only your side of the case, you have not really sold it. That's because when your audience hears the other side of the story, it will be more easily "unconvinced" than if it had heard both sides originally. In other words, if you think that your audience originally heard, knows of, or will eventually hear arguments against you, it will pay you to devote some time to the opposition. Give your audience some mental ammunition with which to defend the position you hope it will take. . . .
>
> Do not make a strong case, just mention enough

of the negative to alert your audience to their existence. The purpose is to insulate your audience against having the idea penetrate from another source.[2]

8. You are not asking for a handout. Your proposal has something to offer to the institution. Talk program, not money.

9. Never lose your temper while presenting a proposal. If absolutely necessary, conclude the meeting immediately and agree to meet when you are "feeling better." One woman athletic director says, "I find one of my best weapons is respect. As long as I'm showing complete respect for him, if he loses his temper, it is his fault. So it is always, 'Yes, sir, I beg your pardon. . . .' It's always the utmost courtesy and respect, no matter how angry he gets at me. But once I step out of the room, that's a different matter."

Learn to compromise and to negotiate. These are very key concepts. Holding out for everything you want can be as detrimental as not asking at all—in fact, sometimes more so, because it engenders hard feelings. Men will be willing to give in part way, provided women do too. One woman related, "The athletic director at my school was used to practicing as long as he wanted, when he wanted. He was happy to share when we worked it out, provided he was home for Monday Night Football." Remember to give up something to get something else.

Compromise does not mean you must give up your goals, merely that you are setting back your priorities for a little while. Be smart about negotiating. Women have never learned to negotiate, something that is inherent in a male's upbringing. Notes one woman athletic director, "Women, unless they get their way, get hurt. Males are used to that. 'Give her a new dress, take her out to dinner and shut her up, and I'll make the big decisions.' In sales when they 'close,' they give up a little thing so you are conditioned to give up a big one to them. Where big decisions are being made, we can't go in naive. Know how far you are willing to compromise."

The men must be encouraged to come in with possible alternatives also, because you cannot be the only one willing to sacrifice. That is not a compromise, that's a concession. Consider such deals where the women's department is given 50 percent of the budget, but the men's department clearly needs more than its 50. You do not need a whole 50 percent because the program is not big enough. Yet you anticipate that within the next few years the women's program will grow big enough to need those extra dollars. So, you volunteer to accept only 40 percent in exchange for the men giving you an additional percentage three years down the line. This works, provided this deal is in writing, so that it is a binding contract.

AFTER THE MEETING

Having written agreements and keeping very good notes on what is said and decided in the meeting are protective devices from unscrupulous administrators. Do not go back to an administrator on the basis of memory. Talk from a position of strength. "You were quoted as saying . . ." Once you get him on record, it will insure his continued agreement. When everyone knows the stand he has taken, it becomes embarrassing and emotionally inconvenient for him to change his mind. There are various ways to have him make an agreement public. Writing is one form; ask him to get a memo to everyone involved. In a major project, get the news out through the public relations department. The faster you make it public, the greater your chances of success.

If the meeting results in your proposal being rejected, that does not mean you have to stop there. You can pursue it up through the chain of command to a female board member or some other sympathetic ear. Probably the most effective way to swing the support to your side is to become politically active. Get involved in the campaigns and meet the candidates. At least one woman athletic director at a state university in this country is on a first-name basis with the governor of her state after helping with his campaign. Although she does not necessarily go to him with her requests, she is seldom turned down for anything at her school because the administrators recognize that she could go to him if they said no. Especially where the budget is decided by the state legislature, it is absolutely imperative that you get to know the men who will decide on it. They may not see the value in women's sports without some evidence or they may simply not realize that the budget for the women's program is inadequate as it stands. This means a woman athletic director conceivably can go over her administration's head and get additional funding for her program. THIS HAS HAPPENED. A politician will be particularly attentive if he knows it means votes. One method to do this is to make all the coaches become registrars of voters, so they may register athletes to vote. You must be careful not to sway athletes to a particular party or candidate (this is against the law), but the athletes alone represent a large number of potential voters in the next election.

Getting involved in community organizations such as the state commission on the status of women or the local American Civil Liberties Union also provides added backing. Influential people in the community organizations can often apply pressure to reluctant administrators to consider your proposals. Get the power people behind you.

Persistence. Do not become despondent if administrators turn you down. Go back and try again until they get tired of seeing you. Revise the proposal, try a new approach, add a new alternative. Be like the one athletic director who says, "My batting average is not too hot yet, but if I don't get you in the first round, I'll get you second time around."

PRESSURE GROUPS—PARENTS, COMMUNITY AND COACHES' ASSOCIATIONS

When direct interaction with the administration is not getting the desired result, it is often necessary to take the fight outside of the institution. This is where parents, community members, and alliances of coaches and teachers are particularly powerful. By applying pressure from the outside, they can often force the action that the "insiders" cannot. "Insiders" risk being fired, "outsiders" carry the clout of the taxpayers and the public conscience.

The organization of these units is very similar to that of an "inside" group. However, coaches play a key role in recruiting parents for such organizations. An impassioned speech at a parent-teacher meeting, at a booster's club night or at a contest might light a fire under parents. Otherwise, coaches will have to do the legwork alone—cornering parents at games, sending letters home via their daughters, or calling them on the phone. Usually, the best system is to get one or two very activist parents involved and then refer all other parents to them. Thus, the coach does not jeopardize her job by being recognized as the organizer.

The activist parents can then begin their own recruiting drive. Getting the parents involved usually takes little more than telling them what their daughter is getting and what she deserves (1) in comparison to what the boys have, (2) under Title IX.

Besides meetings, these organizations should set up an effective communication system such as a telephone tree where key members call 10 or 20 other members to get involved in a particular action such as a letter writing campaign, a public hearing, a demonstration, etc. A newsletter is also particularly helpful to keep members apprised of developments.

Letter Writing Campaigns

This can be conducted in several stages—letters to (1) the school administrators, (2) superintendent, (3) board of education/trustees, and (4) legislators. The organization should draw up a sample letter for parents, students and members to use as a model for their own. Members can be supplied with organization letterhead. Coaches may encourage athletes to participate by providing class time and materials for writing. Letter writing must be made as simple as possible for participants; they should be given the names and addresses and any pertinent facts. To cut down on effort, it might be suggested that each person write only one letter but send carbons to the other three sources (principal letter to the legislator, with copies to the board of education and school administrators).

Petitions

Coaches, students and parents can be supplied with printed petition forms with names, addresses and telephone numbers to circulate through schools and the community. The best way to insure a top response is to set deadlines, so that petition carriers work as fast as possible. Otherwise, they often procrastinate.

Speakers Bureau

Enjoying the public support is a key aspect to pressuring an institution. An excellent method to do that is through face-to-face contact with other local organizations. A speakers bureau, which actively seeks speaking engagements to "spread the word," has a tremendous value in a campaign. These same spokespersons are also good candidates to be media spokespersons. The ACLU recommends the following in developing a speakers bureau:

1) Recruit a sufficient number of members (6 to 8 at a minimum) who are willing to speak. Include both experienced and new speakers in this group.
2) Provide a forum for group issue orientation, public speaking training and exchange of expertise.
3) Appoint a coordinator who can arrange scheduling and handle telephone and mail requests for speakers.
4) Utilize Public Service or Community News announcements to advertise this service. Mailings to community groups and churches may also elicit speaking engagements.[3]

Public Hearings and Board of Education Meetings

Boards of Education do not relish the interference of public pressure groups, but that is precisely why they are effective. The first task of the organization is to make the board aware of the problem through letters, phone calls and face-to-face contact. Leaders of the group should invite board members out to lunch in order to more fully acquaint them with the problem.

Little reminders, such as potted plants sent in the name of the group, help familiarize the board members with the organization.

Call to get the board's agenda for an upcoming meeting and then begin to plan the presentation. It may include students, parents, coaches and other influential community members.

Although it is not always the case, it may be unwise to allow students to speak before the school board. Too often they become overly emotional about the issue and cannot see that they are being "set up" by the board members. Says one woman who has since stopped using students, "I've seen very good students torn apart by adults and it's something I no longer care to subject them to. Some adults can be very cruel."

A telephone tree and mailings should be used to recruit large numbers of sympathetic people to attend; however, only a select few should be the spokespersons.

Very likely, the athletic director or coach will find it is necessary to orchestrate the presentation. Choosing the proper speakers is like playing a chess game. Who will best appeal to the board? What type of people do they relate to best? Not only should the organizer be concerned with how articulate her speakers are, but also their physical appearance. First impressions have a lasting effect on individuals. The selected people do not have to be handsome or beautiful, but well-groomed and intelligent-looking.

The speakers need to be capable of saying, "I don't know," if asked a question that might endanger the campaign. Many questions are loaded and they must be able to discern that. None of the speakers should attempt to talk off the cuff. Before the presentation, they need to be given guidelines for constructing their speech. The organizer must say, "This is the point we want to get across. Now here are the facts and tools you can use to make up your presentation. . . ." If there is going to be a series of speakers, it is imperative that they get together to practice and discuss beforehand to make sure they come to the same conclusions. At many poorly organized presentations, speakers cancel each other out because they arrive at different conclusions.

Even those people who are not speaking must be given a bit of coaching. They need to know precisely what their role is—do they cheer, do they hold up placards, do they walk out when the demands are not met? *Everything must be planned.*

After the presentation is over, call all of the people together before they have time to cool off. In the event the request has been rejected or accepted tentatively, the group must plan its next course of action immediately, while it still has momentum and cohesiveness. Listen to the consensus and then act on it.

One of those actions may well be a public hearing. These are particularly useful in awakening the public to the issues and drumming up support. The same type of planning must go into a hearing as goes into a presentation before the board. The ACLU recommends the following steps in putting together a public hearing:

a) Get as many organizations as possible to co-sponsor the hearing. Even if you have been working from an intra-organizational structure you may wish to make the hearing a coalition effort. A broad base of support will encourage public interest and attendance.

b) Invite school and public officials as well as the general public and media. Personal invitations and follow-up calls should be made to these officials to confirm their attendance.

c) Establish a format that will facilitate an orderly and balanced program. If a large number of people are interested in speaking, it may be necessary to establish

a set time limit per speaker. Efforts should be made
to invite participants representing a varied spectrum
of opinions.

d) Vary your group's speakers so that you present authori-
tative statements on the different issues—the disparate
treatment of women in athletics, the physiological and
medical data available, the level of interest in athletics
among women, the data on methods that have been
used successfully by other schools in remedying sex-
discrimination practices.

e) Invite a community leader or offcial to chair the hearings. This will probably ensure a more orderly and cred-
ible hearing than if a person identified with either position were chairing.

f) Arrange to hold your hearing in a well known, centrally
located and neutral place.

g) Flyers, posters, news stories and public service announcements can be used to advertise the hearings.
These materials are usually more helpful in solidifying
commitment to attendance among those already interested than in attracting new participants. Your personal
and organizational contacts generally will draw the major part of the audience.

h) Some members of your group should arrive early. They
can distribute your position paper (make sure there is
a phone number listed where people can reach you),
be accessible to those with inquiries, and lobby uncom-
mitted officials.

i) Send follow-up letters to those who attend encouraging
them to join your group.[4]

Demonstrations

Although demonstrations can be highly effective, there
are several drawbacks to them:

They can backfire by causing more support for the opposition.

They can get out of hand.

They can be so "ordinary" that no media interest is displayed.

They can have small turnouts, showing there really is little support for your campaign.

Despite all of that, they are worth a try, but again, they require hard work and careful planning. This means deciding on what action fits the situation (picketing, boycotting, street demonstrations, marches, etc.), what the demonstration is supposed to achieve, setting some goals for it, planning it, deciding who will lead it, what will occur during it (speeches, chanting, etc.), what kind of precautions and preparations are necessary (getting permits, arriving early, setting up equipment), how to get all the people assembled in the right place (transportation), how to recruit people involved in it (flyers, posters, media), who will act as a security force to make sure nothing gets out of hand. Alternative plans must be prepared for back up, should anything change. Arrange to have a closing statement or activity that sums up the demonstration and leaves the participants with a good, enthusiastic feeling.

Legislative Contact

A flood of letters will indicate to a legislator that his constituency feels strongly about a certain issue, but personal contact with a representative from a large group of unified people means votes to him. He will listen and weigh the issue, the power and number within the organization, and his conscience, before taking action. Thus, lobbying is a very viable vehicle for organizations. Take a collection or levy dues that will provide enough money for a selected leader of the group to go to the capital to discuss the issues. Once personal contact has been established, the representative will be able to phone the legislator prior to major votes or at key times during the year. But it is unlikely the legislator would accept a call from someone he has not met previously.

Threaten to Take Legal Action

When all other avenues have been exhausted, the organization may either file a complaint with any of the governmental agencies or retain a lawyer. The act of threatening to sue can, in many instances, have the same effect on an institution as filing suit, but it must be made clear that your organization is not bluffing.

NATIONAL ORGANIZATIONS

Bringing to bear the weight of a national organization on a relatively small institution or board of education can put the individual organization into a position of superiority—or power. Instead of the institution being all-powerful, it has to answer to a national power.

National Organization for Women (NOW)
5 South Wabash, Suite 1615
Chicago, Illinois 60603

NOW's 800 chapters provide support and services to women in their struggle for equality in athletics. The organization helps individuals to file discrimination complaints and lawsuits, files class action suits and complaints on behalf of those suffering from discrimination, organizes local campaigns against school boards, publicizes the plight of women athletes in a given school district or institution, takes stands on local issues of concern to women athletes and coaches, advocates allowing girls to play on boys teams and even sponsors combined sex sports clubs.

NOW has several task forces, including one on women and sports, which act as lobbying units and clearinghouses in the field. One branch of the organization, the Project on Equal Education Rights (PEER), assists in Title IX enforcement. Additionally, NOW has published some interpretations on the other statistics useful in complaints.

League of Women Voters
Education Fund
1730 M Street N.W.
Washington, D.C. 20036

In several communities the League of Women Voters has taken an active interest in community recreation programs. By inventorying existing programs and surveying residents, they have been able to pinpoint specific needs, including the lack of women's programs in their community. Armed with the facts, the group put pressure on local officials to produce missing programs. As a result, a booklet has been produced by the organization giving further details. Write to the above address for publication #580 and send 25 cents. Local chapters of the League of Women Voters can be of assistance in equality struggles.

Women's Equity Action League (WEAL)
821 National Press Building
Washington, D.C. 20045

WEAL has been extremely active in the field of women's athletics. The organization sponsors a National Clearinghouse on Sex Discrimination in Sports and funds studies citing discrimination in employment and athletics in school districts and institutions on the

local level. Backed by the results of the studies, it files
suits on behalf of a class or individuals. Members are
available to help others lodge complaints and file suit.
Materials are available to aid local organizations in
campaigns against discriminatory agencies. WEAL assists in such matters as overseeing an institution's compliance with Title IX, urging schools to provide facilities for women, pointing out discriminatory practices
by leagues and conferences. Available through the national office are Sports Kits and Title IX Kits for under
$2.50.

National Association of Commissions
  on the Status of Women
926 J Street, Room 1003
Sacramento, California 95814

This agency can direct a person to the individual
state and local commissions, which in turn will investigate matters of discrimination and design projects and
programs to eradicate unequal treatment. Each commission has a pool of resources and can direct an individual or a group to those people who can best help
solve specific problems. Such boards can also take action on behalf of individuals locally. These are highly
visible groups that can demand much media attention.
Bringing the problem to the commissions will spark
media interest.

American Civil Liberties Union
22 East 40th Street
New York, New York 10016

The ACLU has been in the forefront of rights for
w)men for many years, bringing suit for women who
have been the victims of discrimination. Local
branches provide attorneys for discrimination cases.
Additionally, the organization's Women's Rights Proj-

ect explores laws and policies which have an adverse effect on women and decides on the appropriate campaigns, legal or otherwise, to change them. Local offices sponsor Women's Rights Committees that monitor issues and problems concerning women in athletics. The ACLU publishes a number of helpful packets which assist women in crusades against discrimination, including *Sex Discrimination in Athletics and Physical Education* ($1.50), which is widely quoted in these pages.

Educational Professional Organizations

American Association of University Professors
National Education Association
American Federation of Teachers
American Alliance for Health, Physical Education and
   Recreation

These organizations have all taken strong stands against discrimination in hiring, employment, salaries, benefits and sports. They provide a collection of committees, task forces, studies and statements on the status of women. Several have brought suit for discriminatory actions.

STUDENT PRESSURE

In 1974, the University of Minnesota student government was the first to file a suit under Title IX. Prompted by a speech she heard on Title IX, the institution's first female student-body president mounted a campaign to investigate sex discrimination in all departments of the campus. The worst offender was athletics. So, armed with specific examples of discrimination, the student government filed suit. As a result, the institution today has one of the healthiest women's athletics budgets in the nation.

A group of women at Vanderbilt University, Title IX in Tennessee Committee (TNT), alerted HEW to discrimination on campus, and consequently, HEW demanded to see the institution's year-overdue self-evaluation. Within a year, the TNT Committee hired a lawyer in preparation for a meeting with the university's legal staff and administration. The women did not demand *equal* support—just some. With pressure from students, Vanderbilt began to upgrade the program, including appointing a woman as assistant athletic director.

Women students all over the country are taking matters into their own hands. They are tired of being told what they cannot do and cannot have, so they unite in an effort to make the institutions stop ignoring them.

Jan Palchikoff, one of the nation's leading women rowers, is a case in point. In 1969, she entered UCLA with a good background in AAU swimming. Despite her 10 years of experience, there was nothing she could do. The school did not provide a sufficiently competitive women's swim team, yet her AAU teammates, Olympians Steve and Bruce Furniss, were setting national records on the men's swim team across town at USC. Jan quit athletics and became active in politics and the women's movement. Through her activism, she realized that it was not necessary to give up sports entirely; she had another alternative. The following is an account of her creation of the Union of Women Athletes (UWA):

1. In February, 1974, she wrote a letter to all the athletes in the department rallying support for the idea of a unified campaign and sent an invitation to an organizing meeting (Fig. 7.1).

February 6, 1974

Dear UCLA Athlete,

As a participant in the UCLA Women's Intercollegiate Sports program
you are probably aware of the current state of affairs. You are aware of
the lack of adequate equipment and uniforms. You are aware of the lack of
facilities for practice. You are aware of the lack of training rooms and
trainers. You are aware of the inadequate funding for travelling to various
meets and tournaments. You know that some of our coaches work for no pay
and that the rest of them work for very little pay. Preferential enrollment
is not provided for women athletes (as it is for men) to facilitate regular
practice attendance. No doubt you are aware that we do not receive financial
assistance in the form of athletic scholarships. Nor do we receive publicity
in the general press (and more specifically the Daily Bruin) which is representative of our involvement in the world of sports.

We can do something about this situation. We can organize in the form
of a "union of women athletes" and begin working together to help build
the intercollegiate sports program and develop it to its fullest potential.
As a large group we can make demands which will help up-grade the program
and to obtain the things we as athletes need in order to perform to the best
of our ability.

I have spoken to women from several of the sports about the possibility
of organizing such an effort. All of them felt it was necessary.

Please come to our first meeting to discuss the problems and possible
courses of action. The meeting will be on Wednesday, February 20 in the
evening somewhere on campus and after practice. Please call me for the
details and to tell me if you will be able to attend or just to gripe!
I can be reached at 837 7697 between 7:00 pm and midnight on week days
and all day on Saturday and Sunday or leave a message for me at the Women's
Resource Center 825 3945 or at the Women's Intercollegiate Athletic office
MG 118 (address the note to Shirbey Johnson). I'm looking forward to
hearing from you!

Sincerely,

Jan L. Palchikoff
member, UCLA swim team

2. The first meeting was attended by 40 people.
Five "core" people rose to the fore, who agreed to put
in much of the work.

3. The organization affiliated with the campus as
a student organization through the student activities
office. Thus, it was entitled to meeting facilities and
mailings.

4. A letter was mailed to announce the founding
of the UWA, stating the date of the next meeting. It

also included a tear-off at the bottom allowing women
to indicate what days were preferable for meeting.

5. The core group began doing research on the athletic department and its deficiencies. This included obtaining a copy of the budget and the school's statement
of policy on women's athletics.

6. The executive group began making contacts
with key individuals and committees:

the university policies committee

university recreation and athletic policies committee

student registration fee committee

associated student governing body

the women's resource center

chancellor's advisory committee on the status of women

Women on these bodies introduced proposals on behalf
of the UWA, alerted the group to prospective legislation
for and against women athletes, lobbied for the group,
provided guidance and information and directed the
core group to other key people with influence.

7. The organization was informed that there was
an internal move to reorganize the department of wom-
en's athletics. It requested to be allowed some input
into the proposal, either through a meeting or a written
position paper. Letters were sent to key people including the chancellor, vice-chancellor, and student body
president. The administration instead merely agreed
to read certain sections of the report to the UWA.

8. Shortly thereafter, in May, the program was announced at a press conference. Jan stood at the front
door handing out a press release to media representatives. It stated, in brief, "The Union of Women Athletes
also endorses the proposed UCLA athletic policies on
principle. But we cannot endorse any program, inde-

pendent or not, which in practice, because of inadequate funding, will continue the tradition of sex discrimination in the world of sport." Jan further elaborated the Union's objections: "When a new department is created, one-third of the budget automatically goes toward administrative costs, another one-third to scholarships, the last one-third toward such things as travel, uniforms, coaching salaries, facilities. When you break down that last one-third, it comes out to the exact same amount they spent on operating costs the year before. Everybody who looked at it critically could have seen that, but they were all so impressed with the tripling of the previous budget, they didn't bother to investigate further." A few of the reporters picked up the story.

9. While this campaign was ensuing, the Union took on the campus paper. Jan personally spoke with the sports editor to make him realize the teams should no longer be referred to as "The Bruin Dolls." She and a student council representative measured the number of inches in coverage the paper had given to women's sports and men's sports for four months to point up the inequities. A resolution was presented to the student government asking it to encourage the campus paper to cover women's sports more adequately. Subsequently, coverage did improve and the Union sent a letter commending the *Daily Bruin* to the "Letters to the Editor" column.

10. The administration tried valiantly to work around this "radical" group of feminist athletes by creating an athletes' advisory council, hoping to get some middle-of-the-road representation. However, all of the women representatives of the teams selected to the council were also Union members.

11. The Union was being misinterpreted, so Jan

and the other core members developed some position papers to alert outsiders to the organization's exact stand on issues.

12. Over the course of that summer after the formation of the Union, the core group continued meeting administrators on issues from female athlete's input into the proposed women's program to the school's Title IX recommendations. They also met with student government officers in an effort to gain support. In August, the Women's Resource Center on campus, in conjunction with the Union, sponsored a conference on women's intercollegiate athletics attended by representatives from seven Southern California institutions. Lastly, Jan met with the chairperson of the search committee which was to select the candidates for the directorship of the women's program about having women athletes involved in the selection process.

13. In the fall of 1974, a major issue presented itself. After the crew placed sixth in the nationals, the women's crew coach, who was a law student, requested more money. His salary demands, by administration standards, were outrageous—about $2,000 after his previous pay of $750, which worked out to approximately 93 cents an hour. He was fired, but the team members were not notified until they arrived at the boathouse one day to find a note posted on the door: "The women's crew program has been cancelled until further notice." A replacement coach, hired by the vice-chancellor, Norman Miller, was brought in over the protests of the athletes. He had coached men, but had tremendous trouble relating to women. The women felt he jeopardized the continued development on the women's crew program. The administration refused to see the women, so they set about making a great deal of noise. They contacted several news stations, and had parents write letters to the chancellor.

The vice-chancellor refused to meet with the crew team representatives, so the women organized a campaign where 40 people hand-delivered protest letters to Miller's secretary within half an hour, all of them requesting a receipt that their letters had been received. Constantly, they were turned away from Miller's office to talk to subordinates, but their questions all went unanswered. Angered at the deadends, the women finally managed to schedule a meeting with Miller. Three representatives presented him with a letter stating precisely what they wanted to know. The letter also stated, "The questions are specific and we would appreciate specific answers. If you cannot answer the questions now, we will be happy to wait quietly here in your office or come back in half an hour to receive the answers." He agreed to answer the questions, and immediately after he responded, the women sent him a letter noting their understanding of his statements, along with the comment, "If any statements are incorrect, please notify me by mail so we can iron out our inconsistencies. This will prevent any further miscommunication. . . . If we do not hear from you by (date), we will assume that you are in agreement with the contents of this letter." (Fig. 7.2). Palchikoff also knew how to effectively keep the issue alive through the media. She wrote editorials for the *Daily Bruin* and kept the local press up on the developments. Local television reporters were constantly calling the chancellor's office to find out why the school refused to comply with the Union's request. Finally, a meeting with the chancellor was arranged. Afterward, he was also sent a confirming letter.

Under pressure from the women, the new coach resigned. While the institution searched for a replacement, the women crew members circulated a petition which read, "We, the undersigned, support UCLA's

Jan L. Palchikoff
722 Hill Street   apt. E
Santa Monica, California

November 4, 1974

Chancellor Charles E. Young
2147 Murphy Hall
Campus

Dear Chancellor Young,

Here is a letter of confirmation of the conversation which took place in your
office on October 31, 1974 between you, Steve Halpern, Lori Luck, Shelley
Wandzura, and myself. If any statements are incorrect, please notify me by
mail so we can iron-out our inconsistencies. This will prevent any further
miscommunication. The following is our understanding of the statements you
made during our meeting.

1. You personally would look over the material we gave you and that you would
get back to us personally on Monday, November 4, 1974.

2. We raised substantial points regarding future policy that merit further
consideration and examination and that you would discuss these points with
Dr. Norman P. Miller and Steve Halpern.

3. You see no need to involve a person outside of the Department of Women's
Intercollegiate Sports to evaluate the situation regarding women's crew.

4. Regarding the new crew coach, that no one knows whether he will be good
or not.

If we do not hear from you by Monday November 11, 1974 we will assume that you
are in agreement with the contents of this letter. Thank you for you consideration.

                              Sincerely,

                              Jan L. Palchikoff
                              for UCLA Women's Crew

cc: Steve Halpern

women's crew in their efforts to upgrade the women's
crew program. We also request that Chancellor Charles
E. Young postpone the hiring of a coach for at least
one week, during which time the athletes will have
an opportunity to present their opinions for serious
consideration; that the coach be provided with at least
a minimum wage; that the athletes' welfare be the primary concern in making any decisions relevant to this
matter; and that Larry Daugherty (the original coach)
be reconsidered for the position of head coach of
UCLA's women's crew." As a result of a series of meet-

ings, the women were requested to submit recommendations on the qualifications of a prospective crew coach, the methods to subsidize the coach's salary and the ways to recruit the coach. The final outcome was that the original coach was rehired at the salary he had requested.

14. Jan was gaining practice at campus politics. At one point in all of this, the administration agreed to send the crew team to the nationals if it did well in the regionals. Two weeks before the women were due to leave, they were told there was not enough money to send them. Palchikoff slyly remarked, "You had better find the money to send us because if you do not, this will not look very good in the press." Two student government representatives were with her at the time. The school came up with the funds.

15. In April, 1975, Jan filed a complaint with HEW and announced it with a press conference. She regretted that she had waited that long, saying, "One piece of advice I can give anybody is to do this the first thing, not the last." Simultaneously, she wrote to the senators, congressmen, and lieutenant governor explaining that she had filed the complaint. She told them she understood the political ramifications, and recognized that the issue could be buried since she was only one individual against the whole institution, unless they helped her keep it alive. She says, "I was aware of the political pressure the university could exert to slow the investigation down and I wanted them to please inquire on my behalf as to the progress of the complaint." Consequently, she received copies of all correspondence between the legislators and the university administration.

When Palchikoff graduated, she was given the outstanding senior award by the Alumni Association for her efforts to upgrade the women's program. She considered the Union's greatest achievements to be establishing the athletes' advisory council and prompting student involvement. Palchikoff observed:

> Finally women athletes were saying, "We want to have something to say about what is going on." It started to get the administration thinking in terms of what we wanted and needed. We were beginning to be consulted on things like scholarships and priorities. None of this was haphazard. It was very calculated, so that we could stay involved with all units that had anything to do with the department. Any time a policy or issue came up, we contacted everybody involved. There was a lot of research. I must have spent six hours every day at it, in meetings, making phone calls. It got so that people came to me asking what buttons to push in the administration to get something done. We just took statements out of administrators' letters and policy papers and basically told them, "This is what you said on this date and this is what you are not doing. Let's make it jive or you're going to lose credibility." I never benefitted from what we did because I graduated, but my 12-year-old cousin who is a hot shot in sports sure won't have to go through what I did when she gets to the university.

For those getting involved in a student pressure campaign Palchikoff makes the following suggestions:

A. Meetings with university officials
   1. Always take someone with you to meetings. This is for your own protection. It is a good idea to have someone present as a witness. This is not an act of hostility, as you will soon find out that many times the official may have someone from his or her staff present.
   2. Send follow-up letter to offer thanks for spending the time with you and to confirm in writing anything of significance which was discussed. This will help avoid misunderstandings about each other's positions.

B. Always go through established university channels for problem solving. Start at the bottom and work up. This way you will have done everything according to official procedure.

C. Maintain all contacts through correspondence or phone calls. Send copies of letters, results of meetings, etc. to your contacts, especially within the university. This way you can be sure they are getting your side of the story.

D. Don't be afraid to use the press. Keep the media aware of your problems, concerns and progress.

E. Use your student government. They are usually well informed about university administrative structure and procedure and will know which administrators are easy to work with and which ones will be difficult.

F. *DON'T GIVE UP.* You may be surprised and offended at the number of people who will tell you that you are only hurting women's athletics. "Don't rock the boat." Experience tells me that the only way to get what we want is to demand it, especially where women's rights are concerned. The trick is to learn how to demand in a diplomatic manner.[5]

CHAPTER 8

The Laundry List

Title IX guarantees women athletes opportunities to certain specific services, facilities and benefits, but it does not tell them how to go about getting them. Those areas are:

1. Equipment, supplies and uniforms
2. Scheduling of games and practices, season length, number of games
3. Travel and per diem allowances
4. Opportunity of students to receive coaching
5. Academic tutoring and other academic services
6. Facilities
7. Medical, health and training facilities and services
8. Housing and dining facilities and services
9. Publicity and public relations services
10. Employment: assignment and compensation of administrators, coaches and officials
11. Financial aid to athletes; athletic scholarships
12. Administrative structures of male and female programs (within institutions)
13. Athletic associations and sports governing organizations

In the previous sections we looked at the most effective ways to gain access to equitable or comparable treatment—legal and governmental options, pressure tactics, proposals. All of those methods are applicable for obtaining the rights noted in the laundry list; however, many institutions have found some additional methods.

I. EQUIPMENT, SUPPLIES AND UNIFORMS

The better the team is, the more leverage you will have. In one school, the girls' gymnastics mats were continually being spirited away by the boys' wrestling team. The woman athletic director went to the administration with her complaint, and since her team was far superior to the boys' wrestling team, she was given priority over the mats. As a result, she was able to establish guidelines for use of the mats that applied to both teams. The men were forced to abide by her standards.

When a team plays well enough to consistently make the championships, administrators will be more cognizant of the way the athletes look, because they will be seen by hundreds or perhaps thousands of people at playoffs. Pointing out the shabby appearance of a team prior to the playoffs may well lay the groundwork for better uniforms the next year, especially if the core of the team is returning and has a good chance for another playoff appearance.

A little money can also be used to make more money. Take for example the institution which had about $600 in its budget at the end of the year. The woman coach who controlled the budget for both the men's and women's departments noted that the boys had two pitching machines costing $1,350 each. The girls desperately needed a softball machine. So she went to her administration saying, "The cost of a softball machine is going up, but right now it is only $850. The boys have two at $1,350. You do not think our request is unreasonable in light of that, do you? Well, we only have $600. Can you come up with the last $250?" She got her pitching machine.

At one school where the women athletes were deprived of both shoes and practice uniforms, the athletes were told by the coach to go home and put their objections on paper. During budget talks, the athletes made an appointment to talk to the university president, and presented him their documents. They received their increase.

Some school districts have planning guides and standard equipment lists which note what facilities and equipment a new school or program must have to begin operation. Many times these lists are only for males, because they have not been updated in years. Local women's coaches' associations and women league representatives can start a movement to urge the district to update or provide a planning guide and standard equipment list for female athletes. This guarantees that the district is required to furnish all items on the list, and that when worn out, they will be replaced with operating funds from the student body or institution.

League rules can often be an asset in obtaining quality equipment. If the league rules state that volleyball games will be played with a certain brand volleyball only, all schools in the league must order that type of ball. The same is true of uniform specifications.

Some of the equipment may be gotten from the men's department. One sharp woman athletic director went to the male basketball coach/athletic director asking his advice on whether to continue to have her

© 1979 United Features Syndicate, Inc.

girls play with rubber balls. When he realized how sophisticated the girls' team was becoming, he voluntarily gave the woman coach a $50 leather ball. She also managed to receive practice jerseys and an unused pitching machine (subsequently altered for softball) the same way, by simply asking for suggestions.

The employment of an equipment person is also often a problem. Women coaches at one school convinced the principal that the locker room/equipment room could not remain unattended while they were out on the field, nor could it be locked because athletes needed to gain access. Therefore, an additional part-time person was essential.

II. SCHEDULING OF GAMES AND PRACTICES, SEASON LENGTH, NUMBER OF GAMES

Season of Sport. One of the hottest controversies in girls' athletics today, this problem seems almost insoluble. No matter how it is worked out, somebody is inevitably unhappy—athletes, women coaches, men coaches, state high school associations, principals. The problem results from the fact that the rapid growth of women's sports has put enormous conflict on facility usage. So, administrators have sought to equalize opportunities for females to use facilities, while inadvertently cutting down on those opportunities. They did such things as:

1. Move women's sports (never men's) from their traditional seasons to relieve the facility crunch. As a result, they overlapped sports. For example, basketball is changed to overlap some of the weeks of field hockey, thus preventing young women who are both field hockey and basketball players from playing both sports. Three-sport athletes became one- or two-sport players. In one state, it practically destroyed the field hockey program. Additionally, coaches who handled both sports were forced to choose one over the other, which effectively cut their coaching stipend in half.

2. Combine all the men's and women's seasons in each individual sport (tennis in spring, basketball in fall, etc.). This resulted in the elimination of several boys' frosh-soph, B and C teams in order to accommodate girls' teams in the facilities. It did facilitate use of one coach to handle both teams, but as some have noted, it is easier for a single coach to have a girls' team in one season and a boys' team in the other, in order to provide more personal attention to each student.

Those changes often failed to take into account the reasons why these sports had traditional seasons (it was not exactly pleasant to play softball in the snow or have field hockey turn into ice hockey), and that women placed different emphasis on certain sports (volleyball is a major sport for women, whereas it is minor for men). For women it was like moving football to the summer. Some of the season-of-sport calendars were designed to cut down interscholastic teams and increase intramural competition; however, schools with over-stretched budgets wondered where the money would come from in order to start intramural programs. Also, many of the sports began during the playoffs of other sports.

Much of the problem was that many of the schedules were arranged predominantly by men who saw their own sports as sacred and untouchable. Not sufficiently united on what they did want as an alternative, women could not wield an influence on them.

There is no reason to settle for an unacceptable season of sport. The first and foremost task is for each woman administrator at every school to meet with her principal to explain why the calendar causes hardships, and request he convey those feelings at the league level and then pass them on to the state association governing body.

Women coaches and female athletes can also mount letter writing campaigns; they can strike, protest, petition. However, the most effective method is to present an alternative calendar which is fair to athletes of both sexes. "If you can make a better mousetrap. . . ." as the saying goes, do so. Another way to focus attention on the problem is to simply arrange with all of the other coaches in the region to hold certain sports when they are convenient to all, regardless of sanctioned seasons. This will force principals to look closely at the situation (although it could cause censure). Dropping sports, even with a lot of hoopla, may get nowhere unless they are sports highly supported by the community. For example, in certain areas of the country where there are strong youth soccer leagues, parents become irate when soccer programs for their daughters are eliminated. Utilize parents on season of sport campaigns and other related issues.

Here are some things to consider in drawing up an alternative season of sport:

1. Is it absolutely necessary that JV teams play during the same season as varsity? Instead of putting girls' basketball in the spring and boys' basketball in the fall, put both varsity teams in the spring and JV teams in the fall. This enables coaches to buy one less set of uniforms and equipment for each gender.

2. Are three seasons applicable or are four perhaps more practical for your area? Some school districts find a quarter system more equitable, but others find it too complicated.

3. Can certain parts of the state (because of climate) have the option to select seasons other than those sanctioned by the state association?

4. Can boys' and girls' seasons be staggered in order to afford best use of facilities? (Girls' season is half over when boys' begins.) This allows girls to be gearing up for playoffs, when they need the most intensive use of facilities, at a time when boys are just warming up.

5. Must the JV teams play inside the gym or can they practice on outside courts? In previous years, girls were forced to play outside and boys were allowed inside. This was unfair because it represented sexual discrimination. But what if both boys' and girls' JV teams practiced outside? It may not be the best opportunities for them, but it is fair for both sexes.

Length of Season. Suggest to the district office that it draw up rulebooks and schedules which pair boys' and girls' schedules together. Thus, if there are inequities in the number of contests, length of season, or number of practice contests, they are readily visible. This can also be done by a coaches' association and then passed on to principals.

Adding a Sport. This can be accomplished by citing an institutional student survey showing interest in a sport that the school does not offer. Parents and students can play an important part in lobbying for the sport through a booster club, parent campaign, student pressure group, etc. To get a new sport sanctioned by the state association, gather supporting evidence that there is interest in it (surveys, number of students competing within the community, athletic director's testimonials that the sport is being requested at the schools). Figure out ways to put together the sport inexpensively. Go into the meeting with the work half done already. This will speed up the evaluation process on the part of the administrators.

III. TRAVEL AND PER DIEM ALLOWANCE

Letting women athletes drive to events in cars is extremely risky in terms of possible accidents as well as the legal ramifications of such accidents. Women can help to put a stop to these practices by constantly reminding administrators of liable laws. Send them copies of newspaper clippings where students were injured, or where parents sued; do a comprehensive study of liable cases relating to students driving to contests. (See *Functional Administration in Physical and Health Education,* M. L. Johnson, Houghton Mifflin, 1977, and *Administrative Practices in Boys and Girls Interscholastic Athletics,* John H. and William A. Healey, Charles C. Thomas, 1976.) If the board of education is unaware that the women's program is forced into using this mode of transportation, the risks should be pointed out.

Travel problems must not only be pointed out in a general sense, but a specific one. Take note of the day the bus was overcrowded and then memo the administration, "Regarding my previously voiced con-

cern about our travel situation on our trip Jan. 25, we
had 45 students on a 30-passenger bus. Is there something we can do about this in the future?"

One form of transportation which the men in college athletic departments frequently employ is the
courtesy car, an auto on loan from a local car dealer
at no cost to them or the department. Often these cars
have a sign on the door that reads, "Courtesy of Hank's
Chevrolet," thereby providing free advertising and a
good public relations tool. Even now, when women are
adopting so many of the practices used in the men's
departments, they have failed to use this as a viable
way to cut costs. Courtesy cars can be used for recruiting, scouting, business trips, support staff business, etc.

Mary Alice Hill, associate athletic director at San
Diego State, realized that the only ways she would get
a courtesy car would be to:

a) wait until the department got around to making arrangements for it, or
b) go out pounding on doors herself.

She did the latter. She began sending out letters
to local dealers to see if they were interested (Fig. 8.1).
With the letter, she included a copy of the football program which had pictures of the dealers who had been
loaning the football team cars over the previous year.
A few days after the dealers received her letter, she
called each one to explain the program. The dealers
would receive:

1. A picture in the football program
2. Free tickets to all sports events (men's and women's)
3. Mention of the company's generosity at the 40 banquets
   the coaches and administrators speak at each year
4. Free advertising on all television interviews for wom-
   en's sports

ATHLETIC DEPARTMENT

SAN DIEGO STATE UNIVERSITY   SAN DIEGO, CA 92182
PHONE 714 - 286-5163

The Courtesy Car Program at San Diego State University is designed to provide immediate transportation to some critical areas of our program; these areas are Administration, Coaches & Support Staff and the sports that must do heavy recruiting. Basically, this program provides the means for full time staff to accomplish the tasks that are critical for continuation of the total program.

1. The Athletic Department and the Associated Students will provide the licensing and registration of these vehicles as per contract.
2. Each person is responsible to the dealer in case of accident. Accidents must be promptly reported to the dealer, Athletic Department and the Graduate Manager's Office. A $100.00 deductible policy for these vehicles is in effect and the responsibility for this first one-hundred dollars shall rest with the individual who has accepted the vehicle on the "loaned" basis.
3. The car will be returned to the dealer at the dealer's request. Arrangements for a new model or loaner will be made between the coach and the dealer.

Benefits to the dealers:

1. There is a picture in the Aztec Football Program; this is distributed at all Aztec home games.
2. Free tickets to the dealer for all events, both men & women.
3. Administration & Coaches speak to approximately 40 different groups per year and would mention the contributing dealers.
4. TV interviews concerning the program for Women's Athletics, opportunities to mention the name of contributing dealers.

This would be a very big first for the dealers as it would be the first time a Women's Athletic program was provided with Courtesy cars in the State of California. This alone would merit a great deal of publicity.

BADMINTON	BASEBALL	BASKETBALL	CROSS COUNTRY	FIELD HOCKEY
FOOTBALL	GOLF	GYMNASTICS	SOCCER	SOFTBALL
SWIMMING	TENNIS	TRACK & FIELD	VOLLEYBALL	WATER POLO

Courtesy of San Diego State University.

She briefly summarized the institution's obligations and the nature of the contract. Then she noted
that it would be a first in the state; no other women's
program had courtesy cars. Lastly, she volunteered to
come down and show them the department's standard
courtesy car contract.

Now many of her coaches drive courtesy cars. Hill
makes a point of having her coaches call the dealers
every few weeks to see if they want tickets, which creates a positive atmosphere for future agreements.

IV. COACHING

Getting the proper number of part-time and full-time
coaches is probably one of the women's athletic director's most difficult tasks, because the administration
always feels there is some way to "make do." They
can let the men coach women athletes, combine teams
(male and female, varsity and JV), they can force physical educators to coach against their will. But add more
positions—never!

In California, the California Women's Coaches
Academy was instrumental in pushing the Los Angeles
City Schools to add the paid position of assistant softball coach. This was done through many of the techniques cited in the previous sections—letter writing campaigns, personal contact with board members, HEW
complaints, etc. Women's coaching organizations can
be an excellent vehicle for urging state associations
and school districts to provide adequate coaching jobs.

One factor which may work to the women's program's advantage is the number of "hidden" coaches
in a boys' football or basketball program. Frequently,
the boys' department claims to have fewer coaches
than it actually does. An athletic director reports that
she began to investigate the *real* number of coaches

in the boys' program by first asking for rosters of coaches. She received four completely different lists from the head coach, the athletic director, the secretary, and payroll. Then she went out to observe practice and count coaches, many of whom were very young and worked for very little money. Prepared with her completed list of football coaches, she went into a meeting with the administration requesting additional funding for female coaches. The administrators responded that the boys' program had a number of coaches equal to the girls'. She, in turn, commented, "That may be ture, but I've learned something interesting. They are using two extra people. They seem to be coaches; they are out there with whistles around their necks running drills, but they are listed as instructional aids. Now if we could get some extra people as instructional aids, that would really help." The woman was very successful in her campaign, and recommends that women athletic directors go out and count coaches. If you see one you do not know, ask who he is. Be tactful when presenting the information; do not act like a "muckraker" revealing corruption.

When institutions lose coaches, but have no positions to offer in physical education, it often provides a better incentive for the district or school to open up nontenured positions. Women have also made such suggestions as having the boys' JV basketball coach brought over to coach the girls' team. In one case, the athletic director was given a go-ahead to hire a female coach the next day.

Encouraging administrators to expand a part-time coaching job to a full-time requires some strategy. It should be noted that a full-time person can help with much of the administrative paperwork and that part-timers create overcrowded facilities because they generally can only practice during prime time. There are

a number of other objections to part-time coaches
which may be used in reiterating the need to expand
the position, including citing a lack of loyalty and
coaches' unavailability to students during the day.
However, it is not necessary to lobby for a big jump
from a part-time position to full-time all at once. The
athletic director can recommend providing a gradual
increase from ¼ load to ½ to ¾, and finally full-time
over three or four years. Another way to insure a part-
timer a place on the staff is to look around the institution for other positions (teaching or otherwise) for
which the person may qualify. When hiring part-timers look for people who can also teach, should a position open up. The administration should be aware that
the program with a predominance of part-timers suf-
fers in terms of morale and continuity because they
will usually be looking around for a better full-time
position and this, subsequently, causes a big turnover
in the program.

V. ACADEMIC TUTORING AND ACADEMIC SERVICES

This is usually one of the easiest services to obtain
because tutoring is commonly available to all students
through a learning skills center or other related office.
However, it may take a little effort to convince the
counseling office to send computer readouts of the students' grades to the women's department as well as
the men's. Should this become a problem, go to an administrator high in the institution and explain the dan-
gers to the program of accidentally playing an ineligi-
ble student.

Usually a more serious problem is helping students to get books, since the AIAW forbids the school
from including books in a scholarship. One female athletic director discovered the most effective way of in-

suring the women students books was to volunteer to take over the book loan program for the entire department. Thus, she could reserve a certain number for women athletes instead of having them all doled out to male athletes first.

VI. FACILITIES

The willingness to accept terrible practice hours, to practice outside or in lousy facilities will demonstrate to administrators the women athletes' dedication to their sport. A few months of this is enough to show that the teams deserve better treatment. One of the assumptions is that women are not serious about sport and therefore do not deserve serious consideration for use of facilities. This strategy corrects that impression, but it is unlikely the situation will change unless the woman athletic director can gently point out the sacrifice and request better conditions.

Another option is for the athletic director to subtly suggest that since the women's team cannot obtain reasonable practice time at home, it can just rent the junior high down the street. That should get the administrators where it hurts—in their wallets.

The Los Angeles City Schools have a practice which is very effective in bringing pressure to bear on administrators to either upgrade their facilities for women or to provide more time in the facilities. It is a facility survey that evaluates which schools in each league have unacceptable facilities or playing schedules. The list is published so that all coaches may present it to their principals (Fig. 8.2).

Obviously, the preferable way to gain access to facilities is to work out a schedule peacefully and cordially with the male athletic director, but sometimes that is not possible. As an alternative, a woman may

LOS ANGELES UNIFIED SCHOOL DISTRICT
Student Auxiliary Services Branch
INTERSCHOLASTIC ATHLETICS

January 1977

SUBJECT: FACILITY PROBLEMS AND MODIFICATIONS (AND LEAGUE REPRESENTATIVES)

LEAGUE	NAME/SCHOOL	FACILITY PROBLEMS	MODIFICATION
CITY-WEST	Linda Elliott Palms Jr. High	University has no gym, is trying for Webster Jr. High's gym. Dorsey, Crenshaw, and Venice – No six-foot clearance (approx. five feet). Westchester – Beams We want to play off the ceiling – no replays.	None
CITY-EAST	Karen Chang Roosevelt High	J.V.'s play first. Low ceilings – replay. Hangings – replay.	Low ceilings will be a replay.
MID-CITY	None	Low ceiling at Manual Arts and Jefferson. Walls too close at Jefferson, Hollywood, and Los Angeles.	Four present. Three would rather play off ceiling (keep rule as is). One wants it to be replay off low ceiling.
HARBOR	Sandi O'Bitz Gardena High	Conflicts with student basketball teams in using large gyms. We may request some schedule changes if conflicts are found (in meeting with Athletic Director). The other coaches agree they will not play in Gardena's small gym due to safety factors.	None.
VALLEY-WEST	Mr. Hubbard Taft High	None.	By the book.
VALLEY-EAST	Ruth Halsey Poly High	Verdugo Hills – Having problems with Mt. Gleason Jr. High. Discussed possible change in schedule of switching Wednesday home games to Mondays.	None.
VALLEY-NORTH	Carol Ann Kos San Fernando High	None.	Monroe and Kennedy have short courts. Service areas extend into court areas. San Fernando has no gym.

SUBMITTED BY: Coaches at pre-season meeting.

For assistance, please call Patricia Harvey, Specialist, Interscholastic Athletics, at 625-6447.

APPROVED: JIM CHEFFERS, Director, Interscholastic Athletics

DISTRIBUTION: G.I.A. Volleyball Coaches

send a note to the athletic director (after talks have broken down), the vice-principal and principal noting that having girls practice until 10 every night is educationally unsound. A second choice is to not wait until the male athletic director gets around to working out a schedule. Do it yourself. Prepare a schedule that you feel fits the needs of all concerned, check with the coaches to rally their support, and then present it to him or his superior. Do not go in demanding time. Say something like, "We seem to have a conflict of schedules here. I drew this one up, but it has not been accepted by Jim. Do you think you can look it over and suggest any alternatives? Here are the notes from nearly all the coaches indicating they feel this is viable."

One other tactic that may very well get women's teams into the "good" gym is again a matter of money. Administrators who wish to make the women's program self-sufficient cannot do that by putting the basketball team in a gym that does not even have bleachers or a scoreboard. They must make the package attractive to spectators. This can be used as a lever.

When men coaches demand to use facilities or equipment normally reserved for females, it is only fair that girls have the opportunity to use the corresponding boys' facilities, such as using the opposite sex's locker rooms for a visiting team room. If the male coaches put up a fuss at this argument, discuss the matter with an administrator.

VII. MEDICAL, HEALTH AND TRAINING FACILITIES AND SERVICES

A few years ago, noted woman trainer Holly Wilson surveyed women athletic administrators about whether they saw a need to have a trainer. Nearly three-quarters of the women agreed there was a need, but half of them were resistant to hire one themselves, because there was not enough money in the budget; they felt coaches who supplied first aid were just as competent and there was a low number of injuries, most of which were minor.[1]

It is highly unlikely that Wilson would receive the same answers today. Women's athletics has blossomed and with it has been a drastic increase in the number and severity of injuries. Coaches have proven themselves to be poor substitutes for trainers in preventing injuries and caring for injured students. Liability suits are making coaches wary, but there is only so much they can do without proper training. In fact, several tests have shown that physical educators know very little about what are the best modern procedures in caring for athletic injuries. They are hopelessly behind the times. Many administrators with misplaced priorities add a sport from excess money in the budget instead of protecting athletes already in the program by hiring a trainer. Actually, they are not alone; few men's programs have a full-time certified trainer either. Only 1 percent of the high schools in the United States have a certified trainer.

Why is a trainer so important? She can:

1. Prepare proper conditioning programs to prevent injuries.
2. Free a coach to concentrate on coaching instead of splitting her duties between training and coaching.
3. Be the objective voice that makes a coach refrain from putting an injured athlete back into a game.
4. Help lower the school's athletic injury and liability insurance.
5. Save the school money because she has a better knowledge of the precise needs of a training room. Coaches only guess.

6. Recognize the severity of injuries on the spot and know when a youngster needs a doctor. She is less likely to make mistakes of judgment that a coach might make.
7. Meet any laws a state might make demanding schools to have certified trainers.
8. Create a closer relationship to athletes and parents than many coaches, thereby improving public relations for the school.
9. Do some things a doctor can do, especially if she has a physical therapy license.
10. Be on the lookout for specific trends in injuries which may indicate problems in the facilities or the coach's practice techniques.
11. Prepare a staff of student trainers who can travel with each team.
12. Make use of the most modern and progressive measures to protect the life and health of the athletes.
13. Get athletes back into condition sooner after an injury.

Until school administrators, athletic administrators, coaches, and parents realize these factors, they will continue to offer the lame excuse, "We cannot afford it." On the contrary, they cannot afford not to. They, along with physicians, other athletic health care specialists and trainers, are the ones who must carry the ball in a campaign to obtain a trainer.

Dr. Paul M. Steingard, the director of the Sports Medicine Clinic of Phoenix, told a panel of doctors discussing the need for trainers as reported in *The Physician and Sports Medicine* magazine, "I think it is extremely difficult to sell a trainer to a high school whether you talk certification or not. School boards are so preoccupied with financial distress that introducing a new program or a new concept to them frequently meets with resistance because of the finances involved. It has been our experience that if we want to introduce a new concept, we can gain much more by going to the State Department of Education, rather than to the individual school board."[2]

In their campaign, Dr. Steingard and his colleagues united the state medical associations behind them, and extracted an offer from Arizona colleges to produce the necessary number of athletic trainers if the State Department of Education should decree that each school must have a certified trainer. Both of these factors weighed heavily in their favor.

North Carolina is an excellent example where this type of state department approach has succeeded. The department's Sports Medicine Division has been responsible for developing a framework of teacher-trainers, scheduling sports medicine courses, encouraging the state's universities to offer an undergraduate and graduate curriculum in training, co-sponsoring student-trainer workshops within the state coaches' association, putting on clinics for coaches illustrating the value of trainers to the staff, promoting more activity between the doctors and sports personnel at the schools, locating team doctors, developing television tapes for teacher-trainers which are shown on the state educational network, and initiating research.

The state of Texas went one step further. The legislature mandated that all schools must have a certified trainer, and that trainers must be licensed by the state.

For some time, the United States contemplated the Dellums Bill which would have forced each school to hire a trainer by 1980, but it was finally defeated, partly because of lobbying by the National Federation which held that few schools had the funds to support such a law.

Obviously, a law would be the most effective way to insure young athletes of proper health care, but the impetus for such laws or policies must come from every level—legislators, state and local school administrators, parents, coaches, etc. It must be a united effort.

Joe Borland, physical therapist and athletic trainer in Southern California, says, "The weakest link in having a quality athletic training program has been lack of community involvement. If the parents get involved, the monies will be easier to obtain. The parents are the ones that must come to the superintendent or the principal and ask, 'How come we don't have this? Why are we spending money elsewhere?' They have to put the fear of God in the board. If they settle for anything less than training personnel that is all they will ever get. One school system gave the schools $300 for a trainer. Now those people can't get any more and it's been 10 years. The district says, 'We've already given you $300; that's all you wanted and that's all you get.' "

But getting the parents concerned is the most important task. That can be done by trainers presenting demonstrations to the parents, explaining what they do, and by athletic directors telling a few horror stories about youngsters who have suffered severe injuries because no adequate trainer was available. Mostly, parents are just ignorant of the need for trainers. Schools, coaches' associations, athletic director associations, and local units of the National Athletic Trainers Association (NATA) should begin to sponsor seminars for parents, coaches who are not solidly behind the campaign for trainers, school board members, state department employees and legislators. They should be equipped with up-to-date statistics on athletic injuries in the state and district. Members of state athletic associations and athletic school board committees can make strong recommendations to their superiors for mandatory trainers.

Through the various associations, coaches and athletic directors can call for a statewide symposium on athletic training or a statewide conference or committee to put together a report on a proposed training program. The California Interscholastic Federation Southern Section prepared just such a document which several athletic administrators utilized to convince the school boards that trainers were necessary.

Doctors play a vital role in urging schools to adopt such practices. School boards assume that members of NATA have a vested interest and they may well be skeptical of the value of a trainer unless it is backed up by physicians whom most boards consider the ultimate experts in health care. Thus, it is important for coaches or administrators seeking training programs to rally the local doctors behind the cause. Utilize the team doctors as focal points. Let them act as liaison to professional medical associations.

On a local level, coaches can be especially persuasive. By going before school boards and confessing their lack of knowledge about athletic injuries and their fears about taping their own athletes, they can convince board members to see the spectre of liability cases and the keen need to take action immediately. (Coaches would not be casting a shadow on their own abilities; they have an expertise in coaching. They are not taught to be, nor hired to be, trainers.)

Ultimately, the question of money arises. Where will it come from? How much will be necessary? Coaches and athletic directors pressing for trainers can advance their causes by having the answers at hand for school boards. This takes some research. It requires finding out what funds are available, what other districts are doing, looking for innovative solutions, coming up with alternatives, and finding ways of creating new sources of funding. By presenting all of this information to the board, divided into several alternative plans for action, the board is relieved of the responsibility and may even discover some solutions which it might have overlooked. The demands for funding must be placed into perspective. Asking for $20,000 for a trainer might draw an immediate negative response. However, board members must be made to see that it is actually only $20 per student in a program that serves 1,000 athletes. Surely, parents and board members cannot consider that exhorbitant for the benefits the students are receiving.

VIII. HOUSING AND DINING FACILITIES AND SERVICES

Housing is frequently assigned to students long before letters of intent are signed. It is a good practice to become friendly with housing officials so that they understand your position and hold open however many spaces your athletes may need.

IX. PUBLICITY AND PUBLIC RELATIONS

One of the best ways a woman athletic director can insure adequate sports information service is to look for potential candidates when a sports information director (SID) job is about to open. That way, when the position is announced, she has one or two candidates, male or female, who are extremely interested in women's athletics to present to the administration or athletic director.

At one state university the position of sports information director was completely abolished. As a result, the athletes presented a unified force before the administration, claiming they had no intention of playing before empty stands. They were not interested in getting the outside public to attend games, but they were concerned about getting students into the gym. On that basis, the position was reinstated with a part-time student in the role of SID assigned to emphasize school-oriented coverage.

X. EMPLOYMENT: COACHES COMPENSATION

Women's tennis coach Judy Dixon, who led Yale teams to a 33–9 record in four seasons recently, resigned her position and sued the university for sex discrimination. The men's tennis coach earned close to $1,000 more annually for performing the same duties.

Cries of discrimination of this nature are very common. Male counterparts charge that men should receive a larger stipend for such ludicrous reasons as:

1. they coach revenue-producing sports (women don't)
2. their season is longer
3. they are under pressure to win (women aren't)
4. they have families to support; they are the "bread win-ners" of the household (women aren't)

The school district's argument or defense is most often predicated on an assumption or feeling, rather than fact. It often contends that its women coaches do not spend as much time coaching as their male counterparts, that they have fewer responsibilities and coach shorter seasons; therefore, women coaches work fewer hours. If, in fact, that charge is true, it is a fair argument *only if* judged on clock hours; however, if the stipend is based on the length of seasons and the men's seasons are longer, the lengths have to be altered so they are comparable.

It is advised that a council comprised of men and women be formed to develop the criteria used to deter-mine unbiased salary schedules for coaches. The index may be based on ratios which include such factors as qualifications and experience of the coach. The council should develop a job description for each coach which delineates his or her responsibilities and assignments. In addition to the index, the job description must be considered carefully (but only if it is accurate) when determining individual salaries.

The base coaching salary should be dependent on length of the sport season. Given this premise, the salary could then be computed as follows: A given number of dollars multiplied by the number of weeks in the season (*"x" no. $ x no. wks.*). In addition to the *base* salary, the coach could be awarded supplemental dollars as warranted by the following factors:

1. Type of activity being coached (major vs. minor sports, intramurals vs. interscholastic or intercollegiate competition)
2. Experience of coach (number of years coaching)
3. Coach's training (qualifications, credentials, specialization)
4. Responsibility for personnel (extent to which overseeing of other coaches, trainers, equipment personnel, or other staff is required)
5. Responsibility level (head coach or assistant; junior varsity or varsity)
6. Complexity of duties (number, importance and frequency of decisions made and problems dealt with)

XI. ATHLETIC SCHOLARSHIPS

At institutions where the school provides only a few scattered scholarships to each women's sport, such as three in volleyball, it should be pointed out to administrators that the practice can backfire. The result is combining three highly-skilled scholarship players and three non-scholarship (probably far out-classed) ath-

letes on the floor together. This has the effect of lowering the morale of the very good players, and making
the non-scholarship athletes feel inferior. Schools
should allot scholarships for the starting team, at least.

A gradual increase in scholarship money can be
worked out also. The ultimate goal would be the ratio
of scholarships per athlete in the men's department
to that of the women's department. Over the course
of three years, it climbs steadily toward that figure.

The answer to increasing scholarship dollars is
effective fund raising.

XII. ADMINISTRATIVE STRUCTURES

The key factor in administrative structures is whether
women coaches (or concerned and fair male coaches)
have an opportunity to utilize their judgments on what
benefits female athletes. Whoever is representing the
women's program must be given the power to protect
its interests and expand its capacity. Usually, the best
way to accomplish this is to have a woman who is
assistant or associate athletic director.

A very effective method which is used by some
women to create the position is to do the job for no
or very low pay for some time, then, ask to be paid.
If the administration refuses to pay for the service, it
will find that the woman is really indispensable when
the work falls on the shoulders of the women coaches
or male athletic director. A related strategy is just to
wait until all the chores for women's athletics pile up
on the male athletic director and then "volunteer" to
take much of it off his hands in exchange for a stipend.
Part-time administrators, who wish their jobs to be expanded to full-time administration, can threaten to
leave the school because other full-time jobs have been
offered elsewhere. To do this, of course, a woman must

be very sure that she is highly respected by the administration, or else she is taking a big risk.

Oftentimes, the reason administrators say they will not hire women to oversee combined programs is that they haven't enough experience. This can be remedied by coaxing a male athletic director into providing an internship at no pay for one year. Thus, when a job is opened a woman can maintain she has experience. Another way for a woman to get the necessary experience is to act as a "crossover" assistant athletic director, working on the problems of both the boys' and girls' programs. Under this system, the male and female can alternate in overseeing events—one week she does the boys' basketball game and the next week he does, etc.

Women who are in supposedly equivalent positions to the male athletic director often find they are compelled to report to a person different from the one their male counterparts do. This should be corrected by going to the chief administrator, pointing out the inconsistency, and, if necessary, refusing to continue the practice.

Another way that women athletic directors are slighted is the lack of an office. Ask to share an office with the athletic director or seek the addition of a used trailer where both administrators can be located. A woman must make it known that her job is not less difficult than the male athletic director and therefore she needs the same amount of concentration. She requires an opportunity to have phone calls in private and to shut out people when she wishes to close the door. Here again, it is important to propose a location for the office, so that administrators see that it has been thoroughly thought through.

One woman athletic director says people have a tendency to lump the boys' and girls' programs together. If she does not remind them that the girls' program is totally separate from the boys', her job will be the first to go at budget cut time. She says, "Once you give way to the idea they are one and the same program, you lose control of your own program. If the mail comes in addressed to "The Athletic Director," who gives them the right to send it to him and not me? It's the little things that make an impression on people and that's why I harp on the little things."

General Strategies

A few techniques can be used by women to gain equality in any one of these areas. One is to volunteer for the position of affirmative action coordinator in the district, or ask to get on the Title IX committee. The more committees a woman can become active on, the more leverage she has, but these two committees carry extra clout in a district or school.

Secondly, she can continually remind the administration of the success of the program based on a compendium of newspaper clippings from the local press. This is impressive when administrators are doing budget talks. The more successful the program, the more money it gets, although it is a very unfortunate truism.

Last, women can do as they wish with the little money they are given and then present the administration with a finished product. For example, the women at a high school in Southern California put together an excellent girls' program on virtually no funding. After two years of operation, they went to the administration with a request for official recognition via a budget. They could prove to the administration (1) there was interest in each sport, (2) the women had the expertise, (3) they would be willing to coach, (4) there was a need for the program, and (5) they were already participating in an established league. With student, parent and teacher support behind them, the women won their case.

WISHFUL THINKING: THE IDEAL ATHLETIC MODEL

If endless dollars were available and men treated women as equals, both psychically and practically, then the Ideal Athletic Model could be a reality. But we all know that today it is realistically impossible to expect those factors to exist, given the limited funding which faces institutions and the innate prejudices in society developed throughout history. This is not to say the Ideal Athletic Model could not someday come true. It should provide a goal for which all people— men and women—in athletics can aim. The selected criteria for the Ideal Athletic Model is predicated on a concern for the athlete's welfare—personal, emotional, educational and physical. What is suggested herein takes into consideration the best of all possible worlds for student athletes.

In the Ideal Athletic Model, an equal number of men and women would represent athletic programs at the national, state, conference, and league level. That would mean that all governing bodies would be single units with bicameral divisions. Thus, the men and women would periodically meet separately and together. Such equality would apply to coaching committees or organizations, athletic directors, faculty representatives and institutional administrators. Wherever athletics were to be discussed, an equal number of representatives of men's and women's programs would be present. This plan provides for cohesiveness and supportiveness, so that men and women bolster each other, help each other and work with each other instead of quarreling. It would insure that representatives would be concerned for the total program, and that no one gender could dominate the other.

The athletic department at the institution would serve all students regardless of sex. Its administrative structure would take one of the three following approaches:

1. There would be co-athletic directors, one of each sex, who would not be confined to administrating sports of one gender only. Each would handle all teams of certain sports. For example, she would have basketball, baseball-softball, field hockey-ice hockey; he would have volleyball, football, gymnastics, track, etc.

2. The athletic department and physical education department would be one unit. A person of one sex would be the physical education chair, and a person of the other sex would be the athletic director. They would be each other's bosses. For example, when the male athletic director would teach in the department, he would take orders from the female physical education chair; when she coached, she would take orders from the athletic director. This would force them to work together cooperatively or accept the consequences of retaliation for dirty deeds done to each other. It would put them on equal footing. Either one could fire or reprimand the other. In this type of situation, it could also be established that the male and female switch positions yearly, so that each gained expertise in athletics and physical education administration.

3. There would be one athletic director and an assistant of the opposite sex. However, the top position would not depend on gender only, but on the competen-

cies of each individual. The criteria for athletic director would not include years of coaching, but instead
such factors as experience in administration, professional preparation, etc.

The woman who would take a job in this framework would be fully as competent as any male administrator. A scholarship available for women to study
within the field would have allowed her an opportunity
to enter a master's or doctoral program with a specialization in athletic administration. In the course of her
educational program, she would have had an opportunity to gain experience through an internship program
at a school or in a national body. With demonstrated
skill in the field, she would be given the same power
previously awarded to any male administrator and the
opportunity to report directly to the same institutional
administrator. Her pay would reflect her position, not
her sex.

The position she assumes would be a full-time job
with no teaching or coaching duties, but her previous
coaching and teaching experience would enable her
to relate well to her staff. Without the additional tasks,
she would be free to concentrate on the growing job
of running an athletic department. She would be entitled to any and all services provided by the institution
to administrators of her level, such as secretarial help,
unlimited phone expenses, etc. Additionally, she would

have her own office, located near any male administrator as well as the combined-sex coaching staff. This would facilitate communication.

Last, she would have an opportunity to advance in the administration—from assistant to athletic director, from athletic director to dean, if she so desired. And her application would be solely judged on her qualifications, not her sex.

In the Ideal Athletic Model, all support services would be shared equally. If there is only one business manager or one fund raiser, his or her time would be given equally to athletes of each sex. In the event two people are hired, one could be assigned to the projects and problems of each gender.

The budget would cover all teams, but it would be comparable for men and women athletes. Where there were two teams in the same sport, their budgets would be identical. Women would be required to fundraise no more than the men. The fund-raising machinery and the fund-raising organizations would apply to both sexes. Women's sports would begin to bring in revenue in the form of gate receipts comparable to the revenue produced by men's contests.

All support from the administration—financial, philosophical and practical—would be solidly behind the program as a whole. Winning would be deemphasized in order to place importance on the value of sport as an educational experience for students. The philosophy that the student comes first and the athlete second would filter down from the very top and infiltrate the athletic program. All procedures and paperwork would be non-sexist, applying to *all* athletes.

Considering the administration's concentration on serving the athletes, there would be programs provided at a variety of levels—intercollegiate or interscholastic, club sports and intramural.

The athletic department would not be bound by traditional values about single-sex teams. New options would be open. It would analyze and consider the wisdom of taking the following approaches to sports:

1. Separate but equal teams—This would provide for sex-separated teams which, under the law, could be construed as "inherently unequal" and could hurt the participants psychologically, educationally and socially. However, court cases have upheld separate-but-equal as acceptable in athletics because of the physiological difference between males and females. This is acceptable, provided that both sexes are treated equally.

2. One or two coed teams—A coed team is one where half of the positions would be held open for members of each sex. This would be fair especially in individual sports where men compete against men and women compete against women; their scores are totalled. Objections can be raised when team sports are considered because males may feel they are being held back by females. It may reinforce the feelings of female inferiority. Ability will not be the primary criteria for making the team. Additionally, unless positions are guaranteed in the starting lineup, males will logically have most or all of the spots. This could be guarded against by instituting rules similar to those used by the International Volleyball Association, where two females must be on the court at all times. Rules would have to be modified to make this system work.

3. One or two mixed teams—Essentially, this would come down to two largely all-male teams, because women would be unable to compete equally with the men in winning positions on the team.

4. One varsity mixed team, two single-sex teams—

Although expensive, the system would allow top-level women an opportunity to play with the best males, and still provide slightly lesser male and female athletes a chance to play without the risk that people of the opposite sex would dominate their team. However, it is possible that this could also develop into two male teams and a female team, but at least women would have a chance to play at a high level.

5. One coed team and two single-sex teams—Also expensive, it would insure a more equitable balance.

6. One mixed varsity team and one open to only women—This could be construed by its critics to be discriminatory against men and also injurious to the women's teams because the most outstanding female athletes would be drained off by the mixed team. The effect, however, would likely be to provide a predominantly male team with a very few top-grade women athletes and a female team protected from male domination.

7. Two predominantly one-sex teams—These could include up to 20 percent of the minority sex, but over that percentage, additional coed, male or female teams must be added. This would insure that people of equivalent skill could align, regardless of sex, but it also would protect female teams from the domination of males.

Component Plan I—This would have two predominantly one-sex divisions on each team. The scores of both would be totalled for the team score. The only drawback to this system would be that each element would be dependent on the success of the other; however, that usually leads to the superior element making an effort to improve the inferior one.

Component Plan II—In this system there would be one division where women could earn one or two spots open to athletes of the highest skill level, a second division which would be predominantly single-sex, and a third coed division. In individual sports such as golf, tennis, swimming, and gymnastics, the three teams would be divided according to this system; in team sports, the various traditional sports would form a cluster—baseball, softball and coed softball; hockey, field hockey and soccer; football, flag football and touch football, etc. Thus, the first team would be predominantly male, the second predominantly female, and the last coed. Again, the scores would be totalled for a final tally.

The Ideal Athletic Model would also take a novel approach to coaching in order to erase the inequities between male and female coaches. The athletic director could choose to operate the program in such a way that one person is in charge of all the teams of one sport (varsity and junior varsity, male, female or coed), but that person would be selected regardless of sex. The female head track coach might then employ several male assistants to coach the various teams. Or the athletic director could decide to bring in co-coaches (this may require splitting the stipend), where the female coach with less experience can gain from the benefit of the male coach, but still have the equivalent authority. Another choice would be to hire a male head coach and female assistant for the boys' tennis team and then make the female the head coach and the male the assistant for the girls' team.

The female coaches selected for the job would have been prepared through excellent coaching classes they took in college or intensive in-service programs. Either way, all coaches in the program would be certified. There would be an adequate number of female coaches and a sufficient number of assistant coaches to fill the needs of the students. Each of these coaches would be cognizant that their job is to serve the students and not to build a sports empire. Winning is not the goal. None of the coaches would be compelled to coach sports in which they do not specialize or choose to participate, because there would be enough coaches to cover each sport. No more three- or four-sport coaches. When coaches take the position, they would have an opportunity to select whether they wish to be full-time coaches and go on the coaching track or part-time teacher-coaches and go on the tenure track. Coaches would be awarded sufficient release time to do their job properly, including one extra conference hour daily to perform duties related to coaching. All coaches would be ethical and informed of rules and regulations both at the high school and college level. No "walk-on" coaches would be hired; only trained people who have an allegiance to the institution. Continual clinics and in-service programs would be available and coaches would have entry fees for these and professional association meetings paid by the department. Some travel costs might also be covered.

All coaches would be paid adequately and equitably, receiving salary commensurate with their qualifications, demonstrated skill, amount of commitment (time) and work load. Raises would be based on coaches' contributions to the program, rather than on win-loss record. Offices would be shared by male and female coaches in the same sport, allowing them to build a rapport that would make it easy to work together.

Students would be entitled to a season of sport that denies no student an opportunity to compete and also a comparable schedule of games which would provide relatively the same quality of competition, the same number of contests, the same length of season and the same visibility. Visibility would be assured with back-to-back male-female contests, combined-sex state championships, scheduling women's competition at prime time, allowing women to participate in international competition, playing in large arenas such as Madison Square Garden, and the generating of interest through national and regional sports polls. An example is the National Women's Basketball Poll, begun by Mel Greenberg of the *Philadelphia Inquirer.*

The facilities would be of the best quality and plentiful enough for equitable practice and game times, so that no teams would be forced to use them at unreasonable hours. There would be enough space in gymnasiums, fields, courts, locker rooms, weight rooms, visiting team rooms, storage areas and laundry rooms. These could be for combined use or separate use as long as they were equally well equipped. Space would be planned for future expansion.

Female athletes would travel in the same style as the males (bus or plane), and they would have the same priority, so that they were not the last to be picked up for games. The games would be arranged so that the athletes could obtain comparable competition within a designated geographic area. Women coaches as well as men would be entitled to courtesy cars. Athletes of both genders would stay at quality motels and receive equal per diem.

In order to provide the best coaching, coaches would have access to film and video tape equipment. All athletes would receive the best quality and quantity of uniforms, supplies and equipment and on the same frequency. A full-time equipment person would be provided for each of the equipment cages.

At least two trainers, plus assistants, would be funded for the program, one of which would be specially assigned to women's teams. There would be a coed training room or two separate equitable training rooms equipped with all the modalities and supplies necessary to provide first-class care. All athletes would also have the service of a team doctor and be insured under the athletic program's insurance policy.

Competent officials—male and female—with proper training and experience would be utilized by the league for games. Those officials would be paid equally, regardless of sex. Evaluated frequently, they would be required to renew their certification periodically.

Scholarships to all athletes would be on the basis of need in order to help alleviate many of the under-the-table abuses (though certainly not all could be controlled), but recruiting could be better kept in hand if all schools could offer the same. Then students would be forced to pick institutions because of the important criteria: the coach's personality, the quality of education, etc. However, coaches would be provided adequate funding to cover their travel to assess talent. Academic tutoring would be equally available to all students, and neither sex would have priority to get used books on loan. The entire department would have access to academic counseling and computer information systems. Each of the students would be housed in dorms on campus or in nearby apartments, but would not be segregated from other students. If a training table is provided for one team, it would be open to all. Athletes of both genders would receive equal awards. Those awards would be of a practical nature, deemphasizing winning and emphasizing the character-building aspects of competition. Additionally, the awards would not be costly, nor would they be coveted for size, but for the aesthetic value of them instead. All sports banquets would be sexually integrated, as would letterclubs and student athletic councils.

The sports information service would provide

equal time and energy to the women's programs as to the men's. However, the public relations and publicity campaign would be specially designed for the women's program, since the same approaches frequently are not as effective for the women's program as the men's.

DISCRIMINATION IN SPORT: THE BEGINNING OR THE END?

It has been said that strength comes through struggle; the struggle has been in Congress, the courts, the Department of HEW. Although we still have a long way to go, we have come a long way from confinement in bloomers to justice in gym shorts.

That struggle has opened the doors for massive growth for women. It forced us to use our intelligence, to learn the men's secrets of success and to develop some new ones of our own. It freed us to explore alternatives to conventional methods of change.

Through the struggle, we have also had the opportunity to meet other men and women who share the same ideals. As one looks back at the strides women have made in athletics and the alliances developed along the way, there exists a pride in significant accomplishment. Looking ahead is far more discouraging.

Title IX may never be invulnerable to the attacks by the NCAA and the anti-Title IX lobby. Protecting it may be an unending battle. Despite limited resources that threaten to cause retrenchment and the failure of the Equal Rights Amendment to garner the necessary support, women cannot afford to lose hope or to stop working toward equality.

Without the vision of men and women who realize what women's athletics can be, we would still be at the car-wash or bake-sale stage. It takes courage to

make those ideals a reality. Courage opens the door
to the future and, as George Allen has said, "The Future
is Now."

The task women face is doubly hard because it
not only means mapping a strategy for equality, but
trying to sidestep the mistakes made by our male pre-
decessors. Devising means for change and advocating
a new way will inevitably be met with resistance. The
revolutionary is seldom a popular figure.

Yet, the important factor to remember is that no
woman is alone in the struggle for equality. Each little
effort, as well as each major campaign, gets us closer
to the goal. Whether waged independently, or collectively with women in national organizations, professional societies, athletic leagues or others in the institution, each contribution will have an effect on the future
of women's sports.

The direction that sport will take for men and
women alike should not be determined only by the laws
set forth by the court, nor by the playing rules and
regulations, but rather, by what goes on daily in the
gymnasium and on the athletic field. The real challenge is in implementing sound programs which as-
sure positive sport experiences for *all* young people.
It is a prodigious task, especially for athletic administrators who are so wrapped up in the daily routine
that it is hard to break away and establish new systems.

There are no easy solutions to providing programs
that are absolutely fair for both males and females.
Some sacrifices have to be made by both, merely as a
result of the shortage of funds. It is an unfortunate
fact of life. No one can determine how to eliminate
all the inequities because in granting rights, some have
to be taken away from those holding them initially.
Bringing about fairness calls for creative ingenuity,

a deep reservoir of patience, and an extreme willingness to cooperate. True equality may not occur without
a miracle or two, but then some miracles are (wo)man-
made.

Intercollegiate Athletics: Sex Discrimination

Federal Register / Vol. 44, No. 239 / Tuesday, December 11, 1979 / Rules and Regulations   **71413**

DEPARTMENT OF HEALTH, EDUCATION, AND WELFARE

Office for Civil Rights

Office of the Secretary

45 CFR Part 86

Title IX of the Education Amendments of 1972; a Policy Interpretation; Title IX and Intercollegiate Athletics

AGENCY: Office for Civil Rights, Office of the Secretary, HEW.

ACTION: Policy interpretation.

SUMMARY: The following Policy Interpretation represents the Department of Health, Education, and Welfare's interpretation of the intercollegiate athletic provisions of Title IX of the Education Amendments of 1972 and its implementing regulation. Title IX prohibits educational programs and institutions funded or otherwise supported by the Department from discriminating on the basis of sex. The Department published a proposed Policy Interpretation for public comment on December 11, 1978. Over 700 comments reflecting a broad range of opinion were received. In addition, HEW staff visited eight universities during June and July, 1979, to see how the proposed policy and other suggested alternatives would apply in actual practice at individual campuses. The final Policy Interpretation reflects the many comments HEW received and the results of the individual campus visits.

EFFECTIVE DATE: December 11, 1979

FOR FURTHER INFORMATION CONTACT: Colleen O'Connor, 330 Independence Avenue, Washington, D.C. (202) 245-6671

SUPPLEMENTARY INFORMATION:

I. Legal Background

A. The Statute

Section 901(a) of Title IX of the Education Amendments of 1972 provides:

No person in the United States shall, on the basis of sex, be excluded from participation in, be denied the benefits of, or be subjected to discrimination under any education program or activity receiving Federal financial assistance.

Section 844 of the Education Amendments of 1974 further provides:

The Secretary of (of HEW) shall prepare and publish * * * proposed regulations implementing the provisions of Title IX of the Education Amendments of 1972 relating to the prohibition of sex discrimination in federally assisted education programs which shall include with respect to intercollegiate athletic activities reasonable provisions considering the nature of particular sports.

Congress passed Section 844 after the Conference Committee deleted a Senate floor amendment that would have exempted revenue-producing athletics from the jurisdiction of Title IX.

B. The Regulation

The regulation implementing Title IX is set forth, in pertinent part, in the Policy Interpretation below. It was signed by President Ford on May 27, 1975, and submitted to the Congress for review pursuant to Section 431(d)(1) of the General Education Provisions Act (GEPA).

During this review, the House Subcommittee on Postsecondary Education held hearings on a resolution disapproving the regulation. The Congress did not disapprove the regulation within the 45 days allowed under GEPA, and it therefore became effective on July 21, 1975.

Subsequent hearings were held in the Senate Subcommittee on Education on a bill to exclude revenues produced by sports to the extent they are used to pay the costs of those sports. The Committee, however, took no action on this bill.

The regulation established a three year transition period to give institutions time to comply with its equal athletic opportunity requirements. That transition period expired on July 21, 1978.

II. Purpose of Policy Interpretation

By the end of July 1978, the Department had received nearly 100 complaints alleging discrimination in athletics against more than 50 institutions of higher education. In attempting to investigate these complaints, and to answer questions from the university community, the Department determined that it should provide further guidance on what constitutes compliance with the law. Accordingly, this Policy Interpretation explains the regulation so as to provide a framework within which the complaints can be resolved, and to provide institutions of higher education with additional guidance on the requirements for compliance with Title IX in intercollegiate athletic programs.

III. Scope of Application

This Policy Interpretation is designed specifically for intercollegiate athletics. However, its general principles will often apply to club, intramural, and interscholastic athletic programs, which are also covered by regulation.[1]

---

[1] The regulation specifically refers to club sports separately from intercollegiate athletics. Accordingly, under this Policy Interpretation, club

Footnotes continued on next page

71414 **Federal Register** / Vol. 44, No. 239 / Tuesday, December 11, 1979 / Rules and Regulations

Accordingly, the Policy Interpretation may be used for guidance by the administrators of such programs when appropriate.

This policy interpretation applies to any public or private institution, person or other entity that operates an educational program or activity which receives or benefits from financial assistance authorized or extended under a law administered by the Department. This includes educational institutions whose students participate in HEW funded or guaranteed student loan or assistance programs. For further information see definition of "recipient" in Section 86.2 of the Title IX regulation.

IV. Summary of Final Policy Interpretation

The final Policy Interpretation clarifies the meaning of "equal opportunity" in intercollegiate athletics. It explains the factors and standards set out in the law and regulation which the Department will consider in determining whether an institution's intercollegiate athletics program complies with the law and regulations. It also provides guidance to assist institutions in determining whether any disparities which may exist between men's and women's programs are justifiable and nondiscriminatory. The Policy Interpretation is divided into three sections:

• *Compliance in Financial Assistance (Scholarships) Based on Athletic Ability:* Pursuant to the regulation, the governing principle in this area is that all such assistance should be available on a substantially proportional basis to the number of male and female participants in the institution's athletic program.

• *Compliance in Other Program Areas (Equipment and supplies; games and practice times; travel and per diem; coaching and academic tutoring; assignment and compensation of coaches and tutors; locker rooms, and practice and competitive facilities; medical and training facilities; housing and dining facilities; publicity; recruitment; and support services):* Pursuant to the regulation, the governing principle is that male and female athletes should receive equivalent treatment, benefits, and opportunities.

• *Compliance in Meeting the Interests and Abilities of Male and Female Students:* Pursuant to the regulation, the governing principle in this area is that the athletic interests

Footnotes continued from last page
teams will not be considered to be intercollegiate teams except in those instances where they regularly participate in varsity competition.

and abilities of male and female students must be equally effectively accommodated.

V. Major Changes to Proposed Policy Interpretation

The final Policy Interpretation has been revised from the one published in proposed form on December 11, 1978. The proposed Policy Interpretation was based on a two-part approach. Part I addressed equal opportunity for participants in athletic programs. It required the elimination of discrimination in financial support and other benefits and opportunities in an institution's existing athletic program. Institutions could establish a presumption of compliance if they could demonstrate that:

• "Average per capita" expenditures for male and female athletes were substantially equal in the area of "readily financially measurable" benefits and opportunities or, if not, that any disparities were the result of nondiscriminatory factors, and

• Benefits and opportunities for male and female athletes, in areas which are not financially measurable, "were comparable."

Part II of the proposed Policy Interpretation addressed an institution's obligation to accommodate effectively the athletic interests and abilities of women as well as men on a continuing basis. It required an institution either:

• To follow a policy of development of its women's athletic program to provide the participation and competition opportunities needed to accommodate the growing interests and abilities of women, or

• To demonstrate that it was effectively (and equally) accommodating the athletic interests and abilities of students, particularly as the interests and abilities of women students developed.

While the basic considerations of equal opportunity remain, the final Policy Interpretation sets forth the factors that will be examined to determine an institution's actual, as opposed to presumed, compliance with Title IX in the area of intercollegiate athletics.

The final Policy Interpretation does not contain a separate section on institutions' future responsibilities. However, institutions remain obligated by the Title IX regulation to accommodate effectively the interests and abilities of male and female students with regard to the selection of sports and levels of competition available. In most cases, this will entail development of athletic programs that substantially expand opportunities for

women to participate and compete at all levels.

The major reasons for the change in approach are as follows:

(1) Institutions and representatives of athletic program participants expressed a need for more definitive guidance on what constituted compliance than the discussion of a presumption of compliance provided. Consequently the final Policy Interpretation explains the meaning of "equal athletic opportunity" in such a way as to facilities an assessment of compliance.

(2) Many comments reflected a serious misunderstanding of the presumption of compliance. Most institutions based objections to the proposed Policy Interpretation in part on the assumption that failure to provide compelling justifications for disparities in per capita expenditures would have automatically resulted in a finding of noncompliance. In fact, such a failure would only have deprived an institution of the benefit of the presumption that it was in compliance with the law. The Department would still have had the burden of demonstrating that the institution was actually engaged in unlawful discrimination. Since the purpose of issuing a policy interpretation was to clarify the regulation, the Department has determined that the approach of stating actual compliance factors would be more useful to all concerned.

(3) The Department has concluded that purely financial measures such as the per capita test do not in themselves offer conclusive documentation of discrimination, except where the benefit or opportunity under review, like a scholarship, is itself financial in nature. Consequently, in the final Policy Interpretation, the Department has detailed the factors to be considered in assessing actual compliance. While per capita breakdowns and other devices to examine expenditures patterns will be used as tools of analysis in the Department's investigative process, it is achievement of "equal opportunity" for which recipients are responsible and to which the final Policy Interpretation is addressed.

A description of the comments received, and other information obtained through the comment/consultation process, with a description of Departmental action in response to the major points raised, is set forth at Appendix "B" to this document.

VI. Historic Patterns of Intercollegiate Athletics Program Development and Operations

In its proposed Policy Interpretation of December 11, 1978, the Department

Federal Register / Vol. 44, No. 239 / Tuesday, December 11, 1979 / Rules and Regulations   71415

published a summary of historic patterns affecting the relative status of men's and women's athletic programs. The Department has modified that summary to reflect additional information obtained during the comment and consultation process. The summary is set forth at Appendix A to this document.

VII. The Policy Interpretation

This Policy Interpretation clarifies the obligations which recipients of Federal aid have under Title IX to provide equal opportunities in athletic programs. In particular, this Policy Interpretation provides a means to assess an institution's compliance with the equal opportunity requirements of the regulation which are set forth at 45 CFR 86.37(c) and 86.41(c).

A. Athletic Financial Assistance (Scholarships)

1. The Regulation—Section 86.37(c) of the regulation provides:

[Institutions] must provide reasonable opportunities for such award [of financial assistance] for members of each sex in proportion to the number of students of each sex participating in * * * inter-collegiate athletics.[2]

2. The Policy—The Department will examine compliance with this provision of the regulation primarily by means of a financial comparison to determine whether proportionately equal amounts of financial assistance (scholarship aid) are available to men's and women's athletic programs. The Department will measure compliance with this standard by dividing the amounts of aid available for the members of each sex by the numbers of male or female participants in the athletic program and comparing the results. Institutions may be found in compliance if this comparison results in substantially equal amounts or if a resulting disparity can be explained by adjustments to take into account legitimate, nondiscriminatory factors. Two such factors are:

a. At public institutions, the higher costs of tuition for students from out-of-state may in some years be unevenly distributed between men's and women's programs. These differences will be considered nondiscriminatory if they are not the result of policies or practices which disproportionately limit the availability of out-of-state scholarships to either men or women.

b. An institution may make reasonable professional decisions concerning the awards most appropriate for program development. For example, team development initially may require

spreading scholarships over as much as a full generation (four years) of student athletes. This may result in the award of fewer scholarships in the first few years than would be necessary to create proportionality between male and female athletes.

3. Application of the Policy—a. This section does not require a proportionate number of scholarships for men and women or individual scholarships of equal dollar value. It does mean that the total amount of scholarship aid made available to men and women must be substantially proportionate to their participation rates.

b. When financial assistance is provided in forms other than grants, the distribution of non-grant assistance will also be compared to determine whether equivalent benefits are proportionately available to male and female athletes. A disproportionate amount of work-related aid or loans in the assistance made available to the members of one sex, for example, could constitute a violation of Title IX.

4. Definition—For purposes of examining compliance with this Section, the participants will be defined as those athletes:

a. Who are receiving the institutionally-sponsored support normally provided to athletes competing at the institution involved, e.g., coaching, equipment, medical and training room services, on a regular basis during a sport's season; and

b. Who are participating in organized practice sessions and other team meetings and activities on a regular basis during a sport's season; and

c. Who are listed on the eligibility or squad lists maintained for each sport, or

d. Who, because of injury, cannot meet a, b, or c above but continue to receive financial aid on the basis of athletic ability.

B. Equivalence in Other Athletic Benefits and Opportunities

1. The Regulation—The Regulation requires that recipients that operate or sponsor interscholastic, intercollegiate, club, or intramural athletics, "provide equal athletic opportunities for members of both sexes." In determining whether an institution is providing equal opportunity in intercollegiate athletics, the regulation requires the Department to consider, among others, the following factors:

(1) [3]

(2) Provision and maintenance of equipment and supplies;

(3) Scheduling of games and practice times;

(4) Travel and per diem expenses;

(5) Opportunity to receive coaching and academic tutoring;

(6) Assignment and compensation of coaches and tutors;

(7) Provision of locker rooms, practice and competitive facilities;

(8) Provision of medical and training services and facilities;

(9) Provision of housing and dining services and facilities; and

(10) Publicity

Section 86.41(c) also permits the Director of the Office for Civil Rights to consider other factors in the determination of equal opportunity. Accordingly, this Section also addresses recruitment of student athletes and provision of support services.

This list is not exhaustive. Under the regulation, it may be expanded as necessary at the discretion of the Director of the Office for Civil Rights.[4]

2. The Policy—The Department will assess compliance with both the recruitment and the general athletic program requirements of the regulation by comparing the availability, quality and kinds of benefits, opportunities, and treatment afforded members of both sexes. Institutions will be in compliance if the compared program components are equivalent, that is, equal or equal in effect. Under this standard, identical benefits, opportunities, or treatment are not required, provided the overall effect of any differences is negligible.

If comparisons of program components reveal that treatment, benefits, or opportunities are not equivalent in kind, quality or availability, a finding of compliance may still be justified if the differences are the result of nondiscriminatory factors. Some of the factors that may justify these differences are as follows:

a. Some aspects of athletic programs may not be equivalent for men and women because of unique aspects of particular sports or athletic activities. This type of distinction was called for by the "Javits' Amendment"[5] to Title IX, which instructed HEW to make "reasonable (regulatory) provisions considering the nature of particular sports" in intercollegiate athletics.

Generally, these differences will be the result of factors that are inherent to the basic operation of specific sports. Such factors may include rules of play, nature/replacement of equipment, rates of injury resulting from participation,

---

[2] See also § 86.37(a) of the regulation.

[3] 86.41(c) (1) on the accommodation of student interests and abilities, is covered in detail in the following Section C of this policy Interpretation.

[4] See also § 86.41(a) and (b) of the regulation.

[5] Section 844 of the Education Amendments of 1974, Pub. L. 93–380, Title VIII, (August 21, 1974) 88 Stat. 612.

nature of facilities required for competition, and the maintenance/upkeep requirements of those facilities. For the most part, differences involving such factors will occur in programs offering football, and consequently these differences will favor men. If sport-specific needs are met equivalently in both men's and women's programs, however, differences in particular program components will be found to be justifiable.

b. Some aspects of athletic programs may not be equivalent for men and women because of legitimately sex-neutral factors related to temporary circumstances of a temporary nature. For example, large disparities in recruitment activity for any particular year may be the result of annual fluctuations in team needs for first-year athletes. Such diferences are justifiable to the extent that they do not reduce overall equality of opportunity.

c. The activities directly associated with the operation of a competitive event in a single-sex sport may, under some circumstances, create unique demands or imbalances in particular program components. Provided any special demands associated with the activities of sports involving participants of the other sex are met to an equivalent degree, the resulting differences may be found nondiscriminatory. At many schools, for example, certain sports—notably football and men's basketball—traditionally draw large crowds. Since the costs of managing an athletic event increase with crowd size, the overall support made available for event management to men's and women's programs may differ in degree and kind. These differences would not violate Title IX if the recipient does not limit the potential for women's athletic events to rise in spectator appeal and if the levels of event management support available to both programs are based on sex-neutral criteria (e.g., facilities used, projected attendance, and staffing needs).

d. Some aspects of athletic programs may not be equivalent for men and women because institutions are undertaking voluntary affirmative actions to overcome effects of historical conditions that have limited participation in athletics by the members of one sex. This is authorized at § 86.3(b) of the regulation.

3. *Application of the Policy—General Athletic Program Components*—a. *Equipment and Supplies (§ 86.41(c)(2)).* Equipment and supplies include but are not limited to uniforms, other apparel, sport-specific equipment and supplies, general equipment and supplies,

instructional devices, and conditioning and weight training equipment.

Compliance will be assessed by examining, among other factors, the equivalence for men and women of:
(1) The quality of equipment and supplies;
(2) The amount of equipment and supplies;
(3) The suitability of equipment and supplies;
(4) The maintenance and replacement of the equipment and supplies; and
(5) The availability of equipment and supplies.

b. *Scheduling of Games and Practice Times (§ 86.41(c)(3)).* Compliance will be assessed by examining, among other factors, the equivalence for men and women of:
(1) The number of competitive events per sport;
(2) The number and length of practice opportunities;
(3) The time of day competitive events are scheduled;
(4) The time of day practice opportunities are scheduled; and
(5) The opportunities to engage in available pre-season and post-season competition.

c. *Travel and Per Diem Allowances (§ 86.41(c)(4)).* Compliance will be assessed by examining, among other factors, the equivalence for men and women of:
(1) Modes of transportation;
(2) Housing furnished during travel;
(3) Length of stay before and after competitive events;
(4) Per diem allowances; and
(5) Dining arrangements.

d. *Opportunity to Receive Coaching and Academic Tutoring (§ 86.41(c)(5)).*
(1) Coaching—Compliance will be assessed by examining, among other factors:
(a) Relative availability of full-time coaches;
(b) Relative availability of part-time and assistant coaches; and
(c) Relative availability of graduate assistants.
(2) Academic tutoring—Compliance will be assessed by examining, among other factors, the equivalence for men and women of:
(a) The availability of tutoring; and
(b) Procedures and criteria for obtaining tutorial assistance.

e. *Assignment and Compensation of Coaches and Tutors (§ 86.41(c)(6)).*[6] In

general, a violation of Section 86.41(c)(6) will be found only where compensation or assignment policies or practices deny male and female athletes coaching of equivalent quality, nature, or availability.

Nondiscriminatory factors can affect the compensation of coaches. In determining whether differences are caused by permissible factors, the range and nature of duties, the experience of individual coaches, the number of participants for particular sports, the number of assistant coaches supervised, and the level of competition will be considered.

Where these or similar factors represent valid differences in skill, effort, responsibility or working conditions they may, in specific circumstances, justify differences in compensation. Similarly, there may be unique situations in which a particular person may possess such an outstanding record of achievement as to justify an abnormally high salary.

(1) Assignment of Coaches—Compliance will be assessed by examining, among other factors, the equivalence for men's and women's coaches of:
(a) Training, experience, and other professional qualifications;
(b) Professional standing.
(2) Assignment of Tutors—Compliance will be assessed by examining, among other factors, the equivalence for men's and women's tutors of:
(a) Tutor qualifications;
(b) Training, experience, and other qualifications.
(3) Compensation of Coaches—Compliance will be assessed by examining, among other factors, the equivalence for men's and women's coaches of:
(a) Rate of compensation (per sport, per season);
(b) Duration of contracts;
(c) Conditions relating to contract renewal;
(d) Experience;
(e) Nature of coaching duties performed;
(f) Working conditions; and
(g) Other terms and conditions of employment.
(4) Compensation of Tutors—Compliance will be assessed by examining, among other factors, the equivalence for men's and women's tutors of:

---

[6] The Department's jurisdiction over the employment practices of recipients under Subpart E, §§ 86.51–86.61 of the Title IX regulation has been successfully challenged in several court cases. Accordingly, the Department has suspended enforcement of Subpart E. Section 86.41(c)(6) of the regulation, however, authorizes the Department to

consider the compensation of coaches of men and women in the determination of the equality of athletic opportunity provided to male and female athletes. It is on this section of the regulation that this Policy Interpretation is based.

(a) Hourly rate of payment by nature of subjects tutored;
(b) Pupil loads per tutoring season;
(c) Tutor qualifications;
(d) Experience;
(e) Other terms and conditions of employment.

f. *Provision of Locker Rooms, Practice and Competitive Facilities (§ 86.41(c)(7))*. Compliance will be assessed by examining, among other factors, the equivalence for men and women of:
(1) Quality and availability of the facilities provided for practice and competitive events;
(2) Exclusivity of use of facilities provided for practice and competitive events;
(3) Availability of locker rooms;
(4) Quality of locker rooms;
(5) Maintenance of practice and competitive facilities; and
(6) Preparation of facilities for practice and competitive events.

g. *Provision of Medical and Training Facilities and Services (§ 86.41(c)(8))*. Compliance will be assessed by examining, among other factors, the equivalence for men and women of:
(1) Availability of medical personnel and assistance;
(2) Health, accident and injury insurance coverage;
(3) Availability and quality of weight and training facilities;
(4) Availability and quality of conditioning facilities; and
(5) Availability and qualifications of athletic trainers.

h. *Provision of Housing and Dining Facilities and Services (§ 86.41(c)(9))*. Compliance will be assessed by examining, among other factors, the equivalence for men and women of:
(1) Housing provided;
(2) Special services as part of housing arrangements (e.g., laundry facilities, parking space, maid service).

i. *Publicity (§ 86.41(c)(10))*. Compliance will be assessed by examining, among other factors, the equivalence for men and women of:
(1) Availability and quality of sports information personnel;
(2) Access to other publicity resources for men's and women's programs; and
(3) Quantity and quality of publications and other promotional devices featuring men's and women's programs.

4. *Application of the Policy—Other Factors (§ 86.41(c))*. a. *Recruitment of Student Athletes.*[7] The athletic

recruitment practices of institutions often affect the overall provision of opportunity to male and female athletes. Accordingly, where equal athletic opportunities are not present for male and female students, compliance will be assessed by examining the recruitment practices of the athletic programs for both sexes to determine whether the provision of equal opportunity will require modification of those practices. Such examinations will review the following factors:
(1) Whether coaches or other professional athletic personnel in the programs serving male and female athletes are provided with substantially equal opportunities to recruit;
(2) Whether the financial and other resources made available for recruitment in male and female athletic programs are equivalently adequate to meet the needs of each program; and
(3) Whether the differences in benefits, opportunities, and treatment afforded prospective student athletes of each sex have a disproportionately limiting effect upon the recruitment of students of either sex.

b. *Provision of Support Services.* The administrative and clerical support provided to an athletic program can affect the overall provision of opportunity to male and female athletes, particularly to the extent that the provided services enable coaches to perform better their coaching functions.
In the provision of support services, compliance will be assessed by examining, among other factors, the equivalence of:
(1) The amount of administrative assistance provided to men's and women's programs;
(2) The amount of secretarial and clerical assistance provided to men's and women's programs.

5. *Overall Determination of Compliance.* The Department will base its compliance determination under § 86.41(c) of the regulation upon an examination of the following:
a. Whether the policies of an institution are discriminatory in language or effect; or
b. Whether disparities of a substantial and unjustified nature exist in the benefits, treatment, services, or opportunities afforded male and female

athletes in the institution's program as a whole; or
c. Whether disparities in benefits, treatment, services, or opportunities in individual segments of the program are substantial enough in and of themselves to deny equality of athletic opportunity.

C. *Effective Accommodation of Student Interests and Abilities.*

1. *The Regulation.* The regulation requires institutions to accommodate effectively the interests and abilities of students to the extent necessary to provide equal opportunity in the selection of sports and levels of competition available to members of both sexes.
Specifically, the regulation, at § 86.41(c)(1), requires the Director to consider, when determining whether equal opportunities are available—

Whether the selection of sports and levels of competition effectively accommodate the interests and abilities of members of both sexes.

Section 86.41(c) also permits the Director of the Office for Civil Rights to consider other factors in the determination of equal opportunity. Accordingly, this section also addresses competitive opportunities in terms of the competitive team schedules available to athletes of both sexes.

2. *The Policy.* The Department will assess compliance with the interests and abilities section of the regulation by examining the following factors:
a. The determination of athletic interests and abilities of students;
b. The selection of sports offered; and
c. The levels of competition available including the opportunity for team competition.

3. *Application of the Policy— Determination of Athletic Interests and Abilities.*
Institutions may determine the athletic interests and abilities of students by nondiscriminatory methods of their choosing provided:
a. The processes take into account the nationally increasing levels of women's interests and abilities;
b. The methods of determining interest and ability do not disadvantage the members of an underrepresented sex;
c. The methods of determining ability take into account team performance records; and
d. The methods are responsive to the expressed interests of students capable of intercollegiate competition who are members of an underrepresented sex.

4. *Application of the Policy— Selection of Sports.*
In the selection of sports, the regulation does not require institutions

---

[7] Public undergraduate institutions are also subject to the general anti-discrimination provision at § 86.23 of the regulation, which reads in part:
"A recipient * * * shall not discriminate on the basis of sex in the recruitment and admission of

students. A recipient may be required to undertake additional recruitment efforts for one sex as remedial action * * * and may choose to undertake such efforts as affirmative action * * *"

Accordingly, institutions subject to § 86.23 are required in all cases to maintain equivalently effective recruitment programs for both sexes and, under § 86.41(c), to provide equivalent benefits, opportunities, and treatment to student athletes of both sexes.

71418   **Federal Register** / Vol. 44, No. 239 / Tuesday, December 11, 1979 / Rules and Regulations

to integrate their teams nor to provide exactly the same choice of sports to men and women. However, where an institution sponsors a team in a particular sport for members of one sex, it may be required either to permit the excluded sex to try out for the team or to sponsor a separate team for the previously excluded sex.

a. Contact Sports—Effective accommodation means that if an institution sponsors a team for members of one sex in a contact sport, it must do so for members of the other sex under the following circumstances:

(1) The opportunities for members of the excluded sex have historically been limited; and

(2) There is sufficient interest and ability among the members of the excluded sex to sustain a viable team and a reasonable expectation of intercollegiate competition for that team.

b. Non-Contact Sports—Effective accommodation means that if an institution sponsors a team for members of one sex in a non-contact sport, it must do so for members of the other sex under the following circumstances:

(1) The opportunities for members of the excluded sex have historically been limited;

(2) There is sufficient interest and ability among the members of the excluded sex to sustain a viable team and a reasonable expectation of intercollegiate competition for that team; and

(3) Members of the excluded sex do not possess sufficient skill to be selected for a single integrated team, or to compete actively on such a team if selected.

5. *Application of the Policy—Levels of Competition.*

In effectively accommodating the interests and abilities of male and female athletes, institutions must provide both the opportunity for individuals of each sex to participate in intercollegiate competition, and for athletes of each sex to have competitive team schedules which equally reflect their abilities.

a. Compliance will be assessed in any one of the following ways:

(1) Whether intercollegiate level participation opportunities for male and female students are provided in numbers substantially proportionate to their respective enrollments; or

(2) Where the members of one sex have been and are underrepresented among intercollegiate athletes, whether the institution can show a history and continuing practice of program expansion which is demonstrably responsive to the developing interest

and abilities of the members of that sex; or

(3) Where the members of one sex are underrepresented among intercollegiate athletes, and the institution cannot show a continuing practice of program expansion such as that cited above, whether it can be demonstrated that the interests and abilities of the members of that sex have been fully and effectively accommodated by the present program.

b. Compliance with this provision of the regulation will also be assessed by examining the following:

(1) Whether the competitive schedules for men's and women's teams, on a program-wide basis, afford proportionally similar numbers of male and female athletes equivalently advanced competitive opportunities; or

(2) Whether the institution can demonstrate a history and continuing practice of upgrading the competitive opportunities available to the historically disadvantaged sex as warranted by developing abilities among the athletes of that sex.

c. Institutions are not required to upgrade teams to intercollegiate status or otherwise develop intercollegiate sports absent a reasonable expectation that intercollegiate competition in that sport will be available within the institution's normal competitive regions. Institutions may be required by the Title IX regulation to actively encourage the development of such competition, however, when overall athletic opportunities within that region have been historically limited for the members of one sex.

6. *Overall Determination of Compliance.*

The Department will base its compliance determination under § 86.41(c) of the regulation upon a determination of the following:

a. Whether the policies of an institution are discriminatory in language or effect; or

b. Whether disparities of a substantial and unjustified nature in the benefits, treatment, services, or opportunities afforded male and female athletes exist in the institution's program as a whole; or

c. Whether disparities in individual segments of the program with respect to benefits, treatment, services, or opportunities are substantial enough in and of themselves to deny equality of athletic opportunity.

VIII. The Enforcement Process

The process of Title IX enforcement is set forth in § 86.71 of the Title IX regulation, which incorporates by reference the enforcement procedures applicable to Title VI of the Civil Rights

Act of 1964.[8] The enforcement process prescribed by the regulation is supplemented by an order of the Federal District Court, District of Columbia, which establishes time frames for each of the enforcement steps.[9]

According to the regulation, there are two ways in which enforcement is initiated:

• *Compliance Reviews*—Periodically the Department must select a number of recipients (in this case, colleges and universities which operate intercollegiate athletic programs) and conduct investigations to determine whether recipients are complying with Title IX. (45 CFR 80.7(a))

• *Complaints*—The Department must investigate all valid (written and timely) complaints alleging discrimination on the basis of sex in a recipient's programs. (45 CFR 80.7(b))

The Department must inform the recipient (and the complainant, if applicable) of the results of its investigation. If the investigation indicates that a recipient is in compliance, the Department states this, and the case is closed. If the investigation indicates noncompliance, the Department outlines the violations found.

The Department has 90 days to conduct an investigation and inform the recipient of its findings, and an additional 90 days to resolve violations by obtaining a voluntary compliance agreement from the recipient. This is done through negotiations between the Department and the recipient, the goal of which is agreement on steps the recipient will take to achieve compliance. Sometimes the violation is relatively minor and can be corrected immediately. At other times, however, the negotiations result in a plan that will correct the violations within a specified period of time. To be acceptable, a plan must describe the manner in which institutional resources will be used to correct the violation. It also must state acceptable time tables for reaching interim goals and full compliance. When agreement is reached, the Department notifies the institution that its plan is acceptable. The Department then is obligated to review periodically the implementation of the plan.

An institution that is in violation of Title IX may already be implementing a corrective plan. In this case, prior to informing the recipient about the results of its investigation, the Department will determine whether the plan is adequate.

---

[8] Those procedures may be found at 45 CFR 80.6–80.11 and 45 CFR Part 8 1.

[9] *WEAL v. Harris*, Civil Action No. 74–1720 (D. D.C., December 29, 1977).

If the plan is not adequate to correct the violations (or to correct them within a reasonable period of time) the recipient will be found in noncompliance and voluntary negotiations will begin. However, if the institutional plan is acceptable, the Department will inform the institution that although the institution has violations, it is found to be in compliance because it is implementing a corrective plan. The Department, in this instance also, would monitor the progress of the institutional plan. If the institution subsequently does not completely implement its plan, it will be found in noncompliance.

When a recipient is found in noncompliance and voluntary compliance attempts are unsuccessful, the formal process leading to termination of Federal assistance will be begun. These procedures, which include the opportunity for a hearing before an administrative law judge, are set forth in 45 CFR 80.8–80.11 and 45 CFR Part 81.

IX. Authority

(Secs. 901, 902, Education Amendments of 1972, 86 Stat. 373, 374, 20 U.S.C. 1681, 1682; sec. 844, Education Amendments of 1974, Pub. L. 93–380, 88 Stat. 612; and 45 CFR Part 86) Dated: December 3, 1979.

Roma Stewart,

Director, Office for Civil Rights, Department of Health, Education, and Welfare.

Dated: December 4, 1979.

Patricia Roberts Harris,

Secretary, Department of Health, Education, and Welfare.

Appendix A—Historic Patterns of Intercollegiate Athletics Program Development

1. Participation in intercollegiate sports has historically been emphasized for men but not women. Partially as a consequence of this, participation rates of women are far below those of men. During the 1977–78 academic year women students accounted for 48 percent of the national undergraduate enrollment (5,496,000 of 11,287,000 students).[1] Yet, only 30 percent of the intercollegiate athletes are women.[2]

The historic emphasis on men's intercollegiate athletic programs has also contributed to existing differences in the number of sports and scope of competition offered men and women. One source indicates that, on the average, colleges and universities are

providing twice the number of sports for men as they are for women.[3]

2. Participation by women in sports is growing rapidly. During the period from 1971–1978, for example, the number of female participants in organized high school sports increased from 294,000 to 2,083,000—an increase of over 600 percent.[4] In contrast, between Fall 1971 and Fall 1977, the enrollment of females in high school decreased from approximately 7,600,000 to approximately 7,150,000 a decrease of over 5 percent.[5]

The growth in athletic participation by high school women has been reflected on the campuses of the nation's colleges and universities. During the period from 1971 to 1976 the enrollment of women in the nation's institutions of higher education rose 52 percent, from 3,400,000 to 5,201,000.[6] During this same period, the number of women participating in intramural sports increased 108 percent from 276,167 to 576,167. In club sports, the number of women participants increased from 16,386 to 25,541 or 55 percent. In intercollegiate sports, women's participation increased 102 percent from 31,852 to 64,375.[7] These developments reflect the growing interest of women in competitive athletics, as well as the efforts of colleges and universities to accommodate those interests.

3. The overall growth of women's intercollegiate programs has not been at the expense of men's programs. During the past decade of rapid growth in women's programs, the number of intercollegiate sports available for men has remained stable, and the number of male athletes has increased slightly. Funding for men's programs has increased from $1.2 to $2.2 million between 1970–1977 alone.[8]

4. On most campuses, the primary problem confronting women athletes is

---

[3] U.S. Commission on Civil Rights. Comments to DHEW on proposed Policy Interpretation: Analysis of data supplied by the National Association of Directors of Collegiate Athletics.

[4] Figures obtained from National Federation of High School Associations (NFHSA) data.

[5] *Digest of Education Statistics 1977–78,* National Center for Education Statistics (1978), Table 40, at 44. Data, by sex, are unavailable for the period from 1971 to 1977; consequently, these figures represent 50 percent of total enrollment for that period. This is the best comparison that could be made based on available data.

[6] Ibid. p. 112.

[7] These figures, which are not precisely comparable to those cited at footnote 2, were obtained from *Sports and Recreational Programs of the Nation's Universities and Colleges.* NCAA Report No. 5, March 1978. It includes figures only from the 722 NCAA member institutions because comparable data was not available from other associations.

[8] Compiled from NCAA *Revenues and Expenses for Intercollegiate Athletic Programs,* 1978.

the absence of a fair and adequate level of resources, services, and benefits. For example, disproportionately more financial aid has been made available for male athletes than for female athletes. Presently, in institutions that are members of both the National Collegiate Athletic Association (NCAA) and the Association for Intercollegiate Athletics for Women (AIAW), the average annual scholarship budget is $39,000. Male athletes receive $32,000 or 78 percent of this amount, and female athletes receive $7,000 or 22 percent, although women are 30 percent of all the athletes eligible for scholarships.[9]

Likewise, substantial amounts have been provided for the recruitment of male athletes, but little funding has been made available for recruitment of female athletes.

Congressional testimony on Title IX and subsequent surveys indicates that discrepancies also exist in the opportunity to receive coaching and in other benefits and opportunities, such as the quality and amount of equipment, access to facilities and practice times, publicity, medical and training facilities, and housing and dining facilities.[10]

5. At several institutions, intercollegiate football is unique among sports. The size of the teams, the expense of the operation, and the revenue produced distinguish football from other sports, both men's and women's. Title IX requires that "an institution of higher education must comply with the prohibition against sex discrimination imposed by that title and its implementing regulations in the administration of any revenue producing intercollegiate athletic activity."[11] However, the unique size and cost of football programs have been taken into account in developing this Policy Interpretation.

Appendix B—Comments and Responses

The Office for Civil Rights (OCR) received over 700 comments and recommendations in response to the December 11, 1978 publication of the proposed Policy Interpretation. After the formal comment period, representatives of the Department met for additional discussions with many individuals and

---

[9] Figures obtained from *AIAW Structure Implementation Survey Data Summary,* October, 1978, p. 11.

[10] 121 Cong. REc. 29791–95 (1975) (remarks of Senator Williams): Comments by Senator Bayh, Hearings on S. 2106 Before the Subcommittee on Education of the Senate Committee on Labor and Public Welfare. 94th Congress, 1st Session 48 (1975): "Survey of Women's Athletic Directors," AIAW Workshop (January 1978).

[11] See April 18, 1979. Opinion of General Counsel. Department of Health, Education, and Welfare. page 1.

---

[1] *The Condition of Education 1979,* National Center for Education Statistics. p. 112.

[2] Figure obtained from Association for Intercollegiate Athletics for Women (AIAW) member survey. *AIAW Structure Implementation Survey Data Summary,* October 1978. p. 11.

71420   Federal Register / Vol. 44, No. 239 / Tuesday, December 11, 1979 / Rules and Regulations

groups including college and university officials, athletic associations, athletic directors, women's rights organizations and other interested parties. HEW representatives also visited eight universities in order to assess the potential of the proposed Policy Interpretation and of suggested alternative approaches for effective enforcement of Title IX.

The Department carefully considered all information before preparing the final policy. Some changes in the structure and substance of the Policy Interpretation have been made as a result of concerns that were identified in the comment and consultation process.

Persons who responded to the request for public comment were asked to comment generally and also to respond specifically to eight questions that focused on different aspects of the proposed Policy Interpretation.

Question No. 1: Is the description of the current status and development of intercollegiate athletics for men and women accurate? What other factors should be considered?

Comment A: Some commentors noted that the description implied the presence of intent on the part of all universities to discriminate against women. Many of these same commentors noted an absence of concern in the proposed Policy Interpretation for those universities that have in good faith attempted to meet what they felt to be a vague compliance standard in the regulation.

Response: The description of the current status and development of intercollegiate athletics for men and women was designed to be a factual, historical overview. There was no intent to imply the universal presence of discrimination. The Department recognizes that there are many colleges and universities that have been and are making good faith efforts, in the midst of increasing financial pressures, to provide equal athletic opportunities to their male and female athletes.

Comment B: Commentors stated that the statistics used were outdated in some areas, incomplete in some areas, and inaccurate in some areas.

Response: Comment accepted. The statistics have been updated and corrected where necessary.

Question No. 2: Is the proposed two-stage approach to compliance practical? Should it be modified? Are there other approaches to be considered?

Comment: Some commentors stated that Part II of the proposed Policy Interpretation "Equally Accommodating the Interests and Abilities of Women" represented an extension of the July 1978, compliance deadline established in § 86.41(d) of the Title IX regulation.

Response: Part II of the proposed Policy Interpretation was not intended to extend the compliance deadline. The format of the two stage approach, however, seems to have encouraged that perception; therefore, the elements of both stages have been unified in this Policy Interpretation.

Question No. 3: Is the equal average per capita standard based on participation rates practical? Are there alternatives or modifications that should be considered?

Comment A: Some commentors stated it was unfair or illegal to find noncompliance solely on the basis of a financial test when more valid indicators of equality of opportunity exist.

Response: The equal average per capita standard was not a standard by which noncompliance could be found. It was offered as a standard of presumptive compliance. In order to prove noncompliance, HEW would have been required to show that the unexplained disparities in expenditures were discriminatory in effect. The standard, in part, was offered as a means of simplifying proof of compliance for universities. The widespread confusion concerning the significance of failure to satisfy the equal average per capita expenditure standard, however, is one of the reasons it was withdrawn.

Comment B: Many commentors stated that the equal average per capita standard penalizes those institutions that have increased participation opportunities for women and rewards institutions that have limited women's participation.

Response: Since equality of average per capita expenditures has been dropped as a standard of presumptive compliance, the question of its effect is no longer relevant. However, the Department agrees that universities that had increased participation opportunities for women and wished to take advantage of the presumptive compliance standard, would have had a bigger financial burden than universities that had done little to increase participation opportunities for women.

Question No. 4: Is there a basis for treating part of the expenses of a particular revenue producing sport differently because the sport produces income used by the university for non-athletic operating expenses on a non-discriminatory basis? If, so, how should such funds be identified and treated?

Comment: Commentors stated that this question was largely irrelevant because there were so few universities at which revenue from the athletic program was used in the university operating budget.

Response: Since equality of average per capita expenditures has been dropped as a standard of presumed compliance, a decision to pursue this issue is no longer necessary on this issue.

Question No. 5: Is the grouping of financially measurable benefits into three categories practical? Are there alternatives that should be considered? Specifically, should recruiting expenses be considered together with all other financially measurable benefits?

Comment A: Most commentors stated that, if measured solely on a financial standard, recruiting should be grouped with the other financially measurable items. Some of these commentors held that at the current stage of development of women's intercollegiate athletics, the amount of money that would flow into the women's recruitment budget as a result of separate application of the equal average per capita standard to recruiting expenses, would make recruitment a disproportionately large percentage of the entire women's budget. Women's athletic directors, particularly, wanted the flexibility to have the money available for other uses, and they generally agreed with including recruitment expenses with the other financially measurable items.

Comment B: Some commentors stated that it was particularly inappropriate to base any measure of compliance in recruitment solely on financial expenditures. They stated that even if proportionate amounts of money were allocated to recruitment, major inequities could remain in the benefits to athletes. For instance, universities could maintain a policy of subsidizing visits to their campuses of prospective students of one sex but not the other. Commentors suggested that including an examination of differences in benefits to prospective athletes that result from recruiting methods would be appropriate.

Response: In the final Policy Interpretation, recruitment has been moved to the group of program areas to be examined under § 86.41(c) to determine whether overall equal athletic opportunity exists. The Department accepts the comment that a financial measure is not sufficient to determine whether equal opportunity is being provided. Therefore, in examining athletic recruitment, the Department will primarily review the opportunity to recruit, the resources provided for recruiting, and methods of recruiting.

Question No. 6: Are the factors used to justify differences in equal average per capita expenditures for financially

Federal Register / Vol. 44, No. 239 / Tuesday, December 11, 1979 / Rules and Regulations   **71421**

measurable benefits and opportunities fair? Are there other factors that should be considered?

Comment: Most commentors indicated that the factors named in the proposed Policy Interpretion (the "scope of competition" and the "nature of the sport") as justifications for differences in equal average per capita expenditures were so vague and ambiguous as to be meaningless. Some stated that it would be impossible to define the phrase "scope of competition", given the greatly differing competitive structure of men's and women's programs. Other commentors were concerned that the "scope of competition" factor that may currently be designated as "non-discriminatory" was, in reality, the result of many years of inequitable treatment of women's athletic programs.

Response: The Department agrees that it would have been difficult to define clearly and then to quantify the "scope of competition" factor. Since equal average per capita expenditures has been dropped as a standard of presumed compliance, such financial justifications are no longer necessary. Under the equivalency standard, however, the "nature of the sport" remains an important concept. As explained within the Policy Interpretation, the unique nature of a sport may account for perceived inequities in some program areas.

Question No 7: Is the comparability standard for benefits and opportunities that are not financially measurably fair and realistic? Should other factors controlling comparability be included? Should the comparability standard be revised? Is there a different standard which should be considered?

Comment: Many commentors stated that the comparability standard was fair and realistic. Some commentors were concerned, however, that the standard was vague and subjective and could lead to uneven enforcement.

Response: The concept of comparing the non-financially measurable benefits and opportunities provided to male and female athletes has been preserved and expanded in the final Policy Interpretation to include all areas of examination except scholarships and accommodation of the interests and abilities of both sexes. The standard is that equivalent benefits and opportunities must be provided. To avoid vagueness and subjectivity, further guidance is given about what elements will be considered in each program area to determine the equivalency of benefits and opportunities.

Question No. 8: Is the proposal for increasing the opportunity for women to participate in competitive athletics appropriate and effective? Are there other procedures that should be considered? Is there a more effective way to ensure that the interest and abilities of both men and women are equally accommodated?

Comment: Several commentors indicated that the proposal to allow a university to gain the status of presumed compliance by having policies and procedures to encourage the growth of women's athletics was appropriate and effective for future students, but ignored students presently enrolled. They indicated that nowhere in the proposed Policy Interpretation was concern shown that the current selection of sports and levels of competition effectively accommodate the interests and abilities of women as well as men.

Response: Comment accepted. The requirement that universities equally accommodate the interests and abilities of their male and female athletes (Part II of the proposed Policy Interpretation) has been directly addressed and is now a part of the unified final Policy Interpretation.

Additional Comments

The following comments were not responses to questions raised in the proposed Policy Interpretation. They represent additional concerns expressed by a large number of commentors.

(1) *Comment:* Football and other "revenue producing" sports should be totally exempted or should receive special treatment under Title IX.

Response: The April 18, 1978, opinion of the General Counsel, HEW, concludes that "an institution of higher education must comply with the prohibition against sex discrimination imposed by that title and its implementing regulation in the administration of any revenue producing activity". Therefore, football or other "revenue producing" sports cannot be exempted from coverage of Title IX.

In developing the proposed Policy Interpretation the Department concluded that although the fact of revenue production could not justify disparity in average per capita expenditure between men and women, there were characteristics common to most revenue producing sports that could result in legitimate non-discriminatory differences in per capita expenditures. For instance, some "revenue producing" sports require . expensive protective equipment and most require high expenditures for the management of events attended by large numbers of people. These characteristics and others described in the proposed Policy Interpretation were

considered acceptable, non-discriminatory reasons for differences in per capita average expenditures.

In the final Policy Interpretation, under the equivalent benefits and opportunities standard of compliance, some of these non-discriminatory factors are still relevant and applicable.

(2) *Comment:* Commentors stated that since the equal average per capita standard of presumed compliance was based on participation rates, the word should be explicitly defined.

Response: Although the final Policy Interpretation does not use the equal average per capita standard of presumed compliance, a clear understanding of the word "participant" is still necessary, particularly in the determination of compliance where scholarships are involved. The word "participant" is defined in the final Policy Interpretation.

(3) *Comment:* Many commentors were concerned that the proposed Policy Interpretation neglected the rights of individuals.

Response: The proposed Policy Interpretation was intended to further clarify what colleges and universities must do with their intercollegiate athletic programs to avoid discrimination against individuals on the basis of sex. The Interpretation, therefore, spoke to institutions in terms of their male and female athletes. It spoke specifically in terms of equal, average per capita expenditures and in terms of comparability of other opportunities and benefits for male and female participating athletes.

The Department believes that under this approach the rights of individuals were protected. If women athletes, as a class, are receiving opportunities and benefits equal to those of male athletes, individuals within the class should be protected thereby. Under the proposed Policy Interpretation, for example, if female athletes as a whole were receiving their proportional share of athletic financial assistance, a university would have been presumed in compliance with that section of the regulation. The Department does not want and does not have the authority to force universities to offer identical programs to men and women. Therefore, to allow flexibility within women's programs and within men's programs, the proposed Policy Interpretation stated that an institution would be presumed in compliance if the average per capita expenditures on athletic scholarships for men and women, were equal. This same flexibility (in scholarships and in other areas) remains in the final Policy Interpretation.

Appendix

245

Federal Register / Vol. 44, No. 239 / Tuesday, December 11, 1979 / Rules and Regulations

(4) *Comment:* Several commentors stated that the provision of a separate dormitory to athletes of only one sex, even where no other special benefits were involved, is inherently discriminatory. They felt such separation indicated the different degrees of importance attached to athletes on the basis of sex.

Response: Comment accepted. The provision of a separate dormitory to athletes of one sex but not the other will be considered a failure to provide equivalent benefits as required by the regulation.

(5) *Comment:* Commentors, particularly colleges and universities, expressed concern that the differences in the rules of intercollegiate athletic associations could result in unequal distribution of benefits and opportunities to men's and women's athletic programs, thus placing the institutions in a posture of noncompliance with Title IX.

Response: Commentors made this point with regard to § 86.6(c) of the Title IX regulation, which reads in part:

"The obligation to comply with (Title IX) is not obviated or alleviated by any rule or regulation of any * * * athletic or other * * * association * * *"

Since the penalties for violation of intercollegiate athletic association rules can have a severe effect on the athletic opportunities within an affected program, the Department has re-examined this regulatory requirement to determine whether it should be modified. Our conclusion is that modification would not have a beneficial effect, and that the present requirement will stand.

Several factors enter into this decision. First, the differences between rules affecting men's and women's programs are numerous and change constantly. Despite this, the Department has been unable to discover a single case in which those differences require members to act in a discriminatory manner. Second, some rule differences may permit decisions resulting in discriminatory distribution of benefits and opportunities to men's and women's programs. The fact that institutions respond to differences in rules by choosing to deny equal opportunities, however, does not mean that the rules themselves are at fault; the rules do not prohibit choices that would result in compliance with Title IX. Finally, the rules in question are all established and subject to change by the membership of the association. Since all (or virtually all) association member institutions are subject to Title IX, the opportunity exists for these institutions to resolve

collectively any wide-spread Title IX compliance problems resulting from association rules. To the extent that this has not taken place, Federal intervention on behalf of statutory beneficiaries is both warranted and required by the law. Consequently, the Department can follow no course other than to continue to disallow any defenses against findings of noncompliance with Title IX that are based on intercollegiate athletic association rules.

(6) *Comment:* Some commentors suggested that the equal average per capita test was unfairly skewed by the high cost of some "major" men's sports, particularly football, that have no equivalently expensive counterpart among women's sports. They suggested that a certain percentage of those costs (e.g., 50% of football scholarships) should be excluded from the expenditures on male athletes prior to application of the equal average per capita test.

Response: Since equality of average per capita expenditures has been eliminated as a standard of presumed compliance, the suggestion is no longer relevant. However, it was possible under that standard to exclude expenditures that were due to the nature of the sport, or the scope of competition and thus were not discriminatory in effect. Given the diversity of intercollegiate athletic programs, determinations as to whether disparities in expenditures were nondiscriminatory would have been made on a case-by-case basis. There was no legal support for the proposition that an arbitrary percentage of expenditures should be excluded from the calculations.

(7) *Comment:* Some commentors urged the Department to adopt various forms of team-based comparisons in assessing equality of opportunity between men's and women's athletic programs. They stated that well-developed men's programs are frequently characterized by a few "major" teams that have the greatest spectator appeal, earn the greatest income, cost the most to operate, and dominate the program in other ways. They suggested that women's programs should be similarly constructed and that comparability should then be required only between "men's major" and "women's major" teams, and between "men's minor" and "women's minor" teams. The men's teams most often cited as appropriate for "major" designation have been football and basketball, with women's basketball and volleyball being frequently selected as the counterparts.

Response: There are two problems with this approach to assessing equal

opportunity. First, neither the statute nor the regulation calls for identical programs for male and female athletes. Absent such a requirement, the Department cannot base noncompliance upon a failure to provide arbitrarily identical programs, either in whole or in part.

Second, no subgrouping of male or female students (such as a team) may be used in such a way as to diminish the protection of the larger class of males and females in their rights to equal participation in educational benefits or opportunities. Use of the "major/minor" classification does not meet this test where large participation sports (e.g., football) are compared to smaller ones (e.g., women's volleyball) in such a manner as to have the effect of disproportionately providing benefits or opportunities to the members of one sex.

(8) *Comment:* Some commenters suggest that equality of opportunity should be measured by a "sport-specific" comparison. Under this approach, institutions offering the same sports to men and women would have an obligation to provide equal opportunity within each of those sports. For example, the men's basketball team and the women's basketball team would have to receive equal opportunities and benefits.

Response: As noted above, there is no provision for the requirement of identical programs for men and women, and no such requirement will be made by the Department. Moreover, a sport-specific comparison could actually create unequal opportunity. For example, the sports available for men at an institution might include most or all of those available for women; but the men's program might concentrate resources on sports not available to women (e.g., football, ice hockey). In addition, the sport-specific concept overlooks two key elements of the Title IX regulation.

First, the regulation states that the selection of sports is to be representative of student interests and abilities (86.41(c)(1)). A requirement that sports for the members of one sex be available or developed solely on the basis of their existence or development in the program for members of the other sex could conflict with the regulation where the interests and abilities of male and female students diverge.

Second, the regulation frames the general compliance obligations of recipients in terms of program-wide benefits and opportunities (86.41(c)). As implied above, Title IX protects the individual as a student-athlete, not as a basketball player, or swimmer.

(9) *Comment:* A coalition of many colleges and universities urged that there are no objective standards against which compliance with Title IX in intecollegiate athletics could be measured. They felt that diversity is so great among colleges and universities that no single standard or set of standards could practicably apply to all affected institutions. They concluded that it would be best for individual institutions to determine the policies and procedures by which to ensure nondiscrimination in intercollegiate athletic programs.

Specifically, this coalition suggested that each institution should create a group representative of all affected parties on campus.

This group would then assess existing athletic opportunities for men and women, and, on the basis of the assessment, develop a plan to ensure nondiscrimination. This plan would then be recommended to the Board of Trustees or other appropriate governing body.

The role foreseen for the Department under this concept is:

(a) The Department would use the plan as a framework for evaluating complaints and assessing compliance;

(b) The Department would determine whether the plan satisfies the interests of the involved parties; and

(c) The Department would determine whether the institution is adhering to the plan.

These commenters felt that this approach to Title IX enforcement would ensure an environment of equal opportunity.

Response: Title IX is an anti-discrimination law. It prohibits discrimination based on sex in educational institutions that are recipients of Federal assistance. The legislative history of Title IX clearly shows that it was enacted because of discrimination that currently was being practiced against women in educational institutions. The Department accepts that colleges and universities are sincere in their intention to ensure equal opportunity in intercollegiate athletics to their male and female students. It cannot, however, turn over its reponsibility for interpreting and enforcing the law. In this case, its responsibility includes articulating the standards by which compliance with the Title IX statute will be evaluated.

The Department agrees with this group of commenters that the proposed self-assessment and institutional plan is an excellent idea. Any institution that engages in the assessment/planning process, particularly with the full participation of interested parties as

envisioned in the proposal, would clearly reach or move well toward compliance. In addition, as explained in Section VIII of this Policy Interpretation, any college or university that has compliance problems but is implementing a plan that the Department determines will correct those problems within a reasonable period of time, will be found in compliance.

[FR Doc. 79-37985 Filed 12-10-79; 8:45 am]

BILLING CODE 4110-12-M

References

Preface

1. Phyllis Blatz, "Equity: How to Achieve It In Your School," California Women Coaches Academy Newsletter (Vol. 11, No. 1, October, 1975).
2. Ibid.

Chapter 1

1. Patricia Geadelmann, Christine Grant, Yvonne Slatton, N. Peggy Burke, *Equality in Sport for Women* (Washington, D.C., American Alliance for Health, Physical Education and Recreation, 1977), p. 2.
2. Candace Lyle Hogan, "Title IX for Coaches: Part I," *Coaching Women's Athletics* (March/April, 1975), p. 78.
3. Nancy Scannell, "Interpreting Title IX is Game in Itself," *The Washington Post* (June 3, 1975).
4. Nancy Scannell, "Bayh Urges Title IX Vote, Cites Implementation Delays," *The Washington Post* (June 24, 1975).
5. Patsy Neal, "The Woman Athlete and Coach in Our Society," *Interscholastic Athletic Administration* (Winter, 1975), p. 7.
6. Geadelmann, et al, *Equality in Sport for Women,* pp. 27–28.

Chapter 2

1. Ernest C. Casale, "Title IX and Its Impact on Men's Intercollegiate Athletics," speech presented on November 11, 1976.
2. Pete Axthelm, "Women Who Win," *Newsweek* (September 8, 1975), p. 51.
3. Ibid.
4. Geadelmann, et al, *Equality in Sport for Women,* p. 38.
5. Axthelm, *Newsweek* (September 8, 1975), p. 51.

6. National Collegiate Athletic Association vs. David Mathews, Secretary of the U.S. Department of Health, Education and Welfare, U.S. District Court (January, 1978).

7. Bob Oates, "NCAA Officials Voice Hostility to Title IX," *Los Angeles Times* (June 14, 1977), p. 3.

8. Alan J. Chapman, Letter to Caspar Weinberger (October 15, 1974).

9. Memorandum to NCAA Chief Executive Officers from John A. Fuzak, President, and Stanley J. Marshall, Secretary-Treasurer (February 13, 1976).

10. Oates, *Los Angeles Times* (June 14, 1977).

11. NCAA vs. David Mathews (January, 1978).

12. Richard Alan Rubin, "Sex Discrimination in Interscholastic High School Athletics," *Syracuse Law Review* (Vol. 25:535, 1974), pp. 535–574.

13. Evelle J. Younger, Opinion of the Attorney General of California (September 27, 1977).

14. Ibid.

15. Courtesy of Lionel Sobel of Beverly Hills, Ca. and Richard Weintraub of the Constitutional Rights Foundation.

16. Patsy Neal and Thomas A. Tutko, *Coaching Girls and Women: Psychological Perspectives* (Boston, Allyn and Bacon, Inc., 1975), p. 119.

17. Charles Maher, "City Preps Face Athletic Isolationsim," *Los Angeles Times* (June 17, 1977).

18. Ibid.

19. Neal and Tutko, *Coaching Girls and Women,* p. 120.

20. Maher, *Los Angeles Times* (June 17, 1977).

21. Neal and Tutko, *Coaching Girls and Women,* p. 121.

22. *Interscholastic Athletic Administration* (Winter, 1975), "Expanding Opportunities for Girls in Athletics," pp. 4–5.

23. Maher, *Los Angeles Times* (June 17, 1977).

Chapter 3

1. Yellow Springs School District Board of Education vs. Ohio High School Athletic Association, U.S. District Court (January, 1978).

2. Rubin, "Sex Discrimination in Interscholastic High School Athletics," p. 574.

3. Sandra Wien, "The Case for Equality in Athletics," *Cleveland State Law Review* (Vol. 22:570, 1973), p. 579.

Chapter 4

1. American Civil Liberties Union, "Sex Discrimination in Athletics and Physical Education," Women's Rights Project (January, 1975).

2. Ibid, pp. 17–18.

3. *CAHPER Journal,* California Association for Health, Physical Education and Recreation (Vol. 39, No. 1, November, 1976), p. 20.

4. Margaret Hennig and Anne Jardim, *The Managerial Woman* (Garden City, New York, Anchor Press/Doubleday, 1977), p. xiii.

5. Neal and Tutko, *Coaching Girls and Women,* p. 17.

6. Thomas Boslooper and Marcia Hayes, *The Femininity Game* (New York, Stein and Day, 1973), p. 183.

Chapter 5

1. Barbara Tschida, "Administering Boys and Girls Sports Programs in the Same Season," speech presented at the National Federation's Fifth Annual National Conference of High School Directors of Athletics (December 10, 1974).

2. Craig Thornburgh, "Sexist Sports Legal," *San Clemente Sun-Post.*

3. Jeff Jacobson and Molly Tyson, "Iowa Fever," *WomenSports* (December, 1977), p. 30.

4. Marcille Gray Williams, *The New Executive Woman* (Radnor, Pa., Chilton Book Company, 1977), pp. 13–20.

5. Dr. Joyce Brothers, "The Woman as Boss," *Mainliner* (March, 1974), p. 35.

6. Williams, *The New Executive Woman,* p. 33.

7. Hennig and Jardim, *The Managerial Woman,* p. 172.

8. Williams, *The New Executive Woman,* pp. 53–54.

9. Robert W. Shomer and Richard Centers, "Differences in Attitudinal Responses Under Conditions of Implicitly Manipulated Group Salience," *Journal of Personality and Social Psychology* (15:2, June 1970), pp. 125–132.

10. Dr. Carol Wolman and Dr. Hal Frank, "The Solo Woman in a Professional Peer Group," *American Journal of Orthopsychiatry* (Vol. 45, No. 1, January, 1975), pp. 164–171.

11. Barbara B. Hollmann and Robert W. Hollmann, "Managing Conflict: A Key Dimension in the Athletic Director's Job," *Athletic Administration* (Fall, 1977, pp. 12–20).

Chapter 6

1. American Civil Liberties Union, "Sex Discrimination in Athletics and Physical Education," Women's Rights Project, January, 1975, p. 5.

2. Patricia Geadelmann, et al, *Equality in Sport for Women.*

3. Ibid.

4. ACLU, "Sex Discrimination," p. 14.

Chapter 7

1. Mortimer R. Feinberg, *Effective Psychology for Managers* (Englewood Cliffs, N.J., Prentice-Hall, Inc., 1965), pp. 148–151.

2. Ibid.

3. ACLU, "Sex Discrimination," p. 6.

4. Ibid, pp. 10–11.

Chapter 8

1. Holly Wilson, "Women Athletic Trainers," *Women's Athletics: Coping With Controversy,* edited by Barbara J. Hoepner (Washington, D.C.,

American Association for Health, Physical Education and Recreation, 1974), p. 111.

    2. "Are Athletic Trainers a Luxury or a Necessity," *The Physician and Sports Medicine* (A McGraw-Hill Publication), 5:51–64 (October, 1977) and 5:76–87 (November, 1977).

Index